Entrepreneur
MAGAZINE'S

LEGAL GUIDE

Asset Protection

- Protect Your Wealth
- Limit Your Exposure to Lawsuits
- Maximize Your Tax Savings

Additional titles in Entrepreneur's Legal Guides
Helen Cicino, Esq.
Managing Editor

Entrepreneur
MAGAZINE'S

LEGAL
GUIDE

Robert F. Klueger
Attorney at Law

Asset Protection

- Protect Your Wealth
- Limit Your Exposure to Lawsuits
- Maximize Your Tax Savings

Publisher: Jere L. Calmes
Cover Design: Desktop Miracles, Inc.
Production: CWL Publishing Enterprises, Inc., Madison, Wisconsin,
www.cwlpub.com

Managing Editor for the Entrepreneur Press Legal Guide Series: Helen Cicino, Esq.

This publication is designed to provide accurate and authoritative information in
regard to the subject matter covered. It is sold with the understanding that the publisher is not engaged in rendering legal, accounting, or other professional services. If
legal advice or other expert assistance is required, the services of a competent professional person should be sought.

> —From a Declaration of Principles jointly adopted by
> a Committee of the American Bar Association
> and a Committee of Publishers and Associations

ISBN-13: 978-1-59918-170-7

Library of Congress Cataloging-in-Publication Data

Klueger, Robert F.
  Asset protection / by Robert F. Klueger.
    p. cm. — (Legal guide)
  ISBN-13: 978-1-59918-170-7 (alk. paper)
  1. Executions (Law)—United States. 2. Fraudulent conveyances—United
States. 3. Estate planning—United States. 4. Debtor and creditor—United
States. 5. Trusts and trustees—United States. I. Title.
  KF9025.K54 2008
  346.7305'2—dc22

                                                      2007051573

Printed in Canada

12 11 10 09 08   10 9 8 7 6 5 4 3 2 1

Dedication

This book is dedicated to Patricia,
the Queen of Peachville

Contents

Preface

Two True Cases

Here are two cases, straight from the files of Klueger & Stein, LLP. Only the names have been slightly altered.

In 1999 we represented a client, American Nurses Registry, Inc. (ANR). ANR provided nurses on a temporary basis to hospitals, nursing homes, and private families. Whether you wanted a nurse for four hours or four months, ANR would immediately fill the need, providing you with a qualified nurse. ANR would handle the tax withholding and filing and provide the workers' compensation and all of the paperwork. ANR was founded and owned by a husband-and-wife team who worked very hard, and by 1999 they operated nurses' registries in four California cities and a fifth in New Orleans.

In that year, ANR was sued by two nurses whom ANR had loaned out to a private home. The homeowners had a child who required around-the-clock care. The child had a rare and communicable disease, and, as is often the case with health care workers, both nurses were infected. They were not hospitalized—they barely evidenced any symptoms—but it appears (although it is by no means certain) that they were infected by the child for whom they cared.

The nurses faced one huge problem: California's workers' compensation law (and the law of every other state) prohibits an employee from suing the employer for employment-related injury or illness. Workers' compensation is a trade-off: an employee need not prove that the employer was negligent, but only that he or she was hurt on the job. In return, the employee receives compensation for medical expenses and lost wages. But the employee cannot sue for "pain and suffering" or punitive damages. Workers' compensation assures that the employee receives a little money easily, but it prevents multimillion-dollar awards.

The fact that the law prohibits suits against employers for workplace injuries didn't stop a smart lawyer. It turns out that both nurses were Nigerians working in the U.S. as resident aliens. So the lawyer alleged that his clients' injuries were really the result of racial discrimination. He alleged that ANR knew the child had a communicable disease, and that rather than send Caucasian nurses to care for the child and risk that they become infected, ANR, acting strictly from racial prejudice, sent two black Nigerians to care for the child.

The two plaintiffs knew—and their lawyer soon learned—that the case was a hopeless tissue of lies. The fact that muddied their chances of success was that by the time these two nurses had been assigned to the child, a long line of nurses had already been assigned to the same child, some black, some brown, some white. Indeed, after these two nurses became infected, replacement nurses—some black, some brown, some white—were assigned to the child. The fact that the owners of ANR were themselves not Caucasians made the plaintiffs' case even less credible.

After these facts came to light, did the plaintiffs' lawyer give up? Not a chance. All of these types of cases are brought under contingency fee arrangements. The lawyer agrees to take a percentage of the settlement or the award and take nothing if there is no settlement or award. That meant that once the ugly facts came to light, the lawyer had made a commitment of time and effort, and had to keep fighting. At that point, it became a war of attrition. The more pain in the way of attorney's fees the plaintiffs' lawyer could inflict, the better the chance of extracting a settlement. Having signed a contingency fee agreement with the lawyer, the plaintiffs didn't care how much blood was spilled; once they signed the contingency fee agreement, they were done.

The second case from our files arose in 2007, and—if possible—is even weirder. Ventura Wire Products, Inc. (VWP) is a small shop operated by a father and son, employing approximately ten employees. It manufactures industrial wire. In 2007, VWP terminated an employee, Julia Lowe. Ms. Lowe had been downloading pornography on VWP's computers after hours and had been using drugs on the premises after hours. That would have been sufficient reason to terminate her, but it wasn't why she was terminated. VWP let her go simply because it engaged in a little downsizing, eliminating hers and two or three other positions. After she was terminated, VWP did not fill the jobs eliminated. Of course, VWP had every right to terminate the employees they let go, since they were all at-will employees: they had no employment contracts and could be terminated for whatever reason the employer chose, or for no reason at all. Needless to say, after Ms. Lowe was terminated, VWP thought they had heard the end of it.

Far from it. It turns out that the owners of VWP were members of the Church of Scientology. Ms. Lowe hired an employment lawyer who threatened to sue VWP. The lawyer alleged that Ms. Lowe's firing had been the result of religious discrimination. Specifically, she alleged that the owners had attempted to induce her client to join their church, and when she refused, they retaliated by firing her.

VWP explained to Ms. Lowe's attorney that religious discrimination had nothing to do with her client's termination. They pointed to the fact that most of VWP's current employees were not members of their church, so that being a member of the church could not possibly be a condition of employment. They also pointed to the incontrovertible fact that once Ms. Lowe had been terminated, her position had not been filled by someone else.

In response to this letter, the attorney backed off. She refused to bring a case on such flimsy allegations. Months passed. Once again, VWP thought they had heard the end of it.

Of course, they were mistaken. They forgot that there are 175,000 practicing attorneys in California, many of whom are, in the words of former Chief Justice Warren Burger, "hungry as locusts." They should have known that there is always an attorney to be found who will take any case, no matter how bogus, if there is the prospect of a few dollars to be extorted. Ms. Lowe found another lawyer who did bring the lawsuit, alleging that Ms. Lowe's termination had been the result of religious discrimination.

The Results

I wish I could tell you that both cases resulted in happy endings for the defendants, but I cannot. Both were settled, the first—against the two Nigerian nurses—favorably to ANR. The second was not settled favorably to VWP. The difference between the two was that ANR had far deeper pockets that VWP. The owners of ANR informed the plaintiffs that they had the money and were willing to pay any price to prevent a judgment from entering against them; VWP didn't have the money to fight and caved in.

In both cases, justice had nothing to do with it.

Bottom Line

Both cases had two things in common: Both cases required (1) a plaintiff to bring a frivolous case and (2) a lawyer to bring a frivolous case.

Both cases are similar in what each plaintiff's lawyer assumed would happen. Each lawyer assumed that a judge would permit a lawsuit, no matter how frivolous, to get to the jury without being laughed out of court. Indeed, the whole game is to "get to the jury." That is usually a good assumption, because most judges are willing to let any case continue. The percentage of cases that are dismissed before they get to the jury is very small, based in large part on most judges' belief that to dismiss a case is to deprive a plaintiff of a divinely created right to have any case heard by a jury.

The second assumption is that once a case gets to the jury, the jury will be willing to overlook the weaknesses of the plaintiff's case and instead use this one occasion to play Robin Hood, i.e., to rob from the rich and give to the poor. That too is a good assumption. Many jurors are willing to give credence to the most ludicrous lawsuit on the assumption that if the case really didn't have any merit, the judge would not let it get to them. In other words, the fact that there is a judge sitting there lends an aura of legitimacy to the case.

The final assumption behind these frivolous lawsuits is that once the judge permits the case to get to the jury, and once the jury is given the opportunity to play Robin Hood, there will be money to collect at the end of the day. One thing never happens: lawsuits are never brought against poor people. A lawyer working on a contingency doesn't bring a lawsuit unless he or she is reasonably certain that there will be a payday. No one works just for the experience or the glory.

We cannot prevent gold-diggers from bringing nonsense lawsuits. We are powerless in the face of 175,000 California lawyers (and over 1,000,000 lawyers nationwide), many of whom will allege anything in the hope of extracting a few dollars from a defendant who knows that he or she will have to pay his or her attorney just to defend the frivolous lawsuit. There is nothing we can do about the judges who are willing to let any case go forward out of some twisted notion of "justice." And we cannot change human nature or the jury system. We cannot change the fact that there are more retired postal workers than there are bank presidents sitting on juries.

But there is one thing we can change. We can assure that even after the lawsuit is brought, and even after it gets to a jury, and even after the jury decides to do its part to equalize the imbalance between the rich and the poor, there is nothing there! We can assure that the judgment is worthless because there are no assets to attach, no money to seize—nothing.

Asset protection is a passion at Klueger & Stein, LLP. It is too easy to allege that an employer terminated an employee as a result of racial prejudice and not the employee's own incompetence. It is too easy to find a lawyer who will bring that case. It is too easy for a judge to allow the case to proceed. It is too easy for the jury to participate in the nonsense out of some misplaced sense of fairness. Where does it become difficult for the plaintiffs?

Here is where it becomes difficult. The following chapters are designed to ensure that with a little careful planning, the cupboard will be empty for the plaintiffs. We will examine what we can do to either ensure that our assets are exempt from seizure or make them so difficult to find and seize that no attorney on a contingency fee arrangement will dare take the case.

About the Author

Robert F. Klueger has been a practicing attorney for more than 30 years, specializing in asset protection, tax planning, and estate planning. He is a Certified California Tax Specialist, one of only 450 of California's 200,000 practicing attorneys to have achieved this designation.

Mr. Klueger received a B.A. from the University of Pennsylvania (1967), a law degree from Fordham Law School (1973), and a masters in taxation from the University of Denver Graduate Tax Program (1980).

A frequent lecturer and author, he is a member of the New York, Colorado, and California bar. Mr. Klueger is a founding partner of Klueger & Stein, L.L.P., Encino, CA. For more information on his firm, please visit **www.maximumassetprotection.com**.

How Dr. Nguyen Lived (and Kept) the American Dream

Binh Nguyen (pronounced "win") was born in Vietnam in 1970. He does not know how he lost his parents, other than that they were killed in the war. His only childhood memories are of an orphanage run by an order of nuns. When Binh was eight years old, he was adopted by a family who lived about as far from Bien Hua, Vietnam as one could possibly get: Anaheim, California.

Betty and Jack Brown made two decisions regarding Binh's name. They decided that his teachers and classmates in Anaheim might have trouble with "Binh," so he became "Ben." They also decided that, to honor the memory of Ben's parents, he would keep his Vietnamese surname. The biggest concern they had on the day they brought Ben home to California was that he would not be able to digest American food. He dispelled that concern the next morning as he dove into a bowl of oatmeal.

There was nothing remarkable about Ben's childhood in Anaheim in the 1980s. Jack, a construction contractor, could afford to send Ben to private schools. Ben had a quick mind and a winsome smile; he was five feet two inches tall, and his female teachers wanted to cuddle him. He made friends easily. He was too small and too frail for sports, but he played the clarinet in the band and was president of the Photography Club. When Ben was about 14, he announced that he was going to become a doctor and that was that. Stanford was followed by UCLA Medical School, an internship, and finally his own family practice in Garden Grove, less than a mile from where he had his first bowl of cereal on that first morning in America.

Ben was somewhat apprehensive that first day he opened his family practice clinic. After all, he would be competing with doctors who did not have a strange last name and who were manifestly not Asian. In order to spread the word that he was open for business, he joined everything: the Rotary, the Garden Grove Chamber of Commerce, Toastmasters, any group that had people who might become patients or refer patients. He handed out business cards for "Dr. Ben." That winsome smile didn't hurt, either.

Soon Ben realized that if you stayed open for business nights and Sundays and if you treated people with a smile, they would keep coming back and would refer their friends as well. Many of his patients were on public assistance; many were immigrants such as he. The record keeping could be a nightmare, but it was fun and rewarding. "You nice man, Dr. Ben," he kept hearing them say.

Jennifer McCarthy also thought he was a nice man. The blondest, bluest-eyed woman who ever attended UCLA rewarded him with two equally blonde, blue-eyed daughters. "I'm a long way from Bien Hua," he used to think.

By the time Ben had been in practice for six years, it was more than he could handle himself. So he bought a medical building, hired two associate doctors, and rented the space he wasn't using to other doctors. He and Jenny were both savers. If something was not absolutely necessary for the practice or the girls, it wasn't bought, and what was left over went into the stock market.

One of his patients, Mrs. Chan, owned a 20-unit apartment building she wished to sell. "You buy it, Dr. Ben. You make lots of money on it. I guarantee." And he did. It was enough to move Jenny and the girls into a $2 million house on five acres in Anaheim Hills. The best thing by far about the house was the terraced back yard that he turned into an arboretum. He would lead guests through the expanses of flowers, trees, and shrubs, pointing out the varieties. After a long week at the office, nothing was better therapy than being alone with some pruning shears or a water hose. It didn't get better than that.

Dr. Nguyen was active in the Orange County Medical Society. One night, following a seminar, he and a few other doctors were sitting around chewing the fat. One of the older doctors, Dr. Phil Shohet, mentioned that one of his former partners—an anesthesiologist—had been sued for medical malpractice. A patient had died on the operating table, and his family had sued the surgeon, the hospital, the referring physician, and Dr. Shohet's partner.

"But why the anesthesiologist?" asked Dr. Nguyen.

"They sue everybody. The more defendants there are, the more is available when they start settling the case," replied Dr. Shohet.

"What happened?" he asked.

"They settled it. But my partner had to dig real deep. Cost him a cool quarter-million. It put off his retirement."

"But what about the malpractice insurance? That's why we buy it," said Dr. Nguyen.

"Not enough," said Dr. Shohet. "He carried only the minimum coverage. The dead guy was some big-time investment banker who was only in his forties. They figured that if the jury found that there was negligence, the award could come into the tens of millions. It could have wiped everyone out."

"They could have taken his home?" asked Dr. Nguyen.

"They would have started with his home," replied Dr. Shohet.

There was a long silence. Then Dr. Nguyen said, in a very low voice: "Wow. It's a good thing I've never been sued."

"You're due, kid," said Dr. Ray Katz. "Everyone with a little dough becomes a target sooner or later. It's just a matter of time. That's why you gotta plan ahead."

"How?" asked Dr. Nguyen.

"Didn't you ever hear of the Cayman Islands, or the British Virgin Islands? What do you think those places are for?"

"But you can't put your home into the Cayman Islands, and I own an apartment building. I can't put that into the Cayman Islands," said Dr. Nguyen.

"Look," said Dr. Katz. "I don't know what they do, but they do it. Trusts. Limited partnerships. Whatever. But by the time you're done, they can't touch your assets. Why do you think they call it 'asset protection?'"

"Do you know of such a person?" asked Dr. Nguyen.

"I more than know one," replied Dr. Katz. "You won't find my name on any assets. Anyone who sues me can go pound sand. I'll fish out the guy's card in the morning and call you."

"Thanks," said Dr. Nguyen.

On the drive home, all Dr. Nguyen could think of was his garden. He could not imagine that anyone could take it. He had assumed that the painfully high malpractice insurance premiums at least gave him the assurance that no one could touch his home, his investments, or his savings. Now he was not so sure at all.

Two weeks later, Dr. Nguyen met with Frank Gad, an attorney in Santa Ana who specialized in asset protection—the name on the card. For the first hour, Gad did nothing but ask questions. He asked where Jenny worked (she didn't, since she was still home with the girls), whether there were any pending lawsuits, the state of Dr. Nguyen's estate planning (he had to admit he did not even have a will), even the strength of his marriage. He then delved into Dr. Nguyen's assets in minute detail, even asking whether Jenny had also signed the bank guaranty on the medical building (he couldn't remember).

After an hour, the suspense was killing Dr. Nguyen. "Mr. Gad," he said, "I understand that we can move my cash and stock portfolio to a foreign country. But you can't move my home to the Cayman Islands and you can't move the building my practice is in to the British Virgin Islands or wherever. What can you do to protect the assets that I care about the most?"

"I was just getting to that," Gad said.

For the next hour, Frank Gad laid out a plan to ensure that if a lawsuit hit, the plaintiffs could not get at any of Dr. Nguyen's assets. And before a month had passed, they had fully implemented the plan.

At the time of the meeting with Frank Gad, Dr. Nguyen's clinic had grown to 11 employees. In addition to the two other doctors, Dr. Nguyen employed five nurses and medical technicians, a receptionist, an office manager, and a billing clerk. Just as all of his patients loved him, so did his employees. He paid as well as anyone. Once a year he took the whole office to an Angels game. The Christmas party was a fun event for everyone, including some of his patients who would know no Christmas but for the party. But shortly after the meeting with Frank Gad, he hired a nurse, Angela Venizelos, who seemed a little strange. Dr. Nguyen heard her asking questions about him and Jennifer. She always seemed to be poking around where she didn't belong. She wasn't so much a bad nurse as an uninterested nurse. To work in a small family practice, you had to be a "people person," and she wasn't. For the first time in his medical career, Dr. Nguyen had to fire an employee.

Dr. Nguyen dreaded the interview in which he had to inform Ms. Venizelos that he was letting her go. His fear of hurting her feelings caused him to make a mistake. Rather than simply inform her that she was not working out, he lied and told her he was downsizing the office.

"I don't believe that for a second," she said, with a vehemence that surprised Dr. Nguyen. "I know the real reason you're firing me."

"You do?" said Dr. Nguyen, unable to hide how defensive he felt.

"Sure. I'm not like the other nurses around here. For starters, I'm not going to put out for the doctors," Ms. Venizelos said, referring to the fact that one of his doctors was openly dating one of the nurses. "And another thing: I'm not going to spill out of my uniform just to please the patients." This was a pointed reference to one of the other nurses. "And I really don't appreciate Dr. Atkinson's little jokes and innuendos." He had no idea what this referred to. "So you can take this job and shove it. But I'm not going to take this lying down." And with that, she stormed out.

Dr. Nguyen was a little shaken by what he had heard. He thought his office was one big happy family. What else was going on under his nose that he didn't know about?

If the interview shook him, the certified letter from Miller, Hoskins, Leavitt & Brown, LLP stunned him. In three single-spaced pages, it informed him that the firm had been engaged by Angela Venizelos to represent her in her wrongful termination claim against him, a claim based upon sex and age discrimination, sexual harassment, and "retaliatory firing." The letter claimed that Dr. Nguyen's office fostered a "climate of discrimination," as evidenced by the fact that nurses could advance only if they provided sexual favors to the doctors, and were terminated if they refused. Ms. Venizelos claimed that the discrimination of which she was a victim had caused her pain and suffering, humiliation, depression, anxiety, fear, and apprehension, as well as having damaged her career as a nurse. Her lawyers informed Dr. Nguyen that if they were successful before a jury of Ms. Venizelos' peers, they were confident that they would be awarded $2 million in compensatory and punitive damages. They informed Dr. Nguyen that, under California law, even if they collected only one dollar on their claim for wrongful termination, Dr. Nguyen would have to pay all of her attorney's fees, which could run to $200,000. Finally, they reminded Dr. Nguyen of what the publicity involving a sexual harassment lawsuit might do to his reputation and his medical practice.

With all this in mind, Miller, Hoskins, Leavitt & Brown, LLP was willing to let Dr. Nguyen off easy. If he would write them a check for $60,000 within the next ten days in full settlement of all of Angela Venizelos's claims, they would not file the lawsuit they had already prepared on her behalf, and Dr. Nguyen could resume his life, a little poorer and a lot wiser.

Dr. Nguyen felt as if he had been punched in the stomach. The letter literally took his breath away. The next thing he did was show the letter to his staff. They could not hide their shock and anger.

"You? Sexually harass anyone? You're the last person anyone could accuse of that, Dr. Ben," said one of the nurses.

"Don't you worry, Dr. Ben, we're all behind you," said another. "You've got nothing to worry about. She was a lazy, rotten nurse and we'll all testify to that."

Dr. Nguyen felt a little better. Acting on a referral from another doctor, he made an appointment to meet with Ronald Fink, a well-known employment lawyer in Los Angeles. But the first thing he learned was something he had suspected: he had no insurance coverage for a sexual discrimination claim. He would be paying Ron Fink from his own pocket, at the rate of $400 per hour.

What was worse, Ron Fink asked him some pointed questions for which he had no answers. "Do you maintain an employee manual?"

"A what?" replied Dr. Nguyen.

"A book that all the employees must read informing them that sexual discrimination is absolutely prohibited in the office, and that anyone who suspects that he or she is a victim of it must report it immediately, giving the name of the office administrator to whom all complaints must be reported."

"No, I don't."

"Do you have any rules posted regarding inappropriate conduct?" asked Ron Fink.

"No. We're a medical clinic, not a locker room."

"I realize that. But the absence of these things will definitely be used against you. It's great that all of your employees are willing to stand by you, but it's not a guarantee of success. Let me tell you about Miller, Hoskins, Leavitt & Brown. They're the real instigators of this claim, not the gal you fired. They specialize in this. She probably went in there asking if she could collect some termination pay, and they filled her head with stuff about being the victim of age and sex discrimination because one of the other nurses was dating a doctor and she wasn't. They'll get at least half of whatever she collects. They'll be delighted to split sixty grand with her for writing a letter."

"But I shouldn't have to pay her anything. I didn't do anything wrong."

"Fine," said Ron Fink. "We'll fight them tooth and nail. But there are no guarantees as to what a jury could do. You're a wealthy guy, and sometimes juries like to play Robin Hood. You never know. Just as a precaution, I think you should consult with an asset protection specialist."

And suddenly, the clouds parted and the sun shone through. "I've already consulted an asset protection specialist," said Dr. Nguyen. "Frank Gad in Anaheim. As far as he is concerned, all of my assets are already protected."

"That's great," said Ron Fink. "It's all I need to know. I'll give the slimeballs at Miller, Hoskins and Company a call. I'll tell them I'm on the case, and that there aren't any assets to go after even if they win. Maybe we can head this off at the start."

Unfortunately, Ron Fink was not able to avoid a lawsuit. One of the first things that Miller, Hoskins, et al. did after Angela Venizelos visited them was to conduct an asset search of Dr. Nguyen. They liked what they found: a multimillion-dollar home, a multimillion-dollar apartment building, a successful medical practice housed in a building Dr. Nguyen owned, and cash to an extent they could only imagine. They simply didn't believe that there were no assets to go after.

Months went by, and Dr. Nguyen heard nothing about the lawsuit. He did have to show up at the Miller, Hoskins offices for his deposition. He was sworn in by a court reporter, and spent the better part of the day answering questions about his employment practices. The only embarrassing thing was having to confess that he lied to Angela Venizelos about why he had fired her. Dr. Nguyen protested that he was only trying to spare her feelings, but it came out sounding like he had something to hide. He had no answer when they said, "You were lying then. How can we be sure you're not lying now to protect your assets?"

Dr. Nguyen was surprised to learn that investigators were knocking on his current and former employees' doors at night, inquiring about how he ran his office. They intimated that if the employees had anything against Dr. Nguyen, they too could become plaintiffs in the lawsuit. It wouldn't cost them anything. If an employee told an investigator that he or she didn't have anything bad to say about Dr. Nguyen, the investigator became insistent, reminding the employee that there was real money in it for anyone who joined the suit, and they wouldn't even have to come to court, since the more people who joined, the less chance there was of it going to trial. Some employees were contacted more than once.

More than a year after the case was filed, and approximately six months before the date of trial, the judge ordered that the parties attend a mediation. Ron Fink explained to Dr. Nguyen that a mediation is an informal meeting designed to produce a settlement. The mediator would have no power to order either side to do anything. It was merely an attempt to point out to each side the weaknesses in their case, with a view toward getting each side closer to the middle.

After going back and forth all day, Ron Fink said he wanted to meet face-to-face with the mediator and Mike Miller, Angela Venizelos's attorney.

"Look," he told Miller and the mediator, "There's an aspect of this case you really ought to consider. The defendant has no assets. There's nothing to go after. If you lose you lose, but even if you win, you still lose. You're looking at an empty pantry."

"That's not what my asset search reveals," said Miller.

"Here's what your asset search should reveal, if you looked a little closer," said Fink. "Dr. Nguyen doesn't own his home. His wife owns his home."

"It's still community property, no matter whose name is on the deed," said Miller.

"Wrong again," said Fink. "Dr. Nguyen and his wife entered into a transmutation agreement, changing their assets from community property to their separate property. And the house isn't even in Jennifer's name anymore. She transferred the house into a qualified personal residence trust."

"Sounds like a fraudulent conveyance to me," said Miller.

"Check your files," replied Fink. "The transmutation agreement and the QPRT were all done well before your client got it into her head to sue Dr. Nguyen. I wouldn't want to hang for as long as it will take you to prove that this was a fraudulent conveyance."

"Well, his wife couldn't take all the assets and leave him with nothing. That would be a fraudulent conveyance," said Miller, but without much conviction.

"She didn't," said Fink. "Dr. Nguyen got the office building and the apartment building. But he doesn't own those assets anymore either. They're owned by a limited liability company. Lots of luck getting at those properties."

"Dr. Nguyen leads a pretty good life. He's got to have assets. We'll take a debtor's exam and find out where the assets are."

"You don't have to take a debtor's exam. I'll tell you right now where the assets are," said Fink, warming to his subject. "Dr. Nguyen was the settlor of a trust located in the Cook Islands, which is located in the South Pacific. The trust owns a company that is located on the island of Nevis, which is located in the Caribbean. The Nevis company maintains a bank account in a private bank in Switzerland. You've heard of Switzerland, haven't you, Mike?"

There was a silence. Then the mediator said, "I would like to speak with Mr. Miller privately."

The mediator reminded Miller that the case was weak on Dr. Nguyen's liability in the first place. Considering the time that Miller would have to put into preparing the case, and the likely outcome, not to mention the chance of collecting anything if they won, Miller, Hoskins might more profitably devote its resources to another case.

"I'll tell you what I'll do for you," said the mediator. "I'll twist the defendant's arm to cough up a few bucks so that you can save some face with your client."

So Angela Venizelos did not receive nothing, but what she received was considerably closer to nothing than it was to $60,000.

About six months after the settlement, Dr. Nguyen attended another medical society luncheon. During the course of the lunch, he met a young doctor who told Dr. Nguyen that he was starting to make some money and was afraid of lawsuits.

"Write down your phone number," said Dr. Nguyen. "I'll call you in the morning. I'm going to give you Frank Gad's phone number."

A Brief Tour of Civil Litigation

I often receive frantic calls that go like this: "I was just in a car accident. Can they take my home?" or "I'm late on a payment to the bank. Can they shut down my business?"

The ability to protect your assets begins with knowing what rights and remedies the creditors possess, and that entails a basic understanding of how a lawsuit works. As we will see in Chapter 4 in our discussion on fraudulent conveyances, what we can do to preserve the assets often depends on how early in the game we do it.

Civil litigation varies from state to state and from county to county within each state; indeed, it can vary from judge to judge within a courthouse. However, the basics tend to be fairly standard from state to state. The litigation road map in this chapter generally applies everywhere.

> At each step along the way, we will focus on one question: "Can the plaintiff seize the defendant's assets now?"

Before the Lawsuit Begins

In most cases, you will know that a lawsuit is coming before it actually arrives. If the promissory note you guaranteed is about to go into default, you will learn of it before the lender does. In some cases, a potential defendant will first learn of a pending lawsuit by receiving a demand letter from the plaintiff's attorney. As we saw in Chapter 1, Dr. Nguyen received a letter demanding settlement of the threatened lawsuit before the lawsuit was filed.

On occasion, a potential defendant will receive a letter from the plaintiff's attorney asking that the letter be forwarded to the defendant's insurance carrier. This usually occurs in the context of automobile accidents or other tort claims. With this letter, the plaintiff's attorney wants to ensure that the insurance carrier receives early notice of the pending lawsuit, so that the insurance carrier can participate in settlement negotiations. If you get such a letter, do what the letter suggests: forward the letter to the insurer. Failure to speedily notify the insurer of the pending claim could result in loss of coverage.

The best time to swing into action to protect your assets is when you think a lawsuit is coming. As we shall see in Chapter 4, planning to protect your assets after the grounds for a lawsuit have arisen might constitute a fraudulent conveyance, but doing the same planning after the lawsuit has been filed will more likely be judged to be a fraudulent conveyance. This will not be the last time in this book that we invoke the asset protection planner's mantra: The best planning is planning that is done early.

Can a creditor seize a debtor's assets before filing a lawsuit? Not likely. Most states have statutes that permit the repossession of a car if the loan is in default, but in most other contexts, a creditor will have to file a lawsuit of some sort in order to seize any of the debtor's assets. Bottom line: It isn't likely that a creditor will be able to seize your assets without you first having some ability to appear in court to prevent it.

The Kickoff: The Summons and Complaint

Every lawsuit starts with the service of a summons and complaint on the defendant. The summons is what it says it is: it commands the defendant to appear in court. The complaint is the plaintiff's recitation of all of the terrible things the defendant did and the relief that the plaintiff asks the court to grant. The relief is usually in the form of a money judgment, but not always: a plaintiff may ask for the return of a particular item of property wrongfully taken, or an injunction to prohibit the defendant from committing a certain act. The summons requires the defendant to respond to the allegations contained in the complaint by filing an answer within a prescribed period of time, usually 30 days.

In order to have any legal effect, the summons must be served on the defendant. If the summons is never served, the court has no jurisdiction over the defendant. Without jurisdiction, the court cannot do the one thing that is the whole point of a lawsuit: enter a judgment against the defendant.

Contrary to popular belief, you can be effectively served with a summons without a process server showing up at your front door and handing the summons to you. Depending upon the type of suit and local law, substituted service, including service by mail, may be permitted. If the defendant is a corporation, limited liability company, or other similar "fictional" entity, who is served? The registered agent is served, i.e., the person the corporation designates to accept the summons. Every corporation or other entity has a registered agent: you cannot form a corporation, limited partnership, or limited liability company anywhere without designating a registered agent to accept the summons.

Can a plaintiff seize your assets by filing a summons and complaint? Only in a few limited situations. In most instances, including standard negligence cases and most business litigation, the plaintiff has to wait for a judgment to begin the process of hunting down and seizing the defendant's assets. Depending on how efficient and overcrowded the local court is, that process could take months or even years.

Prejudgment Attachment

The principal exception to the rule that a plaintiff must wait for a judgment before going after the assets is in the case of prejudgment attachment. Every state except Pennsylvania allows a plaintiff in certain very limited circumstances to tie up a defendant's assets before a judgment is entered. The grounds vary from state to state. Many states, including California, Illinois, and Ohio, permit prejudgment attachment if the defendant is a nonresident or a foreign corporation. (See *California Code of Civil Procedure* §492.010 [West, 1979], *Ill. Ann Stat.* ch. 110 ¶4-101 [Smith-Hurd, 1983], and *Ohio Rev. Code Ann.* §2715.01 [Page Supp. 1990].) Some states, such as Colorado and Arizona, permit prejudgment attachment if the defendant has threatened to remove the property from the state for the purpose of "delaying, defeating or defrauding" a creditor. (See *Colorado R. Civ. P.* 102[c] and *Arizona Rev. Stat. Ann.* §12-2402 [Supp. 1990].) In all cases, the plaintiff must allege and prove to the court's satisfaction that he or she is likely to prevail. That usually means that the defendant will have an opportunity to contest the request for prejudgment attachment.

In most cases, the plaintiff is required to post a bond during the pendency of the lawsuit. This makes sense, since the defendant will be denied the use of his or her property before it is decided that he or she was at fault. If the defendant wins the lawsuit, he or she will be able to seize the bond to the extent that he or she has been damaged by the wrongful attachment of the property.

Prejudgment attachment does not always mean the plaintiff takes the property; it may result in the sheriff seizing equipment or inventory, tying up a bank account, or depositing the property with the court. But it will always prevent the defendant from disposing of the property before the underlying lawsuit is finally decided.

The Lis Pendens

A *lis pendens*, also known as a notice of pendency of action, is a document the plaintiff records with the county recorder. It announces to the world that a lawsuit has been or is about to be filed concerning this particular parcel of real estate. It is a warning to anyone thinking of buying this property (or loaning money against it) that it comes with a lawsuit. Indeed, if you buy real estate in the teeth of a lis pendens, you're running the risk that at the end of the day you may have paid for nothing because someone else has a prior claim to the property.

A lis pendens may properly be filed only in those limited cases that actually involve a particular parcel of property, such as boundary line disputes, easements, or claims for misrepresentation involving the sale of the property. If a plaintiff is injured in a car accident and hopes to one day obtain a judgment and seize the defendant's home with that judgment, the dispute does not involve the defendant's home and filing a lis pendens in such a case would not be proper.

The California Supreme Court recently ruled that a lis pendens was properly filed against a parcel of real estate in a case that did not involve the real estate itself, but involved an allegation that the property had been fraudulently transferred during the pendency of the underlying litigation. However, the court admitted that extending the grounds for a lis pendens might open the floodgates to abuse. (See *Kirkeby v. Superior Court* [33 Cal. 4th 642 (2004)].)

The problem arises from the fact that no one needs permission from a judge to file a lis pendens, and as a result, they are subject to abuse. Creditors often file them in the hope of obtaining leverage against their debtors, since filing a lis pendens makes a parcel of real estate unsalable. Needless to say, if you believe that a creditor has wrongfully filed a lis pendens, you must immediately ask a judge to order it removed. Since a lis pendens says that a lawsuit is pending, a judge will always order it removed if no lawsuit has been filed.

Foreclosure

Millions of people buy homes, and most of them sign mortgages (in some states, deeds of trust), but not being lawyers, most people don't know what they've signed.

When you take out a mortgage, you actually sign two legal documents at the same time. The first is the promissory note, which is the legal promise to repay the loan at the times and in the amounts stated in the note. By itself, the note does not give the lender the right to go against any particular parcel of property if the borrower doesn't pay; it's a general, unsecured promise to repay. The document that gives the lender a security interest in your home is the mortgage. A mortgage gives the lender a lien on the property; it says that if you don't pay the promissory note in accordance with its terms, the lender can foreclose its lien and take the house. The key to the mortgage is that the lender doesn't have to sue you to foreclose. There's no complaint, no answer, and no waiting around for months or years until the judge's calendar clears up. Admittedly, the foreclosure of real estate is not as rapid as the repossession of cars, and your residence cannot be foreclosed upon without your knowledge, but it's a very speedy process nonetheless.

Foreclosure is not limited to real estate. Any debt that is secured can be foreclosed upon. A lien against personal property takes the form of a chattel mortgage or security interest, and the effect is the same as that of a mortgage or deed of trust in the case of real estate.

The Answer

The complaint requires the defendant to serve an answer to the plaintiff, usually within 30 days. Depending on the local court rules, the answer will either respond point by point to each allegation in the complaint or it may simply be a "general denial," which is legalese for "Everything you said in your complaint is baloney!" A general denial can be as brief as two words: "General Denial."

What happens if a defendant who has been properly served with a summons fails to file a timely answer? The plaintiff may file a motion with the court asking for a default judgment, which is legalese for "Game Over; We Win." Armed with a default judgment, a plaintiff can seize assets. Once the judgment is entered, it's not likely ever to go away.

I know of people whose assets are so far beyond the reach of creditors that they are tempted to allow a complaint to go into default. That's a terrible idea. Besides the catastrophic effect that a default judgment will have on a defendant's credit, it may cause every allegation in the complaint—no matter how outlandish—to be deemed admitted. The plaintiff may have hoped to receive only a few hundred or a few thousand dollars, but made inflated claims for millions in the complaint; now he or she will receive a judgment for that amount!

> **Klueger's Iron Rule:** Never, never, never, ever allow a complaint to go into default.

Once the answer has been filed, the long process of litigation begins—a process that will end with the case being settled or, failing that, a trial. The trial will be before a jury or a judge, but in either event the end result will be a judgment for the defendant or for the plaintiff. If the judgment is for the plaintiff, this is the plaintiff's ticket to go after the defendant's assets.

Motions for Summary Judgment

We have seen that a plaintiff may, in certain limited cases, obtain prejudgment attachment of a defendant's assets. Plaintiffs can do this before the defendant has filed an answer, or indeed at any time during a lawsuit. Is there some way a plaintiff can short-circuit that whole process and obtain a judgment after the defendant files an answer?

In some cases, a plaintiff may file a motion for summary judgment. This is legalese for the plaintiff saying, "Judge, even if you believe everything the defendant says in his answer to be true, I'm still entitled to win. There's nothing left in this case to decide." Here's an example: Plaintiff Smith's complaint says that Smith loaned defendant Jones $1,000, which, under the terms of the promissory note Jones signed, was payable on November 1, 2008. November 1 came and went and the debt wasn't repaid. Jones, in his answer, admits that Smith loaned him $1,000, admits that he signed the promissory note, admits that he did not repay the loan on the due date, but alleges that the reason he didn't pay was that he lost his job and didn't have the money. Losing his job may be an adequate defense to Jones' mother, but not to the judge. Since the inability to repay a debt validly incurred is not a legal defense, the judge will grant Smith's motion for summary judgment.

Motions for summary judgment are granted in only a minority of cases, since it takes a particularly inept defense lawyer not to be able to write an answer that throws some legally valid defense into the mix. But it happens.

If the plaintiff's motion for summary judgment is granted, the plaintiff may proceed to record the judgment with the county recorder, and once that happens, the plaintiff is free to start pursuing the defendant's assets. The plaintiff loses nothing if the motion for summary judgment is denied, except perhaps an award of the other side's attorney's fees if the local court rules provide for it.

All about "Discovery"

First-time litigants are often surprised that when they get into a lawsuit, after some initial meetings with lawyers and a flurry of activity, nothing happens for months on end until a few weeks before the trial, when there is another flurry of activity.

The exception is the process of "discovery," which generally takes three forms: written interrogatories, oral depositions, and requests for production of documents. Interrogatories are written questions that one party propounds to the other. The answering party is required to respond under oath. If a party fails to respond, the judge can throw out the case if the plaintiff is the recalcitrant party, or award a judgment against a nonresponding defendant. A request for production of documents is just that: a demand that a list of documents be produced for inspection and copying. A party is generally not required to create a document if the document doesn't exist. Other than that, almost any document must be produced if it is even remotely relevant to the case.

The most onerous form of discovery is the oral deposition. A party called for a deposition is required to appear—usually in the office of the opponent's attorney—and answer questions under oath. A court reporter is usually present who records every question and answer, and the resulting testimony is transcribed into book form. The deposition serves a number of purposes, the principal one being to help the party build a case or defend against the plaintiff's case. Also, anything that a party says in a deposition can be used against that party at the trial. For example, in a car accident case, if the defendant admits to "having a few beers" shortly before the accident, but denies it at the trial, the defendant will not only look like a liar (having made contradictory statements under oath) but will also look foolish to the jury.

For asset protection purposes, there is one thing we need to be vigilant about during discovery: disclosure of the defendant's assets. Plaintiffs often are very eager to learn where the defendant's assets are located. If prejudgment attachment is possible, a plaintiff's lawyer would love to learn what assets there are to be attached. Even if prejudgment attachment cannot be obtained, knowing the extent of the defendant's assets will help the plaintiff in settlement negotiations, and it will give the plaintiff a road map to the assets if he or she wins at trial.

Unless disclosing the whereabouts of the defendant's assets is beneficial (more on that in the following section), we should resist the disclosure of assets during the discovery process. The rationale for refusing to answer questions about the defendant's assets is that it has no bearing on the case. In a car accident case, whether the defendant owns an office building or has equity in his or her home has no bearing on whether the defendant obeyed the rules of the road, had a few drinks before the accident, or was wearing a seat belt.

Mediation (and Settlement Conferences)

We saw in Chapter 1 that Dr. Nguyen and the plaintiff, Angela Venizelos, were ordered by the judge to attend a mediation. In some jurisdictions, judges will order the parties to attend a mandatory settlement conference. "Mandatory" modifies "conference," not "settlement." The parties are not required to settle the case, but they are required to show up.

Depending on the jurisdiction, a mediation will be conducted by a professional mediator or a local attorney not involved in the case. In some courts, the judge will select the mediator. In others, the parties will select a mediator from an approved list.

As we saw in the case of Dr. Nguyen, a defendant who has finalized his or her asset protection planning may use the mediation or the mandatory settlement conference to spill the beans, i.e., to inform the plaintiff that even if he or she wins, there will be nothing to go after.

Asset protection is most effective in tort or other types of cases where there is some insurance coverage, but not enough to satisfy the plaintiff. Let's assume a car accident in which there is a real possibility that the defendant caused the accident and the defendant has $300,000 in liability coverage. Let's also assume that the plaintiff suffered permanent injuries and loss of wages. The plaintiff's attorney believes that a jury might award as much as $500,000. It is likely, in this scenario, that the first thing the insurance carrier will do following its review of the facts is to offer the plaintiff the full $300,000 in coverage, in full settlement of the case. At that point, the plaintiff will look to the defendant to contribute to the settlement out of his or her own pocket.

But assume that the defendant—like Dr. Nguyen—has already protected his or her assets. By informing the plaintiff's lawyer of this fact, we force the plaintiff into a difficult dilemma: take the $300,000 in settlement or risk a trial. No trial is a sure thing, as every trial lawyer will tell you. It's possible that the trial will produce a zero: a defense verdict. It's also possible that the trial may indeed result in a $500,000 judgment, but that means trying to collect the additional $200,000. It's highly likely that the plaintiff's attorney took the case on a contingency, and may not be willing to spend months or years chasing down the incremental $200,000 when the first $300,000 has already been offered. The temptation to take the $300,000 insurance coverage becomes powerful indeed.

The Trial and the Judgment

Little needs to be said about the trial itself. Most civil cases don't get that far: 98 percent of all cases are settled or dropped before trial. One thing that should be noted is that, just as the plaintiff usually has no right to force the defendant to disclose his or her assets prior to trial, he or she generally cannot force disclosure during the trial either.

The winner of a lawsuit, be it the plaintiff or the defendant, is entitled to a judgment. If the judgment is for the defendant, the plaintiff gets nothing. The defendant may be awarded a specific sum as reimbursement for his or her court costs, but this is rare, which is why so many questionable lawsuits are brought with impunity: there is little downside to losing.

If the plaintiff sues for money and prevails, he or she obtains a judgment for a specified sum. In order for the judgment to be effective, the plaintiff must enter it on the judgment roll in the local courthouse. This is notice to the world that the plaintiff has been awarded a judgment against a particular person for a specific amount. The judgment will remain on the records until the defendant pays it; at that time, the plaintiff will be required to file a satisfaction of judgment.

For our purposes, it is important to note that a judgment may be recorded only against the specific defendant who lost at the trial. That means that if the defendant is John Smith Incorporated, a corporation, the judgment is effective only against that corporation and its assets. It is not effective against John Smith the individual or his personal assets, even though he may own all the shares of the corporation and control its affairs.

Entering a judgment against a defendant on the judgment roll doesn't shift any of the defendant's assets to the plaintiff; the plaintiff still must do something more. One of the first, and potentially most lethal, things the plaintiff (now called a judgment creditor) can do is record the judgment in any county where he or she thinks the defendant (now the judgment debtor) owns real estate. Here's how potentially devastating that is: if the judgment is against John Smith Inc., recording the judgment in Los Angeles County will act as a lien against all real estate owned by John Smith Inc. in Los Angeles County. This lien operates exactly like a mortgage. It will prevent the judgment debtor from selling the property until the judgment is paid off, since no one will buy a parcel of property that is encumbered by a lien. What is worse, no one will lend money on the property, because the lender's mortgage will be junior to the judgment lien. And still worse, if there is an existing mortgage on the property, the judgment debtor will in effect be making monthly payments and building up equity for a parcel of property that the judgment creditor may one day take. And even worse yet, the unpaid judgment accrues interest. Remember: the judgment creditor does not have to know the whereabouts of the debtor's real estate in the county for the lien to be effective. Indeed, the judgment creditor doesn't even have to know if the debtor owns real estate in the county.

The lien will attach to all of the real estate in that county titled in the judgment debtor's name, but it will not attach to real estate that is no longer titled in the debtor's name on the day the lien is entered. That means that we must strive to remove real estate from the defendant's name before a judgment becomes effective. This may eventually be deemed a fraudulent conveyance (more on that in Chapter 4), but at least we'll live to fight another day. If a lien is allowed to be recorded against a particular parcel of property, it's "Game Over!" The plaintiff wins.

All of this leads us to Klueger's Axiom.

> **Klueger's Axiom:** Asset Protection is not about preventing a creditor from seizing your assets. It's about preventing a creditor from tying up, i.e., encumbering your assets.

As we have seen, a judgment against John Smith Incorporated shouldn't result in a lien against Mr. John Smith's property, since Mr. John Smith was not the defendant. But what is true in theory doesn't always work out that way in real life. Very often the county recorder's computers will sweep up assets that should not be the subject of a judgment, leaving us to explain to a judge why a lien against a parcel of property should be removed. In our example, John Smith wouldn't have had this problem if he had named his corporation "Schmidlapp, Inc.," which leads us to Klueger's Rule of Names.

> **Klueger's Rule of Names:** Don't make life too easy for your creditors. Don't use your own name for the names of your corporations, limited liability companies, trusts, or anything else that might hold title to your assets.

Appeals

Is it possible to prevent a creditor from going after your assets even after a judgment in the creditor's favor has been entered? Yes. Almost every civil judgment may be appealed to the state (or federal) court of appeals. An appeal is commenced by filing a notice of appeal within a relatively short time after the judgment is entered. Merely appealing the case does not prevent the plaintiff from going after the defendant's assets. What stops the plaintiff is the filing of an appeals bond. Bonding companies that specialize in appeals bonds will issue a bond that must at least cover the amount of the judgment. For example, if the court awarded a judgment for $1 million to the plaintiff, it will require a bond in the principal amount of at least $1 million in order to stay the plaintiff's ability to execute on his judgment. The cost of the bond is entirely a matter of the defendant's creditworthiness. The bonding company may require a security interest in the defendant's real estate to ensure that there will still be assets available if the defendant loses the appeal.

Postjudgment Examinations

A plaintiff who obtains a judgment against a defendant is permitted to conduct a postjudgment examination, often referred to as a debtor's exam, for the sole purpose of determining the location of a debtor's assets. If you're thinking of transferring your assets to someone else following the entry of the judgment and before the debtor's exam, think again. Such a transfer will undoubtedly be deemed to be a fraudulent conveyance. In some jurisdictions, giving notice of the debtor's exam results in a lien on the debtor's assets, preventing the transfer of assets. See, for example, *California Code of Civil Procedure* §708.110 and *New York Civil Practice Law & Rules* §5229.

In most jurisdictions, the debtor's exam is conducted in the courthouse where the trial was held, but not always before a judge. In all cases, the defendant is sworn in, and the plaintiff's attorney inquires as to any assets that the defendant has or may have had. Smart plaintiffs' attorneys will ask about any trusts, limited liability companies, or other entities in which the defendant owns an interest. Of course, the defendant must answer truthfully, since he or she is under oath. When we devise an asset protection plan, we assume that the plaintiff will eventually learn about everything we did.

> **Remember:** Asset protection isn't about hiding your assets. It's about structuring your assets so that even if the creditors know where your assets are, they cannot get at them.

If the plaintiff believes that someone other than the debtor is holding assets belonging to the debtor, the plaintiff may also call that person into court to be examined about those assets.

If the defendant moves out of state, the plaintiff must first domesticate the judgment in the state to which the defendant moved. That usually entails little more than bringing a copy of the judgment to the local courthouse and registering it. If the defendant's assets are in yet another state, the plaintiff can domesticate the judgment in that state as well, and then conduct a debtor's exam in that state. Indeed, there is no limit on the number of places in which a judgment creditor may domesticate the judgment.

Nor is there a limit on the number of times a creditor may conduct a debtor's exam. If one debtor's exam yields no assets, the creditor may call the debtor in for another exam three, four, or six months later, depending on the local court rules.

Conducting a debtor's exam in a foreign country may not be nearly as easy. The United States maintains treaties with some countries to permit the domestication of U.S. judgments there, but by no means does this include every country. As described in Chapter 10, we will form foreign trusts in countries that will not recognize a U.S. judgment.

What happens if the debtor's exam reveals that the debtor (or a third person) possesses assets that are not exempt from seizure? This is where things can get really ugly. If there is a judge present (or available), the creditor may ask that the judge issue a turnover order, ordering the debtor to turn over the asset. Debtors have known to show up for a debtor's exam in a fancy new car and wind up going home on the bus!

CHAPTER 3

An Overview of Asset Protection Planning

I know an attorney in southern California who does a lot of foreign trusts. In fact, if you go to his office seeking a partnership agreement, you'll wind up with a foreign trust. If you want a limited liability company, you'll get a foreign trust. If you need asset protection, you'll get a foreign trust, no matter who you are or where your assets are located. This attorney isn't actually practicing law; he's selling foreign trusts, much in the same way that McDonald's sells hamburgers, except that McDonald's has a larger menu. Of course, on occasion, one of this attorney's clients actually does need a foreign trust; after all, a stopped clock does tell the right time twice each day.

This is no one way to do asset protection. When it comes to asset protection, every person has different needs. A married person with $5 million in cash who resides in California has very different asset protection needs than a single person with $5 million in real estate residing in New York. In the world of asset protection, one size does not fit all.

The Four Variables

Four variables must be examined before we can craft an asset protection plan for a given individual or married couple. That means that foreign trusts don't invariably "work" as asset protection devices, nor do trusts, nor do corporations. Each might work for one person and fail for another. These are the four variables that must be addressed:

- Who is the likely plaintiff?
- Who is the likely defendant?
- What is the nature of the claim?
- What assets are we seeking to protect?

Let's examine each of these variables in depth.

Who Is the Likely Plaintiff?

Many people want asset protection simply because they are wealthy and fear that they're walking around with a target painted on them. A lawsuit is not likely to come from any particular source, but could come from anywhere, and when it comes, they want to be prepared.

However, such people are in a minority. Most people have a sense of the nature of people who will be suing them, if not their actual identities. If you're a neurosurgeon, the plaintiffs are likely to be your former patients. If you're a real estate developer, the plaintiff is likely to be the lender whose loan you personally guaranteed. If you own a 100-unit apartment building, the plaintiffs are likely to be your tenants.

We need to know who the plaintiffs will be because different plaintiffs can be dealt with differently.

Commercial creditors. If a bank lends you money and you don't repay it, the bank will sue you, and they will have no compunction about spending more money than you borrowed to collect the debt. If they didn't, anyone who borrowed a small amount of money would default on the debt, knowing that it would be too expensive for the bank to try to collect. As a result, banks make a wise business decision to try to collect as many debts as they can, even if some collection actions are money losers.

Similarly, if you sell T-shirts with Mickey Mouse's likeness on them without first obtaining a license from Disney, you can safely assume that Disney will sue you, even if you only made a $1,000 profit on the shirts and even if far more than $1,000 will be expended in legal fees to shut you down. The rationale is the same: if they made a business decision not to sue you because you're too small, soon every small fry would be selling Mickey Mouse T-shirts. So Disney sues the big and the small, in the hope of deterring everyone.

I have considerable grudging respect for banks and other business creditors. They can be tenacious in their collection efforts. If you borrow money from a bank and don't repay it, they tend to take it personally. We noted in Chapter 2 that one of the creditor's weapons is a postjudgment debtor's exam. If you owe a large judgment to a bank, you can count on attending debtor's exams until the debt is paid.

Government creditors. It's very different when you're dealing with a government creditor. If the creditor is the IRS or a state taxing authority, you may owe them money, but they didn't actually lend you money, and no one at the IRS is going to lose his or her job if the debt isn't collected. The IRS has two principal weapons at its disposal: the wage levy (more on that later in this chapter) and the lien on real estate. We saw in Chapter 2 that a lien filed in the county where the judgment debtor's real estate is located will tie up the property until the debt is repaid. That's how the IRS collects a lot of taxes. But we also saw that if the debtor has no real estate in his or her name, the lien will not attach.

I often lecture to groups of attorneys. For years, I have been asking two questions in these lectures. First, I ask for a show of hands from all attorneys in the room who have ever attended a debtor's exam. Most attorneys have attended at least one debtor's exam. Next, I ask for a show of hands from attorneys who have attended a debtor's exam called by the IRS. In all the years I have been posing this question, I have only had one or two attorneys admit to attending a debtor's exam conducted by the IRS. Because the IRS generally does not conduct debtors' exams, if they cannot attach assets by means of a lien or a wage levy, they are not likely to collect the debt.

What makes life even more difficult for the IRS is that it is just about the only creditor subject to a statute of limitations on collecting taxes. The statute of limitations on tax debt is 10 years, and it's measured from the date that the tax is assessed. If you file a tax return on April 15, 2008 for the 2007 tax year showing that you owe $10,000, but you don't pay the $10,000, the IRS has until April 15, 2018 to collect the tax. If the IRS hasn't figured out by then where your assets are, you're home free. Remember: the statute of limitations begins to run only on the date of assessment, and there can be no assessment if no tax return is filed. If you never filed a return for a given year, there is no time limit on the IRS's ability to collect.

However, the situation is very different if your government creditor is the Federal Trade Commission (FTC). The FTC is charged with preventing a wide range of consumer fraud. It has an arsenal of powers, including issuing injunctions, seizing the assets it can find, and ordering the turnover of other assets it cannot find, all before a trial. People who have fallen victim to the FTC have found their businesses raided, all of their records and computers hauled away, and their bank accounts frozen before they knew what hit them. There have been instances where the seizure of assets was so thorough that the victims barely had the money to hire attorneys to defend themselves. Bottom line: if you think you might fall victim to the FTC, you need to plan ahead.

Government creditors—especially federal government creditors such as the IRS and the FTC—differ from other creditors in one other important respect: they are generally not subject to state exemptions from attachment and seizure of assets. The reason they are exempt lies in Article IV, Clause 2 of the United States Constitution, the "Supremacy Clause." As a result of the Supremacy Clause, any and every state law that provides an exemption from seizure must give way to any federal statute that permits the seizure of the asset. For example, a state statute may provide a homestead exemption, which prohibits a creditor from seizing a home, at least to the extent that the value of the home does not exceed the state homestead exemption. But the Internal Revenue Code, which has its own set of exemptions, contains no homestead exemption. If the IRS wishes to seize a residence, no state homestead law will stand in the way. As you might expect, the exemptions from seizure contained in the Internal Revenue Code are not nearly as generous as most state exemption schemes.

Similarly, many states either limit or prohibit the garnishment of a debtor's wages. The Internal Revenue Code contains no such limitation. The result is that if the IRS is the creditor, the state limitation has no effect, and the IRS is free to take the lion's share of a debtor's wages.

The Supremacy Clause can work in a debtor's favor. As we shall see in Chapter 5, money that is placed in a retirement plan governed by the Employee Retirement Income Security Act of 1974 (ERISA) is almost always shielded from creditors. ERISA is a federal statute, and most pension plans, 401(k) plans, and profit-sharing plans are governed by ERISA. It will likely trump any state statute that would make the transfer of the money into the retirement plan a fraudulent conveyance.

It gets more complicated when we consider whether a government creditor can take a particular asset. Generally, the federal government is subject to state law notions of whether a person owns an interest in an asset in the first place. For example, if State X says that a debtor owns only a half interest in a parcel of real estate and that a creditor can get at only that half, the federal government is generally subject to that restriction.

Tort creditors. A tort is a civil (as opposed to criminal) wrong. The most prevalent tort is negligence. Libel, slander, battery, and false imprisonment are all torts, but they are not nearly as common as negligence. In almost every tort action, the plaintiff seeks an award of money damages from the defendant.

Plaintiffs in negligence cases are very different from commercial and government creditors. For one, the plaintiff's attorney is usually working the case on a contingency, usually for a third but in some instances as much as half of the proceeds derived from a settlement or a trial. In many cases, the attorney is the real instigator of the lawsuit. Many negligence attorneys advertise for cases, informing the citizens of their "rights." The economics of their legal practices dictate that they must settle the overwhelming percentage of the cases they bring; they would quickly go broke if a majority of their cases went to trial. Negligence cases differ from other lawsuits in one other particular: the defendant often has some form of insurance that will pay all or part of the plaintiff's claim. The plaintiff's attorney's job, therefore, is to get at as much of the insurance coverage as possible in the least amount of time and then move on to the next case. What makes a negligence case even more unusual is that the defendant's attorney is often appointed by the insurance carrier, and the insurance carrier's objective (to keep the insurance payoff as low as possible) and the defendant's objective (to make sure that only insurance money is used to pay the plaintiff) are often in conflict.

If it sounds like protecting your assets from negligence attorneys is usually easier than protecting your assets from commercial plaintiffs, you're right. It is.

Secured and unsecured creditors. If you have ever given a mortgage or a deed of trust to a bank to purchase a home, the bank is a secured creditor. The mortgage permits the bank to take the house if you default in the payment of the promissory note. The bank is not subject to any exemptions created under state law; the bank simply takes the house. Nor does the bank need to sue you to recover the house. Every state provides the bank with a simplified foreclosure proceeding. You may have some defenses against the foreclosure action and, depending on state law, you may have the ability to buy back (redeem) the house in the foreclosure, but your rights are severely limited.

If you haven't signed something that gives a lender a security interest in a particular parcel of property, the creditor is likely to be an unsecured creditor. That means the creditor does not have a right to go against any particular parcel of property. The creditor will have to sue, get a judgment, and then try to enforce the judgment against whatever assets he or she can find. Even after the judgment is recorded, the creditor is still only an unsecured creditor.

Very often, a particular parcel of property is encumbered by both secured and unsecured debts. For example, a buyer may have given a bank a mortgage in order to acquire the property. Later, the same buyer may have borrowed on the property again, in which case the property will be burdened by a second mortgage. If there are unpaid property taxes and a judgment was recorded against the property, all of these debts are junior to the first mortgage, which is the senior lien. If the bank that first loaned funds to buy the property institutes a foreclosure action, the rights of all the other creditors in the property are wiped out. (That's the derivation of the term "foreclosure.") The junior lienors don't lose their rights to be repaid; they just can't go against this particular piece of property.

Whenever we craft an asset protection plan, we need to take the secured creditors into account. Transferring an asset will do nothing to avoid secured creditors; their liens will follow the property into the hands of the transferee.

On occasion, the existence of secured debt will work in our favor, especially if the mortgage was given to someone friendly to the debtor. Even if the asset is more valuable than the amount of the secured creditor's debt, many unsecured creditors will not bother trying to take a parcel of property knowing that it is burdened by another creditor in a superior position.

Who Is the Likely Defendant?

When I meet with asset protection clients and ask them who they think will be the likely defendant, the question surprises them. "Me" is the usual answer: "I'm going to be the defendant—that's why I'm here."

But the question is more complicated than that. As we shall see in greater detail in Chapter 8, if you are a limited partner in a limited partnership, the extent to which the limited partnership will shield your assets, and which assets it will shield, depends on whether the defendant is the limited partnership itself or its partners.

Similarly, certain claims may be brought only against a corporate defendant. The shareholders of the corporation may be immune from suit. More on that in Chapter 7.

As we shall see in Chapter 6, whether a plaintiff can bring an action against both a husband and a wife or is limited to only one of the spouses may make all the difference in the world. In my law practice, I frequently meet with business owners and real estate developers who have guaranteed corporate debts.

I always ask my client, "Did only you sign the guarantee, or did your wife also sign?" Very often the answer is "I don't remember." But the asset protection planning we do might hinge on the answer. If Mr. Businessman was the only guarantor, only he will be the defendant. If he and his wife both signed the guarantee, they will both be defendants, and any planning we undertake to shift assets between the spouses will be fruitless.

What Is the Nature of the Claim?

Just as it is important to get a fix on the likely plaintiff and defendant, it is also important to know as precisely as possible what the lawsuit will be about. Here's an example of how one fact can change everything: If a plaintiff has won a large verdict following an automobile accident, the defendant can discharge, i.e., wipe out the judgment by filing for bankruptcy if the accident did not involve alcohol (see 11 U.S.C. §54). We may not have any intention of filing for bankruptcy, but it may be beneficial to know that the debt is dischargeable when we're negotiating a settlement with the plaintiff's attorneys.

Here are some common variables:

Is the claim civil or criminal in nature? When we discussed government creditors, such as the IRS, the FTC, or any other government agency, we assumed the claim was civil in nature, i.e., the government was suing to recover monetary damages or, at worst, obtain an injunction to prevent the recurrence of some conduct it deems objectionable. But if the case is criminal—i.e., if the government agency wishes to throw the defendant behind bars (whether or not it also wants money)—then everything changes. The reason is that moving assets that are the fruits of a crime or moving assets to prevent the discovery of a crime is money laundering, and money laundering is itself a crime. Money laundering cannot exist in a vacuum; it always exists to aid some other crime. No attorney can advise a client to commit a crime or assist a client in committing a crime. If the claim is criminal, asset protection won't work.

Is there prejudgment attachment? As we saw in Chapter 2, it is usually the case that a creditor must wait until he or she obtains a judgment before going after the assets. That means that time is on our side. But certain other claims are amenable to prejudgment attachment, in which case we will have to move quickly.

How early (or late) are we planning? We'll discuss fraudulent conveyances in greater depth in the next chapter. For planning purposes, we need to know how early or late we're doing the planning, i.e., whether the claim has matured beyond the mere possibility of becoming a judgment, to whether a lawsuit has been threatened, to whether a lawsuit has been filed, to whether the trial has been set, to whether the trial has occurred, to whether a judgment has been entered. The later we do the planning, the more risk we run that what we do

> **Klueger's Shortest Rule of Asset Protection Planning:** Plan early.

will be deemed a fraudulent conveyance. Which brings us to Klueger's Shortest (and best) Rule of Asset Protection Planning.

What Are the Assets We Are Seeking to Protect?

It is usually the case that the key variable is the assets themselves. Most wealthy individuals desiring asset protection own a basket of different assets, some of which are more easily shielded than others. The attorney who sells every client a foreign trust regardless of the nature of the client's assets may be helping some clients, but not others, and there certainly is no planning involved with what he is doing. Before we can plan to protect the assets, we must have a firm fix on what the assets are.

Who owns the asset? On more occasions than you might believe, clients come to me desperate to preserve a particular asset from creditors. A man who has just caused a car accident and who owns a mountain cabin that is the principal joy in his life suddenly perceives that the plaintiff might take the cabin. But when we pull the deed from the county recorder, we find that our client doesn't own the cabin at all: his corporation, or a partnership, or his wife, or his uncle actually owns the cabin. If a spouse, a controlled entity, or a relative owns the asset, a different asset protection plan may be necessary for each. When it comes to real estate, there is no substitute for actually pulling the deed and determining who the owner is.

As we shall see in Chapter 6, if a husband and wife are co-owners, some states that have "tenancy by the entirety" statutes may shield the asset from creditors. But if the same asset is owned by the same spouses in a community property state such as California, a creditor might be able to take the property, even if only one spouse is the debtor. And in yet other states, if two spouses are co-owners and only one spouse is the debtor, the creditor may be able to seize only half the property.

Will the creditor want the asset? It often happens that a client asks me to protect a business from creditors. The business produces a healthy profit for the owner, and if the owner were to sell the business on the open market, the business could fetch a price equal to many times its annual earnings. Whenever the asset that is exposed is a business, I ask my client this question: "What would happen to the business if you walked away?" In other words, is this a type of business that could survive without the services of the entrepreneur who founded it and runs it every day, or would it collapse if the owner leaves?

If the business would fold without the owner, it is not likely that any creditor would want to take the business. It is sometimes difficult for business owners to understand that a business that might generate a hefty price if sold might have no value if taken. If the business were sold, the buyer would require the seller to remain in the business for a few months to provide the buyer with a smooth transition. During this period, the seller would introduce the buyer to the seller's suppliers, key customers, distributors, etc., and train the buyer in all of the nuances of the business. None of that will happen if a creditor takes the business.

If a business is sold, the buyer will likely require the seller to enter into a non-compete agreement with the seller. That won't happen if the business is seized; after the creditor seizes the business, the debtor will be free to open a competing business across the street and invite all of his prior customers to do business with him. The creditor will be left with the expenses of the business, but none of the revenues. Smart creditors don't do that.

However, even if the business is one that a creditor would never take, we still need to be careful, since the business may own an asset that a creditor might want. For example, most businesses have accounts receivable. If the debtor is the business, a creditor might seek to have a receiver appointed by a judge. The receiver takes just enough of the accounts receivable to retire the debt to the creditor and leaves. This does not happen often, since receivers are expensive (the creditor must pay for the receiver) and smart debtors usually can discount and accelerate the payment of receivables before a receiver can be appointed.

It is not just businesses that a creditor might find unpalatable. A parcel of real estate may be "untouchable." For example, one of the worst things that can happen to anyone who owns real estate is to have it become subject to environmental cleanup laws. Under the Comprehensive Environmental Response, Compensation, and Liability Act (CERCLA), the federal government can order a landowner to clean up any contamination on his or her property, whether or not the landowner caused the contamination. Once that happens, not only does the value of the property fall to zero, but no creditor—not even a bank holding a mortgage—will take the property, since anyone who owns the property becomes liable for the debt.

Is the asset exempt? If the asset is exempt, the creditors can't touch it. More on that in Chapter 5. But for planning purposes, the inquiry doesn't stop there. An asset may be exempt from creditors now, but it might not always be. Cash that is safely tucked inside a 401(k) plan or an IRA may suddenly be subject to creditors when the assets are removed from the plan. A residence exempt from creditors in a state with a "tenancy by the entirety" statute may become vulnerable if one of the spouses dies or they are divorced. Finding that assets are exempt is often the beginning of the inquiry, not the end.

How difficult will seizure of the asset be? This may be the real "bottom line" criterion. Certain assets are more easily shielded from creditors than others. As a general rule, real estate is more difficult to protect than cash, stocks, mutual funds, and all other liquid and near-liquid assets, for the simple reason

---

The Asset Protection Planner's Deepest, Darkest Secret Revealed!

There are two types of asset protection: easy asset protection and difficult asset protection. Difficult asset protection involves real estate. Easy asset protection involves everything else.

---

that you can move all other types of assets, but you cannot move real estate. Which brings us to the deepest, darkest asset protection secret.

Not all real estate is the same. A building that is encumbered by a mortgage is worth far less to a creditor than a building that is "free and clear." If the building is encumbered, a creditor who takes the building will either have to pay off the mortgage in full or pay the mortgage as it comes due every month. That might make the building far less attractive. (As we shall see in Chapter 11 in our discussion of "equity stripping," we might place a mortgage on the property to keep a creditor at bay.) Depending on the size of the creditor's claim, the location of the real estate may make the real estate less attractive. A creditor located in Vermont may have no difficulty seizing Vermont real estate—but if the real estate is located in Montana, the creditor might have difficulty even locating the property; in addition, he or she will have to

---

Should Neurosurgeons Own Apartment Buildings?

The value of every investment is, at least in part, a function of its risk. If the risk inherent in an asset is great, the reward must be commensurately great, or no one would make the investment. If two investments brought the exact same rate of return, but one was riskier than the other, no one would buy the riskier investment. Some people buy "junk" bonds—bonds that are not backed up by anything. Other people buy Treasury Bills, or T-Bills, which are backed by the full faith and credit of the United States. For the T-Bills to go into default, the United States of America would have to go belly-up, an unforeseeable event. T-Bills produce lower yields than junk bonds, as everyone expects and accepts. Economists have a technical term for the risk inherent in an asset: the "beta factor," which is the measurement of the riskiness of the asset compared to all other assets.

Real estate also follows the same risk/reward dichotomy. Since operating an apartment building carries greater risks than putting your money into a money market fund, you would expect a greater rate of return from an apartment building than a money market fund.

The limitation of this analysis is that it doesn't take into account who owns the asset and whether the asset can be taken by a creditor. Consider a neurosurgeon who owns an apartment building that produces a 15 percent annual return on investment. He also owns

---

> a money market account that produces a 5 percent annual return. But let us assume that the neurosurgeon has just been sued for malpractice. In weighing the risks and rewards of holding each asset, should we not now compare the relative risk of a creditor taking the apartment building versus the risk of the creditor taking the money market account?
>
> If it is highly likely that the creditor can take the apartment building, it would seem that the apartment building should produce far more than a 15 percent rate of return. If it is also unlikely that a creditor could seize the money market account, would it not make the money market account more valuable than the apartment building?
>
> **Query #1:** When the neurosurgeon is sued, wouldn't he be wise to sell the apartment building and put the proceeds into a money market fund?
>
> **Query #2:** Why don't more neurosurgeons sell their real estate when they are sued?

engage Montana lawyers and might even have to travel to Montana. It might not be worth it.

Don't Forget Income Protection

Consider the case of Mr. Fabulous Athlete, known to his fans, the press, and his entourage as "M-Fab." M-Fab's agent was successful in negotiating a multimillion-dollar salary for M-Fab. With the proceeds, M-Fab acquired homes in Beverly Hills and the Côte d'Azur and a 252-acre ranch in Jackson Hole, Wyoming. He owned a chain of theaters, a sports bar, and a health club. His agent was wise enough to ensure that all M-Fab's assets were protected from creditors' claims right from the start. No one could ever claim that what M-Fab did was a fraudulent conveyance.

Things were going swimmingly until M-Fab acted as a "compensated spokesperson" for a skin care product that not only didn't work—it harmed the skin. It turned out that M-Fab had a hunch that the stuff didn't work, but the pay was too good to complain. When all this came to light, M-Fab was sued, and a huge judgment was entered against him.

M-Fab knew his assets were completely shielded, so he didn't need to worry—or so he thought. Then his agent reminded M-Fab that in one crucial respect, he was no different from any minimum-wage worker in a cannery: he worked on a salary, a salary that was subject to garnishment. Those checks that came in every two weeks were huge, but they were salary checks nonetheless. All the judgment creditors had to do was serve garnishment notices on his employer, New York Knights, Inc., requiring them to turn over a portion of M-Fab's pay to the creditors. What was the chance that New York Knights, Inc. would fail to respond to the garnishment? None whatsoever. The team would do almost anything to keep M-Fab happy, but if they failed to honor the garnishment, they would be liable to M-Fab's creditors. They didn't love M-Fab that much.

In some cases, there are strategies that we can employ to legally circumvent a garnishment. But the point here is that for some debtors who receive regular income by way of a salary from an unrelated employer, asset protection doesn't solve all problems. We still need to deal with the debtor's income.

Don't Forget the Taxes!

Almost every step we take in the asset protection process implicates taxes. That's because asset protection most often entails transferring assets, and when we do that, we need to be careful that we do not incur one form of taxation or another. Most people don't think it's very good planning to incur a present tax in order to avoid a future creditor.

If we sell an asset that has appreciated in value, we will likely incur a capital gains tax, measured by the difference between the sale price of the asset and what the seller paid for it. If we give an asset away, it will likely result in a gift tax. Depending on the state (or even the county) in which the donor resides, a transfer may result in increased property taxes, sales taxes, or transfer taxes. Bottom line: we need to be careful when we transfer assets.

All about Fraudulent Conveyances

Here is the world's most archetypical fraudulent conveyance:

Mr. Jones has just been sued for $10 million resulting from his default on his guarantee of a corporate loan. He immediately quitclaims his home to his nephew, Irving. He withdraws all of his savings from the bank, flies to Patagonia, finds a hollow tree, and stashes all the money. He transfers the ownership of his business to his children.

Will it work? It might. But only if Mr. Jones is lucky enough to have the world's stupidest and laziest creditors.

Before we can craft any asset protection plan, we must consider the fraudulent conveyance laws. If no such laws existed, we wouldn't need attorneys who specialize in asset protection, and we certainly wouldn't need this book. All we would need is a friendly nephew who would be willing to hold on to our assets until the creditor problem blows over. We might be inconvenienced by having a nephew hold on to our assets or our cash, but it beats losing the assets to creditors.

Every inquiry into fraudulent conveyances should be (but often isn't) a two-part inquiry:

- Question #1: What is a fraudulent conveyance?
- Question #2: If a transfer is a fraudulent conveyance, what are the consequences?

Too often, only the first question is raised. I have sat in asset protection seminars where speakers droned on for hours trying to determine the exact nature of a fraudulent conveyance, never considering what it means if a conveyance is one. We won't make that mistake here.

If, after reading this chapter, you scratch your head and wonder, "Exactly what is a fraudulent conveyance?" you won't be alone. No one knows exactly what a fraudulent conveyance is. Some people think that, like pornography, they "know it when they see it." The inherent difficulty in defining a fraudulent conveyance often works to our advantage, because creditors also have difficulty defining a fraudulent conveyance.

The Basics: Two Types of Fraudulent Conveyances

Actual Fraud

Things get complicated right at the start. There are two types of fraudulent conveyances: those involving "actual" fraud and those involving "constructive" fraud. They are very close, and very often indistinguishable. The best definition of actual fraud, contained in the Uniform Fraudulent Transfer Act (UFTA) and incorporated into the laws of many states, is that it is a transfer made with actual intent to hinder, delay, or defraud any creditor of the debtor.

However, not every transfer that hinders, delays, or defrauds a creditor is a fraudulent conveyance. If it were, making a monthly mortgage payment on time would be a fraudulent conveyance if it made life more difficult for other creditors. More is required. In order for a transfer to constitute actual fraud, not only must it be made with the prohibited animus of hindering, delaying, or defrauding a creditor, but the transfer must be made without receiving a reasonably equivalent value in exchange for the transfer or obligation, and either of these two factors must also be true:

- The transferor was engaged or was about to be engaged in a business or a transaction for which the remaining assets of the debtor were unreasonably small in relation to the business or transaction.
- The transferor intended to incur, or believed or reasonably should have believed that he or she would incur, debts beyond his or her ability to pay as they became due.

See, for example, *California Civil Code* §3439.04.

Here's what this means in plain English: it's actual fraud if you give something away without receiving something of equivalent value at a time when you know you won't be able to pay your debts. But even if that is true, it's not actual fraud if you didn't have the requisite bad intent.

It's very difficult to prove actual fraud, for the simple reason that most people don't leave behind notes saying, "I sure hope I can delay or hinder my creditors by doing this." Consequently, the only way to prove actual fraud is by examining the facts and circumstances of the transaction, and for that the courts have, over the years, developed a series of "badges of fraud." If you flunk one or more of the badges of fraud, a court will likely find that there was actual fraud. The problem is that it isn't a simple matter of adding up which you passed and which you failed and toting up the final score. You may flunk only one of the badges of fraud and still be found to have committed actual fraud. In fact, those of us who read all the cases have the sneaking suspicion that the judges decide in advance whether a transaction is a fraudulent conveyance or not and fill in the scorecard later.

Nevertheless, here are the badges of fraud, as they are spelled out in §4 of the UFTA:

Badge #1: Was the transfer to an insider? If the transfer is to a relative, a friend, or someone who is a fiduciary of the transferor, such as a trustee of a trust, it's a transfer to an insider. When people give away assets to hinder their creditors, it's generally to an insider.

Badge #2: Did the debtor retain possession, control, or enjoyment of the asset after the transfer? If you purport to give an asset away, but keep the income or the management of the asset after you purportedly give it away, it raises the question of whether you really gave it away or just pretended to.

Badge #3: Was the transfer disclosed or concealed? If you hide the fact that you transferred an asset, it presumes that you had something to hide. We never do that. If we transfer real estate, the transfer must be recorded with the county recorder. This is usually not a very important factor.

Badge #4: Had the debtor been sued or threatened with a suit prior to the transfer? I think that this is the most important factor when considering actual (not constructive) fraud. Creditors usually also believe this is the critical factor. They generally have no problem going after an asset that was transferred after a lawsuit was filed or threatened. They very often will not go after an asset that was transferred before a lawsuit was on the horizon.

Badge #5: Did the transferor transfer all or substantially all of his assets? This is very close to the "insolvency" inquiry that is at the heart of constructive fraud (more on that below), which causes so much confusion. It's also one of the more important badges of fraud. If a transferor gives everything or almost everything away, it's a sign that the transfer was done for the purpose of defeating creditors.

Badge #6: Did the transferor abscond? I once heard of a man who not only transferred his assets to the Cayman Islands, but transferred himself there as well. That was many years ago, and I haven't heard of it since. This is not an important factor.

Badge #7: Was the value of the consideration received equivalent to the value of the asset transferred or the amount of the obligation incurred? This is one of the key factors. The rationale behind it is that people do not give assets away without receiving equivalent assets in return unless they intend to hinder their creditors. As we shall see shortly, there are defenses to this. Whenever assets are transferred to a trust, it is a transfer without consideration, but such transfers are often made for reasons having nothing to do with asset protection, such as for estate planning.

Badge #8: Was the debtor insolvent or did the transferor become insolvent shortly after the transfer was made? "Insolvent" is a technical term which we shall discuss shortly. Generally, it means having fewer assets than you have liabilities. The presumption is that if you cannot pay your debts when they come due as a result of a transfer, you made the transfer with the intent of not being able to pay your debts.

Badge #9: Did the transferor make the transfer shortly before or shortly after a substantial debt was incurred? If you did, it's presumed you made the transfer so as not to be able to pay the debt.

Badge #10: Were business assets transferred to a lienholder who then transferred them to an insider? This badge is designed to circumvent the "friendly" mortgage. It is not an important factor.

These badges of fraud all have one thing in common: they involve transfers that are not made in the ordinary course of business, and generally do not make sense unless someone is trying to assure that there will be little or nothing left for a creditor.

It is possible to explain away a transfer of assets to a trust, or the wholesale transfer of assets to a corporation or a limited liability company, without the transfer being a fraudulent conveyance. In fact, the accepted reason for incorporating a business is the limited liability that corporations give their owners (more on that in Chapter 7). Something more is required for a transfer to constitute actual (or even constructive) fraud. Generally, if there is something about the transfer that smells—something that makes an impartial observer of the transaction (such as the judge) believe that something fishy went on—the transfer will likely be deemed a fraudulent conveyance.

Constructive Fraud

It is usually very difficult to prove a person's subjective intent, even with the presence of the badges of fraud. It is easier to prove constructive fraud.

Generally, constructive fraud exists if the transferee did not pay a reasonably equivalent value for the asset, and the transferor was insolvent at the time of the transfer or was made insolvent as a result of the transfer.

[It is never the case that someone makes a transfer and then cannot meet his or her normal obligations. Thus, the key to insolvency—at least for purposes of constructive fraud—is whether the sum of the debtor's assets exceeds the value of the debts.]

A Little History

The first law designed to prevent fraudulent conveyances was the Statute of Elizabeth, which was enacted in England in 1571. Under that statute, a transfer was nullified if the transfer was deemed to have been made for purpose of hindering or defrauding a creditor. The penalty under the Statute of Elizabeth was the forfeiture of the asset, with half of the proceeds going to the creditor and half going to the royal treasury!

From 1571 until 1918, fraudulent transfers in the United States were governed by the Statute of Elizabeth. It was codified into law in 1918 with the adoption of the Uniform Fraudulent Conveyances Act (UFCA). The UFCA was replaced by the UFTA in 1984, but Maryland, New York, Tennessee, and the Virgin Islands still have the UFCA. Every other state has adopted some form of the UFTA.

The UFCA is more friendly to creditors, and the UFTA is more friendly to debtors. The principal difference is in how assets and liabilities are counted for determining whether or not a debtor was insolvent.

We do what is sometimes referred to as a "balance sheet analysis," comparing the debtor's assets with the liabilities, to see if the final result is negative (insolvent) or positive (solvent). The analogy is flawed in one key respect: balance sheets reflect the historical value of the assets, i.e., what the owner paid for them. Balance sheets don't tell us what the assets are worth today, and that's what constructive fraud is all about. Consequently, to determine whether a debtor was solvent at the time of the transfer (or whether the debtor was rendered insolvent by the transfer), we must appraise each and every asset.

Unfortunately for debtors, not all assets are permitted to be counted when determining whether a debtor is insolvent. If an asset is exempt from creditors' claims (see Chapter 5), we cannot count the asset. For example, if an asset has a fair market value of $1 million, but state law gives the owner a $150,000 homestead exemption, it only counts as $850,000 for the purposes of the owner's "balance sheet." If the asset is completely exempt, such as an employee's interest in a "qualified" pension or 401(k) plan, then the asset cannot be counted at all. If real estate is held by spouses as "tenants by the entirety" (more on that in Chapter 6) and only one of the spouses is the debtor, the real estate cannot be counted. If property is subject to a valid lien, such as a mortgage, we must reduce the value of the property by the amount of the lien.

What is more troublesome is the matter of the transferor's liabilities. For purposes of the UFCA and the UFTA, liabilities include not only fixed liabilities such as judgment and promissory notes, but also "contingent liabilities," unfixed liabilities that may become fixed later. Let's assume that the debtor was involved in an auto accident. Perhaps the debtor has already been sued, but since there has not yet been a trial, we don't know whether the plaintiff will collect millions, thousands, or nothing. How do we count this contingent liability? For purposes of compiling the debtor's balance sheet, we might have to obtain a letter from the debtor's personal injury lawyer, asking his opinion of the likely outcome of the trial.

Present Creditors and Future Creditors

Does it matter whether a fraudulent conveyance is determined to be the result of actual fraud or constructive fraud? Perhaps not. If the fraud is constructive, only present creditors have any remedies against the transferor or the transferee of the debtor's assets. If the fraud is actual, present and future creditors have remedies. In practice, however, there is less to this distinction than meets the eye.

Present creditors are not limited to those creditors who have sued, or who even have threatened to sue. If the transferor of assets knows that a lawsuit is imminent—or even likely—the creditor is a present creditor. If a surgeon leaves a sponge in a patient's stomach, the patient becomes a present creditor on the day of the operation, not when the patient's lawyer files a lawsuit or even threatens a lawsuit.

Contrary to popular belief, future creditors do not include all those persons who might file a lawsuit in the future. If you transfer your assets to your nephew Irving on a Monday, and you injure someone in an automobile accident the next Tuesday, the person you injured cannot be a present or future creditor with respect to that transfer. That being the case, what is a future creditor? These are the people that you know today will become your creditors because of some action you will take but have not yet taken (even if they cannot know). For example: I know that if I give all my money to my nephew Irving, and then borrow money from my friend Engelbert, I will not be able to repay the debt to Engelbert. Engelbert is a future creditor, not a present creditor. He must prove actual fraud, not constructive fraud. Of course, since I gave all my money to an "insider" (Badge #1), received nothing in return (Badge #8), and became insolvent as a result of the transfer (Badge #9), Engelbert might not have too much difficulty proving that the transfer was fraudulent, albeit only the "constructive" kind.

Defenses to Fraudulent Conveyances

From everything we've said so far, it might appear that it's difficult to defend against a fraudulent conveyance claim. Don't be fooled. Every fraudulent conveyance lawsuit is basically a "smell test." If the transfer can be explained as something other than an attempt to hinder, delay, or defraud a creditor, i.e., if the transfer doesn't reek of being motivated by creditors, a transferor has a good chance of defeating a fraudulent conveyance claim.

It Is Never a Fraudulent Conveyance to Prefer One Creditor over Another

It is the rare debtor who wishes to avoid paying all of his creditors. In fact, most debtors have no problem in paying all of their creditors except one. In Chapter 1, we saw that Dr. Nguyen paid his bills on time and would not think of avoiding any of his legitimate debts. It was only when a frivolous lawsuit appeared on the horizon that he was grateful to have his asset protection plan in place.

It is not a fraudulent conveyance if you owe money to a series of creditors and you pay some and do not pay others, even if paying some means you cannot pay others. The rule applies even if you prepay one or more of your debts to avoid paying a creditor. Here is an example: Assume that Mr. and Mrs. Brown own a residence that has a fair market value of $1 million. There is a $400,000 mortgage on the residence. They live in a state that permits "tenancy by the entirety," which means that as long as they remain married, a creditor cannot take their home. They also have $300,000 in cash and securities, which is not protected from creditors. In order to shield the $300,000, they prepay their mortgage. The result is that they have less cash and more equity in their home, but the $300,000 that would otherwise be exposed is shielded. The transfer of the $300,000 is not a fraudulent conveyance.

It Is Never a Fraudulent Conveyance to Receive Fair Value for an Asset

There are occasions when the easiest and simplest asset protection strategy is to sell the asset for its fair market value. A sale for fair value can never be a fraudulent conveyance. Let's review: a sale for fair consideration cannot constitute actual fraud, since the failure of adequate consideration is one of the prerequisites a claimant must prove when alleging a fraudulent conveyance. Nor will a sale for adequate consideration constitute constructive fraud, because the seller cannot be rendered insolvent by the sale; the seller is receiving one asset (presumably, cash) in exchange for the asset sold.

This can be somewhat problematic if the asset is not sold for cash, but for a promissory note. An example: Assume that Mr. Brown owns a parcel of real estate valued at $1million. If a judgment is entered against him, the creditor will be able to record the judgment, encumbering the property. The creditor might even foreclose on the property, but will not have to, since the property cannot be sold without the creditor first being paid. So Mr. Brown sells the property to his nephew Irving for $1million. Irving doesn't give Mr. Brown $1million, but instead gives Mr. Brown a $1 million promissory note secured by a deed of trust on the property. The note pays interest at 6 percent per year, which, we will assume, is a market rate of interest.

There is now nothing that a creditor can do with respect to the real estate. The best a creditor can do is attach the note payments as they come due, which is far more difficult to do than record a judgment against a parcel of real estate. It's not a perfect solution, but it might be all that's needed to sufficiently soften up a creditor to produce a desired settlement. We noted in Chapter 3 that one of the questions we must ask before we can craft an asset protection plan is "Who is the plaintiff?" If the plaintiff is a tort claimant whose lawyer is working on a contingency, the prospect of having to wait years for the note payments to be paid is not pleasing. It may be just what is needed to settle the case favorably.

The Asset Is Exempt

We will see in Chapter 5 that certain assets, such as funds deposited in "qualified" retirement plans, are so completely shielded from creditors that notions of whether these assets were fraudulently conveyed are irrelevant.

What Is the Effect of a Fraudulent Conveyance?

We began this chapter by noting that the analysis of fraudulent conveyances should (but does not always) involve two questions. The first question is "What is a fraudulent conveyance?" Once it has been established, or assumed, that a transfer is fraudulent, the second question comes into play: "What is the effect of a fraudulent conveyance?" Stated otherwise: "What are a creditor's remedies if there has been a fraudulent conveyance?"

The creditor's remedies are contained in Section 7 of the Uniform Fraudulent Transfer Act. The principal remedy is "the avoidance of the transfer or obligation to the extent necessary to satisfy the creditor's claim." Simply put, this means that if Mr. Brown, who knows that a judgment is about to be entered against him, transfers his bank accounts and the title to his home to his nephew Irving, Mr. Brown's creditors can sue Irving to recover the assets. In other words, Mr. Brown's creditors, who previously had no grounds to sue Irving for anything, now do. Section 7 of the UFTA gives the creditors the right to an attachment "or other provisional remedy" against the transferred asset. Other "provisional" remedies might include an order freezing any further disposition of the asset by Irving, the appointment of a receiver of the asset if the asset is income-producing, or, if feasible, an order requiring Irving to deposit the asset into the registry of the court. Of course, the court might also order Irving to return the transferred asset. If Mr. Brown had transferred some, but not all, of his assets to Irving, a court might enter an injunction prohibiting Mr. Brown from transferring any more of his assets.

These remedies sound pretty gruesome, and sometimes they are. However, if you consider it carefully, you will note that any remedy directed against the transferee (in our example, Irving) requires that the court have jurisdiction over Irving. If the court has no jurisdiction, the remedies are toothless and the issue of fraudulent conveyances is beside the point. Let's assume that Mr. Brown, who lives in California, transfers his savings to Irving, who lives in Maine. If Irving has never set foot in California, and has no plans to do so, a court order directed against Irving to return the transferred asset will be wholly without effect. Of course, a creditor could hire an attorney in Maine and record a judgment in Maine and proceed against Irving in Maine as if Irving were living in California. But that's expensive and time-consuming, and not all creditors are willing to do it. (Know your plaintiff!)

Keep this discussion in mind when you read Chapter 10, where we deal with foreign asset protection planning. Let's assume that Irving doesn't live in Maine. Let's assume that he lives in the Cook Islands. And let's assume further that Irving isn't a person at all, but a trust company organized under the laws of the Cook Islands, which are in many respects very favorable to debtors and very hostile to creditors. When a creditor seeks to go after the transferee, and the transferee lives in the Cook Islands, it really doesn't matter if the transfer was or wasn't a fraudulent conveyance under U.S. law. Now you have an inkling of how foreign trusts work. More on that in Chapter 10.

Planning for Exempt Assets

We noted in Chapter 3 that one of the most important criteria, if not the most important criterion, in crafting an asset protection plan is to determine what are the assets that we are seeking to protect. In many cases, one of the first things we will seek to determine is the existence and extent of any exempt assets, i.e., assets that cannot be taken by creditors. Some exemptions are limited in scope, others (such as state homestead exemptions) limited in amount.

In some cases, we can use exempt assets as a starting point for a broader asset protection plan. Here is a typical example: Mr. Brown resides in California, a state that has a $75,000 homestead exemption for persons under age 65. A $75,000 homestead exemption means that if Mr. Brown has a judgment entered against him and the creditor tries to take his residence from him, the creditor (or anyone else who bids and buys the residence at the sheriff's sale) must first hand Mr. Brown a check for $75,000. Let's assume that Mr. Brown has $75,000 in a bank account, an account that any creditor would have no difficulty seizing. But let's assume that Mr. Brown removes the $75,000 from the bank and buys a home for $500,000, using the $75,000 as down payment and borrowing $425,000 from the bank. We have converted the $75,000 from a nonexempt asset to an exempt asset. Fraudulent conveyance? Not a chance.

It will become readily apparent that all exempt assets are not equal. We begin with the granddaddy of all exemptions—assets held in a "qualified" retirement plan.

Asset Protection and Retirement Plans

Millions of Americans participate in pension plans, 401(k) plans, and profit-sharing plans offered by their employers. The plans provide an easy way for employees to save for retirement, because the money that an employee contributes to his or her account is tax-deductible, and the investments in the plan appreciate on a tax-exempt basis until the account is withdrawn at retirement. These plans also make sense for employers, because the contributions that they make to the plan give them a tax deduction and go a long way toward providing them with a loyal and stable work force. The occasional Enron-like scandal involving the mismanagement of employee retirement plans is the exception to the rule.

All of these plans are governed by the Employee Retirement Income Security Act of 1974 (ERISA). ERISA is administered by the Department of Labor and the IRS. If the IRS approves a plan (making it a "qualified" plan), employers and employees governed by the plan obtain a tax deduction for monies contributed to the plan. No approval, no deductions. It does not take much for a plan to be approved, and most plans are boilerplate. The key to qualification is nondiscrimination. An employer can write a plan that includes only the executives and leaves out everyone else, but it will never get IRS approval, and none of the contributions to the plan will be deductible.

Each qualified plan has two parts. One is the plan itself, and the other is a trust. The trust has a trustee, which is often the employer or an outside plan administrator. The beneficiaries of the plan are the employees who elect to participate in the plan. Some plans provide for contributions from the employer and the employees; others only the employees.

The tax and retirement benefits of ERISA plans are well known to most participants. What is less known is the extent to which employees' plan accounts are absolutely exempt from creditors' claims. The exemption stems from a requirement that each qualified plan must include a provision to the effect that "benefits provided under the plan may not be assigned or alienated." See 29 USC §1056(d)(1). If the plan does not have such an "antialienation clause," the plan will not be approved.

The provision prohibiting plan assets from being "assigned or alienated" means that a creditor of a plan participant cannot get at the participant's retirement account. It means that the account cannot be seized, levied upon, garnished, foreclosed upon, or any of the other remedies that creditors have when they seek to hunt down a debtor's assets. If the employee files a bankruptcy petition, the assets in the ERISA plan are exempt from the employee's creditors in the bankruptcy.

The antialienation clause in every ERISA plan protects every employee, from the lowest drudge in the mailroom to the owner of the corporation who set up the plan.

Which Plans Are Governed by ERISA?

Most retirement plans sponsored by employers are governed by ERISA. But most plans that are maintained by employees are not governed by ERISA, and hence do not have the antialienation protection. The most common of these are Individual Retirement Accounts (IRAs) and Simplified Employee Pension Plans (SEPs). IRAs and SEPs are retirement plans, but they are not governed by ERISA. A creditor can gain access to these funds. However, as we shall see shortly, some states have enacted their own exemptions governing these retirement plans.

Which Claims Are Shielded by ERISA?

ERISA shields an employee from almost all—but not quite all—creditors' claims. For example, ERISA exempts its participants from all civil judgments.

If an employee on a drunken rampage kills a school bus full of children, there may be millions of dollars in damages, but not one cent of his retirement plan is attachable. Don't believe it? Consider this: Mr. O. J. Simpson lost a $29 million judgment to the heirs of Nicole Simpson. He lost his Heisman trophy, but not one dime of his NFL pension, because it is an ERISA-qualified plan. Negligence claims, breach of contract claims, intentional malfeasance of all kinds—it doesn't matter. ERISA shields its participants from all such claims.

ERISA also shields a participant from the creditors of the participant's spouse. This is a somewhat surprising result. Let's assume that Mrs. Jones contributes part of her weekly earnings to a qualified plan maintained by Acme Widgets. Mrs. Jones resides in Texas, which is a community property state. That means that every time Mrs. Jones contributes a dollar to the plan, 50 cents is really Mr. Jones' money. Let's assume that Mr. Jones runs down a school bus full of children. Can the plaintiffs get at the money in Mrs. Jones' retirement account? Not a chance.

ERISA even shields its participants from state claims, even state tax claims. Assume that Mrs. Jones fails to pay her Texas state income taxes. Obviously, Texas law requires every Texas resident to pay income taxes. Texas, like every other state, maintains a small army of tax collectors who have the full power of seizure and levy over those miscreants who fail to pay their fair share of Texas taxes. Can the state of Texas attach her retirement plan account? Once again, not a chance. The reason is that the Supremacy Clause provides that when a federal statute (such as ERISA and its antialienation requirements) and a state statute conflict, the federal statute prevails.

The antialienation prohibition extends even to criminal conduct. In a landmark case, the United States Supreme Court ruled that a union official who had been convicted of embezzlement could not have his retirement plan assets attached to pay for the judgments of his creditors resulting from his criminal conduct (*Guidry v. Sheetmetal Pension Fund*, 493 US 372 [1990]).

What about Fraudulent Conveyances?

May a creditor of a participant in an ERISA plan set aside a contribution to a plan by alleging that the transfer of the funds into the plan was a fraudulent conveyance? What if the employee transferred funds into the plan with full knowledge that the assets remaining outside the plan would not be sufficient to cover the employee's debts?

It doesn't matter. The simple fact is that ERISA is a federal statute, and ERISA will trump any state fraudulent conveyance statute per the Supremacy Clause. It really doesn't matter how flagrant or egregious the transfer was; the creditors will be left holding the bag.

Exceptions and Limitations

We noted that ERISA exempts most—but not all—creditor claims. There are a few limited exceptions.

Let's return to Mrs. Jones, who failed to pay her Texas state income taxes. As we saw, Texas might be able to levy on her wages or take her home and her stock portfolio, but there is nothing Texas can do with respect to her ERISA-qualified retirement plan. However, let's assume that Mrs. Jones also failed to pay her federal income taxes. Does the IRS suffer under the same limitation that the state of Texas does? It does not. The reason is that the Supremacy Clause does not apply to a federal agency such as the IRS.

The one "creditor" who may be able to attach a portion of the employee's qualified plan assets is the employee's spouse in the event of a divorce. ERISA contains a provision permitting a divorce court judge to issue a Qualified Domestic Relations Order, or QDRO. If the QDRO is served upon the administrator of the plan ordering certain assets to be turned over to the employee's spouse, the plan administrator must comply with the order [29 USC §1056(d)(3)(j)]. A QDRO does not give the spouse any rights to the plan assets greater than the employee had. For example, if under the plan the employee would have had to work for the employer for a minimum number of years in order to "vest" in the plan's benefits and thereby obtain the right to make a withdrawal from the employee's account, the employee's spouse will be subject to the same limitation.

One of the most troublesome limitations is the one that requires the plan to have at least one nonowner participant in order for the antialienation provision of the plan to be effective. Here is an example: Dr. White maintains a profit-sharing plan for his dental office. The only participants in the plan are Dr. White and his wife, who works in the office as a receptionist. The plan qualifies as an ERISA plan, and Dr. White may deduct from his taxes the amounts that he contributes to the plan. But if Dr. White is sued, and his creditors obtain a judgment, his creditors will be able to attach the assets in his retirement account, for the sole reason that there are no participants in the plan other than the owner of the business and his wife. The Supreme Court has ruled that if Dr. White has only one nonowner employee in the plan, then all of the employees, including Dr. White and his wife, will be shielded by the antialienation clause. (See re Yates, 541 US 6 [2004].)

Anyone who maintains a qualified plan whose only participants are owner-participants and who wishes to qualify for the asset protection benefits of ERISA must do one thing: hire an employee. It doesn't matter how little the employee is paid relative to the owner-employees, as long as there is one other participant.

Finally, ERISA protects assets in the plan only while the assets remain in the plan. Once the assets are removed from the plan they lose the protection, even if the employee keeps the distributions in a segregated account. What is worse, most plans (and the tax laws) require the participant to remove assets from the plan when the participant retires. To this extent, ERISA is inferior to some state retirement exemptions, which exempt retirement assets from the claims of creditors even after the plan assets have been removed.

Planning with Retirement Plan Assets

There are some—but not many—planning opportunities for retirement plan assets. People who have large ERISA-qualified holdings consider themselves lucky, safe in the knowledge that creditors cannot get at these assets, at least while the assets are safely tucked in the plan.

The most obvious strategy is to maximize your permitted contributions to the plan. This is easier if you control the plan. If potential creditors are a concern, you might consider amending the plan to permit greater contributions, or even creating a new plan. The contributions you will need to make on behalf of your employees may be a small price to pay relative to the protection the plans might afford you.

May I intentionally overfund my contributions to an ERISA plan? Let's assume that Mr. Black has $500,000 in his ERISA-qualified plan. He makes the maximum permitted annual contributions to the plan. He also has $600,000 in a bank account, money that is exposed to creditor claims. May Mr. Black simply shift the $600,000 into his ERISA account? It's a high-risk strategy. For one, the Internal Revenue Code imposes a 10 percent penalty on excess contributions to any ERISA plan (i.e., contributions above the deduction limitation). Admittedly, many people threatened by creditors will be happy to pay the 10 percent penalty if the balance of the contribution is shielded, but it is problematic that the strategy would work. ERISA shields legal contributions; the antialienation clause in the plan may not shield a contribution not permitted by the plan. Of course, it is possible that a creditor may never become aware of the overfunding. Most creditors, knowing how protected ERISA plans are, don't bother to ask when the contributions were made; they simply assume they cannot get at them. But a savvy creditor might ask, and if the contributions are too large and too recent, the creditor might smoke out an illegal overfunding. (Know your creditor!) All of this assumes that Mr. Black controls the plan. If he doesn't, overfunding is not available, for the simple reason that the plan administrator will not accept the excess contribution.

May I transfer assets from an IRA into a qualified plan? We noted earlier that Individual Retirement Accounts (IRAs) are not governed by ERISA, and hence do not enjoy the protection that ERISA plans do. Very often, employers elect to terminate their ERISA plans and, to avoid taxation on the distributed funds, roll the ERISA account into an IRA. Employees often leave an employer, receive a distribution from their 401(k) plan, and roll the proceeds over into an IRA, for the same tax reason. That's smart tax planning, but terrible asset protection planning, since it involves transferring assets from protected to unprotected status. Is it possible to reverse the process and transfer the IRA account into a qualified plan? It is. All that is required is that the plan permit contributions from IRAs.

Asset Protection and Nonqualified Plans

One state—California—provides a statutory exemption for retirement plans that are not covered by ERISA. The statute provides an unlimited exemption for "private retirement plans" (*California Code of Civil Procedure* §704.115[a]). Unfortunately, the statute does not define what a "private retirement plan" is, but the courts have filled in the gaps. Although the California exemption is unlimited, it is narrow in scope. The plan must arise in an employment setting, and the employer must be a corporation. In other words, you cannot go out and simply wrap your savings account into a "private retirement plan" you draft when your creditors come calling. Most importantly, the plan must be designed and used strictly for retirement purposes. If you use the money before you retire, or if you have retired but don't use the assets for retirement needs, there is no way that the plan will qualify.

The California exemption comes in handy in filling in gaps left by ERISA. For example, we noted that an ERISA plan whose only participants are owners and their spouses will not qualify. But California's statute has no such limitation, and a plan created under ERISA and intended for retirement but with only one participant—the owner—will be exempt under California law.

We noted that ERISA exempts plan assets while the assets are still in the plan, but leaves them exposed after the assets are withdrawn. Assets distributed from a California "private retirement plan" remain exempt even after they have been withdrawn (*California Code of Civil Procedure* §703.080). If you withdraw funds from a plan exempt under California law, make sure that you segregate these assets in a separate account. In light of their exempt status, you should use other (nonexempt) funds for normal living expenses before you dip into the exempt assets.

We also noted that ERISA does not exempt IRAs, but some states do. In California, "self-employed retirement plans" and IRAs are exempt only to the extent that the funds are necessary to provide for the reasonable retirement needs of the retiree and the retiree's spouse and dependents (*California Code of Civil Procedure* §704.115[e]). A "self-employed retirement plan" is one provided by an unincorporated employer, such as a Keogh plan that a sole proprietor might provide. What "reasonable retirement needs" are is determined on a case-by-case basis. A 60-year-old retiree with a $25,000 IRA and no other assets other than his or her home will have a far better chance of having the IRA shielded than a 30-year-old with a $25,000 IRA and $1 million in other assets.

In contrast, some states provide an unlimited exemption for IRAs: see *Florida Statutes* §222.21, *Texas Property Code* §42.0021, *New York Civil Practice Laws and Rules* §5205(c), *New Jersey Statutes Ann.* §25:2-1, and *Kansas Statutes Ann.* §60-2308(b).

Even if there is no federal or state exemption, there are circumstances under which it may be impossible for a creditor to get at the assets in a retirement plan. As we shall see in greater detail in Chapter 8, a creditor has no interest in a trust that is superior to a beneficiary's interest; the creditor "steps into the shoes" of the beneficiary. If the plan restricts the beneficiary's access to his account (for instance, by requiring the employee to wait until retirement), then a creditor of the beneficiary will be subject to the same restriction.

The Homestead Exemption

The asset that is nearest and dearest to most people's hearts is their home. But state law shielding the home from creditors varies wildly from state to state, from the minuscule (Arkansas: $25,000) to the unlimited. Unfortunately, most states do little to shield a home from creditors.

Here is how the homestead exemption operates. Let us assume that Mrs. Green resides in Massachusetts, a state that provides a $300,000 homestead exemption (*Massachusetts Laws Ann.* Ch. 188 §1). A creditor files a judgment against Mrs. Green. Her home is valued at $700,000. When the home is sold at auction to satisfy the judgment, the creditor (or anyone else bidding for the home at the auction) must first pay $300,000 to Mrs. Green. Let's assume that there is a $400,000 mortgage encumbering the residence. Anyone (including the judgment creditor) who wishes to buy the residence at the auction must not only give $300,000 to Mrs. Green, but also either pay $400,000 to the mortgage holder or work out a deal with the mortgage holder to pay the principal and interest on the mortgage as it comes due. That's not a very attractive prospect. It's so unattractive that the $300,000 homestead is all that might be needed to dissuade a creditor from attempting to seize Mrs. Green's home. As we shall see in Chapter 11, "equity stripping," i.e., loading debt onto a property, is a strategy often employed to prevent creditors from seizing real estate.

The homestead exemption does not apply if the creditor is the mortgagee (the person who loaned money to the owner and obtained a mortgage or deed of trust in exchange). Let's assume that Mrs. Green defaults on her $400,000 mortgage. When the lender forecloses on the home, the lender is not required to give Mrs. Green $300,000; the lender simply takes the property.

From the standpoint of the homestead exemption, the best places to live are Florida, Texas, Minnesota, Oklahoma, and Kansas, which have unlimited homestead exemptions. An unlimited homestead exemption translates into your creditors never being able to seize your residence. In Florida and Kansas, the unlimited homestead exemption applies to homes on less than 160 acres outside of a city and ½ acre inside a city (*Florida Constitution Art*. X §4 and *Kansas Statutes Ann*. §60-2301). Texas' homestead exemption is available for homes on 200 acres or less if owned by a family and 100 acres if owned by a single person, but only one acre if the residence is in an urban area (*Texas Property Code Ann*. §41.001). Oklahoma's unlimited homestead exemption is for 160 acres outside of a city and 1 acre in an urban area (*Oklahoma Statutes* §31-2). The best of the best are Florida and Texas, because their homestead exemptions are not statutory, but are enshrined in their state constitutions. That means that the homestead is impervious to any notions of fraudulent conveyances. No one can inquire into how or why you obtained the funds to acquire the residence. If it is your residence, it's exempt.

The states vary with respect to their requirements for qualification. Most states require that you be a resident of the state to qualify for the homestead exemption. If you wish to avoid your creditors by buying a $10 million hacienda on 160 acres in central Florida, make sure you become a Florida resident. To be on the safe side, you should do everything that Florida residents do, including registering your car in Florida, obtaining a Florida driver's license, and registering to vote in Florida. Florida even provides a procedure to permit you to qualify before you actually arrive: simply complete a

Declaration of Domicile form and file it with the clerk of the county where the residence is located. The Declaration of Domicile says that even though you may own a home in another state, the Florida home is your primary residence, qualifying you for the homestead exemption.

What Is a Residence for Purposes of the Homestead Exemption?

The houseboat or the mobile home you live in may be as much of a home to you as Hearst Castle was to William Randolph Hearst, but your houseboat or mobile home may not qualify for the homestead exemption. State laws vary wildly as to what qualifies. If you do not live in a conventional home on terra firma, you should check your local law to see if the state homestead statute applies to you at all.

What Happens to the Proceeds from the Sale?

Let's return to Mrs. Green. If her $700,000 home is sold to satisfy a creditor, she will receive $300,000 (the Massachusetts homestead exemption) and her creditor will get the residence. Let's assume that her indebtedness to the creditor remains unsatisfied even after the creditor takes the residence. May the creditor then turn around and go after the $300,000 that Mrs. Green just received? That also depends on state law. Unfortunately for Mrs. Green, Massachusetts does not exempt the homestead proceeds in any way. Contrast this to California, which has a typical statute, exempting the homestead amount ($75,000 for a married couple; $150,000 for a person aged 65 or over) from seizure for a period of six months after the proceeds are received (*California Code of Civil Procedure* §704.720). If Mrs. Green lived in California, she could spend the proceeds (or dispose of them in some other way) during the six-month interval without any fear that the creditor could reach them.

Exemptions from Wage Garnishment

In Chapter 4 we considered Mr. Fabulous Athlete—M-Fab—who shielded all of his assets from creditors, but whose salary was as exposed as any wage earner, which M-Fab was, albeit on a glorious scale.

Fortunately for M-Fab, a federal statute—the Consumer Credit Protection Act—and a variety of state statutes exist that either limit or prevent a creditor from seizing a debtor's wages, a.k.a., "garnishment." The federal statute places a ceiling on the amount that a creditor can remove from any paycheck equal to the lesser of 25 percent of the wage earner's "disposable earnings" or 30 times the federal minimum wage, which is currently $5.15 per hour. "Disposable earnings" means what is left over after deductions for taxes, social security, unemployment insurance, etc. See 15 U.S.C. §1673.

The Consumer Credit Protection Act is not nearly as broad as it could be. It shields wages only from consumer-type debts. It does nothing to shield a debtor from other liabilities, such as tort claims, business defaults, and federal and state taxes.

Many states have antigarnishment statutes, most of which track the federal statute. If the state statute allows a creditor to obtain more from a wage earner than the federal statute, the federal statute will trump the state statute, based on the Supremacy Clause of the United States Constitution. But some state statutes are more generous to debtors than the federal statute, and in those cases the state statute will apply.

The most generous states are Pennsylvania, Texas, and Florida, which prohibit wage garnishments. Texas' prohibition is absolute (*Texas Statutes Ann.* §42.001[b][1]), as is Pennsylvania's (*Pennsylvania Statutes Ann.* tit. 42 §8127). Florida's unlimited exemption is available only to heads of households (*Florida Statutes Ann.* §222-11). In each of these states, wages will be attachable by a claimant for support, the prohibition notwithstanding.

Other states have expanded the federal statute. Typical are New Mexico and Washington, which exempt the greater of 75 percent of each paycheck or an amount equal to 40 times the minimum wage; see *New Mexico Statutes Ann.* §35-12-7 and *Washington Rev. Code* §6.27.150(i).

It is possible to game the system somewhat by increasing the amount that is withheld, which reduces the amount available for garnishment. The over-withholding will produce a tax refund, which is not subject to garnishment.

Avoiding Garnishments

In certain limited instances, it may be possible to avoid garnishments entirely. Here's how.

A garnishment is an order directed at an employer by a creditor. A garnishment basically says, "Dear Acme Widgets: If you have an employee working for you named Arthur Shmidlap, we have a judgment against him. Don't pay him anything more than the state (or federal) exemption, and give the rest to us." But what if there is no such person on the payroll as "Arthur Shmidlap"? In that case, there is nothing to garnish, and Acme Widgets informs the creditor of this fact. Let's assume that the services that Arthur Shmidlap used to perform (before he felt the hot wind of creditors) are now performed by "A.S. Enterprises, Inc." Arthur Shmidlap is an employee, but not of Acme Widgets. He is an employee of A.S. Enterprises, Inc.

Needless to say, this technique cannot be employed if you work on an assembly line at General Motors. But if you are an entertainer or consultant, avoiding a garnishment should not be too difficult.

Another way to avoid a garnishment is to simply go off the payroll. Many business owners are also employees of their closely held businesses. They want to be employees because they will then qualify for the retirement plans and other benefits that are available only to employees. But that means that their pay is subject to garnishment. They can avoid the garnishment by ceasing to be employees, so that when the garnishment hits, there is no "debt" owing from the corporation. Compensation can be bled out of the corporation in any number of ways that are not subject to garnishment, such as loans or stock dividends.

Social Security

A federal statute exempts Social Security benefits from seizure; see 42 U.S.C. §407. But that statute does not apply to federal creditors, such as the IRS. As a matter of practice, the IRS will not seize more than 25 percent of any Social Security payment.

Life Insurance

There is a seemingly endless variety of life insurance products. Nonetheless, life insurance falls into two basic categories: term and whole life.

Term insurance is insurance that offers nothing more than a death benefit. If Mr. Brown owns an insurance policy on his life (making Mr. Brown the insured), which pays $1 million to his nephew Irving upon his death (making Irving the beneficiary), the $1 million is the death benefit.

Let's assume that Mr. Brown loses a lawsuit, and now has a judgment against him. His creditors conduct a debtor's exam and learn of the existence of the life insurance policy. Can they take the life insurance policy? Not a chance. The reason is that there isn't anything to seize. The insurance policy is nothing more than the insurance company's promise to pay an amount in the future to someone else, provided that the insured pays the annual premiums. Now let's assume that Mr. Brown dies, and what was once an insurance policy—a promise to pay in the future—is now $1 million in cold cash. May the creditors of what is now Mr. Brown's estate go after the $1 million in Irving's hands? Not likely, unless the creditor can somehow prove that the purchase of the insurance was itself a fraudulent conveyance.

Whole life insurance is very different, and comes in many different forms, including variable life, universal life, and annuities. What they all have in common is that each policy has two features: a death benefit similar to the death benefit in a term policy and an investment feature. The best way to view a whole life policy is as a term policy with a mutual fund tacked onto it. That mutual fund is often referred to as the cash value or the cash surrender value, and since it is similar to a mutual fund, it is very much attachable by creditors.

The proceeds of a life insurance policy are exempt from income taxes, and with a little planning we can exempt life insurance from estate taxes. (More on that in Chapter 8.) Many states exempt the cash value from creditors' claims. The following states have unlimited exemptions for the proceeds of life insurance:

Alabama	Delaware	Florida
Idaho	Illinois	Indiana
Kansas	Kentucky	Massachusetts
Michigan	Missouri	New Jersey
New Mexico	New York	North Carolina
North Dakota	Ohio	Oklahoma
Oregon	Rhode Island	Tennessee
Texas	Vermont	Virginia
Washington	Wyoming	

Some states have pitifully small life insurance exemptions, such as California's $8,000 ($16,000 for a married couple), Connecticut's $4,000, Georgia's $2,000, and Utah's $1,500. Moreover, you need to read the state statute before you rely on the exemption. Some are restricted to policies where a spouse or child is the beneficiary. Others do not apply to creditors with child support or similar claims.

The Florida Annuities Exemption

I single out the Florida exemption for annuities simply because it's my favorite. We noted that Florida's homestead exemption is not only unlimited, it is a part of the Florida constitution, giving it superior status to any Florida statute, including Florida's version of the Uniform Fraudulent Transfer Act. That means you can build a multimillion-dollar fortress in Florida and thumb your nose at your creditors (and people have).

But once you've taken all your cash and socked it into a big hacienda, how do you buy groceries? No worries, mate. Florida also permits its citizens and residents to buy annuities, and those annuities are completely exempt from creditors (*Florida Statutes Ann.* §222.14). For example, if you take $1 million and give it to an insurance company in exchange for an annuity contract whereunder they promise to pay you $75,000 per year for your and your spouse's joint lifetimes, both the $1 million and the annual $75,000 are both exempt. The issuer of the policy need not be located in Florida; it could be located in Switzerland.

Florida's exemption is so broad that it appears to apply to private annuities that don't involve insurance companies at all. If Mr. Green gives $1 million to his nephew Irving in exchange for Irving's promise to give Mr. and Mrs. Green $75,000 per year for the rest of their joint lifetimes, this arrangement also appears to be covered by the Florida exemption.

Asset Protection for Spouses

We will discuss foreign asset protection planning in great detail in Chapter 10, where we will see that for most assets (except real estate), nothing beats a foreign trust to assure that assets cannot be touched by a creditor. But you may not need to go to the Cook Islands, the Isle of Man, or Liechtenstein to obtain asset protection. With proper planning and a little luck (depending on where you live), the best asset protection plan may begin with the person who occupies the pillow next to you every night—your spouse. However—also depending on where you live—that same person may cause you to become subject to liabilities that could not have been incurred had you never married.

The "where you live" is a function of whether you reside in a "common law" state (also referred to as a separate property state) or whether you reside in a community property state. To make matters worse, the rules vary considerably among the common law states and among the community property states. To complicate matters further, within each state there is an overlay of joint tenancy, tenancy in common, and in some states, tenancy by the entirety that can result in a bewildering array of results. We'll attempt to sort it all out here. One prefatory note: If you're not married, all of your property is your separate property. You cannot have community property without being married. Your "significant other" may be very significant to you, but in the eyes of the law, you are strangers, and with very few exceptions, the two of you have no rights to each other's property and cannot be liable for each other's debts. The notable exception is if you have signed a guarantee or other contract making you liable for your significant other's debts.

Separate Property and Community Property

Nine states are community property states. They are:

- Arizona
- California
- Idaho
- Louisiana
- Nevada
- New Mexico
- Texas
- Washington
- Wisconsin

Puerto Rico is also a community property jurisdiction. Alaska permits spouses to "opt in" to community property. All the rest are separate property states.

All about Separate Property

The key to living in a separate property state is that, with some minor exceptions, a creditor of one spouse cannot go after the separate property of the other spouse. Whether a parcel of property is the separate property of one spouse or the other is determined by whose name appears on the title.

The same rule applies to the earnings of each spouse: the earnings of one are exempt from the claims of the other's creditors. See, for example, *Pennsylvania Statutes Ann.* tit. 23,§4104 and *Illinois Compiled Statutes* ch. 750 §65.

A typical example: Dr. Brown is a neurosurgeon. His wife is a homemaker. Dr. Brown is sued for malpractice, and a $4 million judgment is awarded against him. The titles to their home, their vacation home, and their stock portfolio are in the name of Mrs. Brown. When the plaintiff seeks to enforce the judgment, the plaintiff cannot touch the property titled in Mrs. Brown's name.

This brings us immediately to Klueger's Separate Property Rule.

> **Klueger's Separate Property Rule:** In separate property states, property should be titled in the name of the lower-risk spouse.

This rule isn't foolproof. It puts a premium on Mrs. Brown driving safely. If she becomes the debtor, the plaintiff can go after all of the property titled in her name.

Let's assume that Dr. and Mrs. Brown's marriage fails. Does the fact that all of the property is in Mrs. Brown's name mean she will be awarded everything and he will get nothing? In most separate property states, the answer is no, since all of their property becomes "marital property" the moment that one of them files for divorce. The marital property is subject to equitable division, with the divorce court judge deciding who gets what, based on a number of factors, such as their relative ability to earn income, the length of their marriage, the lifestyle to which they have become accustomed, etc. The problem with this equitable division is that a creditor of one of them may develop the ability to seize marital property that the creditor could not have touched had the property remained the separate property of the other prior to the divorce.

We noted that there are some minor exceptions to the rule that a creditor of one spouse cannot reach the separate property of the other. A common exception is a debt incurred for family necessities, i.e., a debt incurred to support the other spouse or the children, such as for food or medical care. What constitutes "necessities" varies from state to state, but such debts can be considerable. If they include education expenses—as they do in Illinois—the university could proceed against the property of the nondebtor spouse (i.e., the spouse who did not sign the contract obligating the tuition costs).

Another exception is the general rule regarding fraudulent conveyances. If Dr. Brown suddenly finds himself the subject of a lawsuit, the transfer of all of his assets to his wife will not shield those assets; Mrs. Brown is now undoubtedly the transferee of a fraudulent conveyance, and can be sued, not on the underlying debt, but on the fraudulent conveyance. As with almost all asset protection planning, Klueger's Separate Property Rule works only if you *plan early!*

All about Community Property

I practice law in California, a community property state. On more occasions than I can remember, a client has said to me, "That property isn't mine; it's in my wife's name." At that point I have to give the client a little education on community property law, which always leaves the client a little sadder.

In a community property state, property that is "owned" by either or both spouses is presumed to be owned one-half by each spouse, regardless of whose name is on the title. Technically, the "community" owns the asset, and each spouse has an equal interest in the community. If the deed reads "Dr. Brown," the property is owned one-half by Dr. Brown, and one-half by Mrs. Brown. The same is true for earnings and wages. When that client pays for the little education I have provided him by writing a check to "Robert F. Klueger," half of the money is owned—at that very instant—by Mrs. Klueger. The best way to think about community property (at least in California) is to remember that titles don't matter.

What, then, is community property? In all community property states, community property is property that is acquired by either spouse during the marriage. The two notable exceptions are property that one spouse acquires by gift or by inheritance (see, for example, *California Family Code* §770, *Texas Family Code* §5.01(a), and *Arizona Revised Statutes* §25-211). If Mrs. Brown receives a new car from her nephew Irving as a gift, it's her separate property. If she inherits a car when her Aunt Lucy dies, it's her separate property. But just to give you an idea of how state community property laws differ, if Mrs.

Brown is hit by a car in Texas and receives a settlement from the negligent driver, the settlement proceeds are her separate property.

Property that is acquired by spouses during their marriage is presumed to be community property, but property that was owned by a spouse prior to marriage and brought into the marriage remains that spouse's separate property. If that property appreciates during the marriage, the appreciation is also separate property. If separate property is sold during the marriage and other property is acquired with the proceeds, the replacement property remains separate property, provided that the replacement property can be traced to the proceeds of the property that was sold. There is, however, a notable exception to this rule: if separate property is commingled with community property, the separate property loses its separate character and becomes community property.

The classic case of commingling occurs when one spouse inherits property and immediately places the funds in a joint account with the other spouse. But it's possible to commingle assets by accident. Assume that Mr. Brown owned an apartment building prior to marrying Mrs. Brown. They reside in California. The apartment building is, of course, his separate property. Mrs. Brown works as a schoolteacher. Her income is community property. She places her paycheck in a joint account with Mr. Brown. On occasion, they withdraw funds from the joint account to pay for the apartment building's taxes, trash removal, and maintenance expenses. In so doing, Mrs. Brown has made a contribution from her community property to service Mr. Brown's separate property. The result is that she has a community property interest in his separate property. Her interest is not a one-half interest, and were they to divorce, two sets of appraisers and forensic accountants would become richer than they already are in attempting to divine the extent of her interest, but an interest she clearly has. As we shall see shortly, it is an interest that a creditor might seize.

Creditors' Rights to Community Property

We have already seen that, as a general rule, a creditor of one spouse cannot reach the separate property of the other. A creditor's ability to seize community property is both broader and more complicated.

There is no question that if both spouses are liable, a creditor can reach all of the community property, as well as the separate property of both spouses. The complexity arises if only one spouse is a debtor.

In California, the general rule is that a creditor of one spouse can seize all community property, even if the debt arose prior to marriage (*California Family Code* §990). Here's an example that is extreme, but by no means unprecedented: Jill Jones, who works as a dental technician in California, marries Bubba. They open a joint account into which Jill deposits her paycheck. Bubba forgot to mention to Jill on the way to the altar that he owes tens of thousands of dollars in student loans and hundreds of thousands in back taxes. Two weeks after the marriage, the IRS seizes the bank account. Can they do that? Absolutely. The bank account is community property, and a creditor of one spouse may seize all of the community property to cover the premarriage debt of the other (*California Family Code* §910[a]). Here's another example of how bizarre—and arbitrary—the rules can be: if Jill had deposited the paycheck into an account labeled "Jill Jones—Separate Property Account," the IRS would not have been able to seize the account (*California Family Code* §911).

Things get still more complicated in Texas. In Texas, the nondebtor spouse's share of community property is not subject to the claims of the other spouse's creditors if the debt arose prior to marriage. Even if the debt arose after marriage, a nondebtor spouse's share of community property cannot be reached if the nondebtor spouse has exclusive management over the property, provided that the debt arose in a nontort context (*Texas Family Code* §5.61). Property is presumed to be under one spouse's exclusive control if that spouse's name is on the title. If there is no title, it is presumed to be within that spouse's control if the spouse has possession of it (*Texas Family Code* §5.24). This represents a radical shift in the rights of creditors, and makes community property in Texas—at least as far as creditors are concerned—look very much like separate property.

Arizona takes a position somewhere between California and Texas. In Arizona, a spouse's share of the community property is liable for the premarital debts of the other spouse, "but only to the extent of the value of the spouse's contribution to the community property which would have been such spouse's separate property if single" (*Arizona Revised Statutes* §25-215B). Nevada takes a position that is exactly contrary to California's: in Nevada, a spouse's one-half share of community property is not liable for the debts of the other spouse, whether incurred before or after marriage (*Nevada Revised Statutes* §123.050). New Mexico requires a creditor to first go after the separate property of a debtor-spouse, and if the separate property is not sufficient, allows the creditor to go after the non-debtor spouse's one-half interest in the community property, but does not allow the creditor to place a lien on the non-debtor spouse's interest in the marital residence, regardless of how title in the residence is held (*New Mexico Statutes Ann.* §40-3-10A). As noted earlier, the results vary wildly from state to state.

Quasi-Community Property

Just to make matters even more confusing, each of the community property states has a concept known as "quasi-community property." It applies to property that was acquired by a married couple in a non-community-property state. For example, if Mr. and Mrs. Brown, who reside in California, own a parcel of real estate in Pennsylvania, that real estate would be separate property if owned by Pennsylvania residents, since Pennsylvania is a separate property state. But California treats the Pennsylvania property as quasi-community property. The result is that the Pennsylvania property is considered to be community property for all purposes (see *California Family Code* §912). A creditor of either Mr. or Mrs. Brown could seize the entire Pennsylvania property, a result that could not happen if Mr. and Mrs. Brown resided in Pennsylvania.

Joint Tenancy and Tenancy in Common

Regardless of whether spouses live in a separate property state or a community property state, every state allows spouses (and single persons who own property with others) to hold property as tenants in common or as joint tenants, often referred to as joint tenants with right of survivorship. From an asset protection standpoint, the differences are not great, but they are worth noting. What is confusing to many people is that when spouses residing in a community property state hold property together, property held as tenants in common may also be either their separate property or community property, and property held as joint tenants may also be their separate or community property.

Let's assume that Mr. and Mrs. Brown own a 40-acre parcel of real estate. The deed reads "John Brown, a married man, as to a 50 percent interest as tenant in common, and Mary Brown, a married woman as to a 50 percent interest as tenant in common." What is tenancy in common? It means that each of them owns a one-half undivided interest in the whole property. It does not mean that John Brown owns the east 20 acres and Mary Brown owns the west 20 acres. But it does mean that each of them has the right to sell half the property, or to give half the property to his or her heirs in a will. From the deed alone, we cannot tell if the property is their separate property or their community property. In most community property states, there is a presumption that the property is community property if it was acquired by them during marriage. If they reside in California, and the property is community property, a creditor of one of them will be able to seize both halves of the property. As we have seen, it's more complicated in Texas.

Joint tenancy with right of survivorship is still more complicated, and even some lawyers have difficulty understanding exactly what it means. The key to it is the "right of survivorship." Let's assume that the deed reads "John Brown and Mary Brown, joint tenants." John and Mary can each still sell half the property, in which case the joint tenancy will automatically be severed, and the buyer will be a tenant in common with the other of them. But if John Brown dies, he cannot leave half the property to anyone in a will or a trust, because in the event of his death, Mary becomes the sole owner of the property, by virtue of her right of survivorship.

From an asset protection standpoint, joint tenancy produces a quirky result. Let's assume that John Brown—but not Mary Brown—owed federal income taxes from a year prior to the time they were married. The IRS placed a tax lien on property of which both were joint tenants. If the IRS had desired, it could have seized the property, but it failed to do so. John Brown then died.

As a result, Mary Brown owned 100 percent of the property, and the tax lien was extinguished, because the property was no longer owned by the tax debtor.

Joint tenancy is sometimes referred to as the poor man's estate plan; property held in joint tenancy avoids state probate procedures, because the property automatically transfers to the surviving joint tenant. But living trusts also avoid probate, and they afford substantial estate tax and income tax savings that joint tenancy does not.

Fixing the Problem: All about Marital Agreements

It should be obvious by now that living in a separate property state beats living in a community property state, because creditors of one spouse have a far more difficult time getting at the separate property of a nondebtor spouse than creditors do in a community property state. In a separate property state, there is never an issue of "commingling" because there is no community property to commingle with. As long as spouses in separate property states take care to keep the titles to their assets in the name of the lower-risk spouse, they will be able to shield the assets from the liabilities of the higher-risk spouse. If the lower-risk spouse signs no guarantees, obligates himself or herself under no contracts, and drives safely, this may be all the asset protection planning they will ever need.

If you live in a community property state and you are green with envy, take heart. Most community property states provide you and your spouse with a mechanism—a marital agreement—to remove yourselves from the operation of your state community property law. Couples not yet married may enter into a prenuptial agreement, often referred to as an antenuptial agreement. If already married, they can enter into a postnuptial agreement, often referred to as a transmutation agreement. The effect of both is the same: the spouses are governed by separate property principles and not by community property principles. Of course, couples intending to marry in separate property states may enter into premarital agreements, but they do so principally to determine their rights to property between themselves in the event of divorce or in the event of the death of one of them. They have no need to enter into a marital agreement for asset protection.

The Premarital Agreement

Thousands of couples enter into premarital agreements every year. They do so to avoid state laws that are designed to protect a divorced or widowed spouse, but that may be completely inappropriate for many couples. In a typical case, a man and a woman, both having been previously married and each with children of their own, may desire not to obligate themselves to each other in the event of death or divorce. A premarital agreement may be the ideal vehicle to accomplish this goal. Each may waive an interest in the other's present and/or future assets and/or earnings. They might waive whatever rights to inherit their spouse's assets their state law gives them. They might even waive their rights to receive alimony (also known as spousal maintenance) in the event of a divorce. There was a time when state statutes prohibited such waivers, but they are now almost universally permitted. The one thing that cannot be waived in a prenuptial agreement is child support, because the money being given up belongs to neither spouse, but to the child.

For couples residing in a community property state, a premarital agreement has the added benefit of removing the couple from the harsh effects of community property. An agreement that says "What's mine is mine and what's yours is yours" is essentially an agreement to always have separate property. A well-crafted agreement will make it clear that each spouse is liable only for the debts associated with that spouse's income, and that there cannot be any "commingling," since there cannot be any community property.

State laws vary as to what formalities are required for a premarital agreement to be binding. Most states have adopted the Uniform Premarital Agreement Act, which permits a waiver of spousal maintenance (alimony), but not a waiver of child support. At a minimum, there should be full disclosure of each party's assets and liabilities, lest a party later claim that he or she was fraudulently induced to enter into the agreement. It is best that each side be advised by independent legal counsel.

Transmutation Agreements

It is still rare for couples intending to marry to enter into a premarital agreement for asset protection. In the overwhelming number of cases, couples seeking to remove themselves from community property are already married and need a postnuptial agreement in order to transmute their assets from community property to their respective separate property.

Most community property states permit some form of transmutation from community property to separate property. Texas permits spouses to "partition or exchange" their "existing or to-be-acquired" property, making that property the separate property of each of them. Even if property remains the community property of the spouses, an agreement in Texas between the spouses giving one of them the exclusive management and control over an asset will exempt that asset from the other spouse's creditors (*Texas Family Code* §5.52). Nevada simply states that spouses may make contracts with each other with respect to their property (*Nevada Revised Statutes* §123.070). Washington also permits spouses to enter into agreements with respect to their "then owned" or "afterwards to be acquired" property, but goes on to say that such an agreement will not "derogate from the rights of creditors" (*Revised Code of Washington* §26.16.120).

California says the same, more explicitly. California allows spouses to "transmute" their community property into the respective separate property of each of them, and allows spouses to transmute property from separate property into community property. The transmutation of real estate is effective against third parties (i.e., creditors) only if the transmutation is recorded, either by the recordation of the transmutation agreement itself or by means of a recorded deed indicating that the property is now the separate property of one of the spouses (*California Family Code* §850). However, in the next breath, California then says that transmutation agreements are "subject to the laws of fraudulent conveyances" (*California Family Code* §851).

There are no cases interpreting §851 of the California Family Code, but we have a pretty good guess at what it means. Let's assume that Dr. White is a neurosurgeon, and Mrs. White is a homemaker. All of their assets are community property, having been acquired during their marriage. They enter into an agreement transmuting all of their assets—the real estate, the stock portfolio, and all the cash—to Mrs. White as her sole and separate property, leaving Dr. White with his golf clubs and an autographed photo of Bobby Vinton as his sole and separate property. Will that work? We saw in Chapter 4 that the hallmark of a fraudulent conveyance is the transfer of property without the receipt of adequate consideration in return. What did Dr. White receive in exchange for giving up his 50 percent interest in all of the real estate, the stock portfolio, and the cash? Nothing. In fact, Dr. White has been made insolvent by the transfer. If there was ever a fraudulent conveyance, this is it.

Planning with Transmutation Agreements

Giving everything to one spouse and leaving the other spouse with nothing probably will not work. But that doesn't mean we cannot use a transmutation to shield at least 50 percent—if not more—of the community property from the claims of creditors.

Let's take a closer look at Dr. and Mrs. White's assets with a view toward how they might be divided in a transmutation agreement. We will assume that Dr. White is the high-risk spouse and Mrs. White is the lower-risk spouse. It's Dr. White's creditors, not Mrs. White's creditors, that we are protecting against.

Their assets are as follows (for the sake of simplicity, we have eliminated the debt encumbering any of the assets).

Asset	Fair Market Value

Real Estate
    Residence
    Apartment Building
    Vacation Home
	
	$1,000,000
	$2,000,000
	$600,000

Total	$3,600,000
Stocks and Bonds	$2,000,000
Dr. White's 401(k) Plan	$1,000,000
Dr. Gerald White, P.C.	$2,000,000
Cash	$400,000
Total	$9,000,000

Because this is a $0,000,000 estate, all of which is community property, it would appear that we need to give each of them $4,500,000 in order to avoid any challenge that the transmutation is a fraudulent conveyance. In other words, Dr. White and Mrs. White must each release a $4,500,000 interest in half of the assets. Right?

Not exactly. We saw in Chapter 5 that the $1 million in the 401(k) plan is already exempt from the claims of creditors, assuming that Dr. White is not the only participant in the plan. A court will not allow us to consider assets that are already exempt. For our purposes, this is a $8 million estate. We need to transmute those assets into the separate property of each of them. But which assets should we assign to each?

Let's begin with Dr. White's medical corporation. Unlike the 401(k) plan, it's not an exempt asset. If Dr. White desired to retire, he could sell the corporation to a younger doctor or to a medical clinic. The corporation has a fair market value that can be ascertained by means of an appraisal. The corporation may have value to a buyer, but as a practical matter, the corporation has no value to a creditor. If Dr. White were to sell the corporation, a buyer would require Dr. White to remain on the job for a period of time, introducing him to patients so as to assure a smooth transition. Moreover, any purchaser would insist that Dr. White enter into a non-competition agreement to ensure that Dr. White does not turn around and compete with the business he just sold. If a creditor were to seize the business, none of that would happen. The business is an asset that has value, but it's not an asset a creditor wants. We'll leave the medical corporation with Dr. White as his separate property.

We saw in Chapter 2 that some assets are easier to seize than others. The easiest asset for a creditor to seize, and the most difficult to protect, is real estate, for the simple reason that we can't move it. Because it's Dr. White's creditors we are concerned with, the wise strategy is to give Mrs. White a separate property interest in the real estate, and leave Dr. White with a separate property interest in the liquid assets and the business. As a result of the transmutation agreement, each of them has a separate property interest in the following assets.

Mrs. White	
Asset	Fair Market Value
Residence Apartment Building Vacation Home	$1,000,000 $2,000,000 $600,000
Total	$3,600,000

Dr. White	
Dr. Gerald White, P.C.	$2,000,000
Stocks and Bonds	$2,000,000
Cash	$400,000
Total	$4,400,000

It does not appear that the division is equal; Dr. White has $4,400,000 in nonexempt assets, and Mrs. White has only $3,600,000. Isn't this still a fraudulent conveyance? Not really. Remember, in the likely event that the debtor is Dr. White, no one will be heard to say that it's a fraudulent conveyance because Dr. White emerged from the transmutation with more than 50 percent of the assets. Of course, we might face this argument if Mrs. White gets into an automobile accident and she becomes the debtor.

It's obvious that a transmutation agreement is not a magic bullet, because it still leaves assets on the table for a creditor to reach. The $2 million in stocks and bonds and the $400,000 in cash are still there for the taking, not to mention all of the real estate in the event that Mrs. White becomes a debtor. But we have at least removed the easy assets from Dr. White's creditors' grasp.

Nor are we finished. For spouses residing in a community property state, a transmutation agreement is often the starting point of the asset protection planning; it is not the end. As we shall see in Chapter 9, we might place the apartment building in a limited liability company to shield it from creditors. As we shall see in Chapter 11, we might place the residence and the vacation home into a Qualified Personal Residence Trust in order to heighten the asset protection for these assets. As for the cash, it might find its way into a foreign trust; more on that in Chapter 10.

Tenancy by the Entirety

We could have included our discussion of tenancy by the entirety in Chapter 5, because real property held in this form of ownership is an exempt asset. We include it here because tenancy by the entirety exists only for married couples.

In those states that permit tenancy by the entirety, real property titled as such is exempt from the claims of one of the spouse's creditors. Tenancy by the entirety is similar to joint tenancy, except that, unlike in joint tenancy, one of the spouses may not sever the tenancy without the consent of the other. Because the interest of a creditor in a debtor's property can never be greater than the interest of the debtor in that property, the inability of the debtor to sever the tenancy means that the creditor cannot sever the tenancy either. As long as the property is titled as tenancy by the entirety, and as long as the spouses stay married, a creditor cannot seize the property.

The following states (and the District of Columbia) have some form of tenancy by the entirety:

Alabama	Arkansas	Delaware
Florida	Hawaii	Illinois
Indiana	Kentucky	Maryland
Massachusetts	Michigan	Mississippi
Missouri	New York	New Jersey
North Carolina	Oklahoma	Oregon
Pennsylvania	Rhode Island	Tennessee
Vermont	Virginia	Wyoming

Of these states, only Alaska, Hawaii, Tennessee, and Vermont permit tenancy by the entirety for rental real estate; the others limit this form of ownership to the spouses' residence. Moreover, in these four states, the income from the rental real estate is not considered part of the tenancy by the entirety. The income is subject to attachment as separate property.

One notable thing about this list is that all of the states are separate property states; no community property states are on the list.

There are limits to the efficacy of tenancy by the entirety. For one, it will defeat a creditor only if one—but not both—of the spouses is the debtor. (Once again, we are forced back to one of the four questions governing all asset protection planning: "Who is the defendant?") Secondly, it can work only to delay the day that a creditor will get at the asset, since tenancy by the entirety can only exist for married couples, and every marriage must eventually terminate, either by divorce or death. Finally, it is not clear if tenancy by the entirety trumps all considerations of fraudulent conveyances. May you transfer property into tenancy by the entirety to defeat a known creditor? Illinois has a statute that says no, but only to a limited extent. In Illinois, a creditor may reach property transferred into tenancy by the entirety if the transfer was made "with the sole intent to avoid the payment of debts existing at the time of the transfer beyond the transferor's ability to pay those debts as they become due" (*Illinois Code of Civil Procedure* §5/12-112). Clear as mud, isn't it?

Spouses residing in states permitting tenancy by the entirety should consider titling their residences as tenancy by the entirety as early as possible. The law may not presume that real property owned by spouses is tenancy by the entirety unless the deed clearly says so. Once the real estate is safely in tenancy by the entirety, the spouses should leave it there.

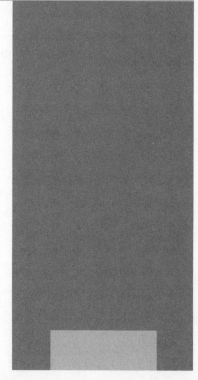

CHAPTER 7

Asset Protection Using Corporations

Corporations have existed for hundreds of years. The Dutch East India Company was chartered by the Netherlands in 1602. In its heyday, it commanded a large chunk of the world's trade, established colonies, subdued native populations, and warred with foreign nations in the process. But corporations were not much needed until the rise of industrialization in the 19th century. Before that, most industry was conducted in private homes by individuals and their families. The business grew and matured as the founder grew and matured, and when the founder died the business died, unless the founder was fortunate enough to have a child or children willing and able to continue the business. Industry was labor-intensive, not capital-intensive.

All that changed with the advent of modern technology and the emergence of the first great industry—the railroads. In order to build a great railroad, you needed lots of money, and in order to raise lots of money, you needed investors. If an investor believed your business venture might be profitable, he or she might be willing to part with some capital for a share of your profits and become a shareholder. The understanding was very straightforward: if the enterprise made money, the investors made money. If the enterprise lost money (or failed completely), the investors stood to lose their investment. That was the risk the investors were willing to run.

But one risk that no investor was willing to run was losing not only his or her investment, but his or her other assets that had not been invested in the enterprise. If the people who ran the business (who most often were strangers to the investors) mismanaged the enterprise, or committed fraud or even theft, investors did not want to be liable. Losing one's investment was bitter enough; no one would invest if someone else's negligence or cupidity resulted in the loss of one's home or savings.

Inherent in the idea of the corporation is limited liability. You might lose your investment, but that's all. All of your other assets are walled off from the corporation's creditors. Corporations are formed for the sole purpose of shielding their shareholders from liability. Is that a fraudulent conveyance? Absolutely not.

What Is a Corporation?

The limited liability that is the raison d'être of every corporation is not achieved by means of a statute. It results from what a corporation is: a legal entity separate from its owners, the shareholders.

Let's assume that three computer programmers, Joe, Jimmy, and Jane, decide to form Three J's Enterprises, Inc. After Three J's is formed, when Joe, Jimmy, and Jane are seated around a table, there are no longer three legal persons in the room: there are four. There are four persons who have legal and constitutional rights, may bring lawsuits and be sued, and are subject to federal and state taxes. The difference between Joe, Jimmy, and Jane on the one hand and Three J's on the other is that only Three J's is engaged in the business of providing computer programming services; Joe, Jimmy, and Jane do not.

There is another fundamental difference between Joe, Jimmy, and Jane on the one hand and Three J's on the other, which is that Joe, Jimmy, and Jane are natural persons; Three J's is a fictional person. Joe, Jimmy, and Jane have arms and brains to conceive of ideas and sign contracts; Three J's can act only through them. Nevertheless, when a prospective customer is taken to lunch by Joe, and given a presentation by Jimmy, and inks a contract with Jane, and shakes hands with all of them, the customer hasn't dealt with them: he's dealt with Three J's, acting in the only way it can, through natural persons.

When Joe, Jimmy, and Jane go into business and buy computers, desks, and pencils, the assets will be owned by Three J's, not them. The workers hired will be the employees of Three J's, not any or all of them. The profits will be earned by Three J's, and the taxes on the profits will the responsibility of Three J's. Most importantly, the debts and liabilities generated from the operations of the business will belong to Three J's, not Joe, Jimmy, and Jane. This limited liability is a direct result of the fact that Three J's is in business and they are not. As we shall see, however, the many exceptions and limitations to this simple principle limit the asset protection effectiveness of the corporation.

How Are Corporations Created?

A corporation can be created in only one way: being granted a charter by the secretary of state or department of corporations of one of the 50 states or the District of Columbia. The state will grant the charter upon the filing of articles of incorporation. Most states require very little to have the articles of incorporation accepted and the charter issued.

A state will require that the name selected not duplicate or be deceptively similar to a name already granted. If you choose a name that has already been taken in another state, the secretary of state will have no way of knowing this, and it is possible that the name you choose may infringe upon the trademark of another corporation. This can be avoided by conducting a nationwide trademark search, either by engaging a trademark attorney or by conducting an online search at the United States Patent and Trademark Office's website, www.uspto.gov.

Many states now provide online preclearance and name reservation service. The secretary of state will also require that the corporation appoint a registered agent who is located at a registered address in the state of incorporation. The registered agent's sole function is to accept a summons and complaint if the corporation is sued.

There was a time when the corporation's articles of incorporation needed to specify the purpose for which the corporation was formed. That was a trap, since any act the corporation performed that was not specified in the articles was deemed to be an *ultra vires* act. The result of ultra vires conduct was that the advantage of limited liability was forfeited, since ultra vires acts were deemed to be the acts of the shareholders, not the corporation itself. Every state now provides that a corporation may be formed for any lawful purpose, resulting in the elimination of the ultra vires trap.

Certain purposes are regulated. For example, Joe, Jimmy, and Jane could not form a corporation for the purpose of operating a bank; special permission from the state banking commissioner is required.

A corporation cannot be formed without the issuance of a charter, but once the charter is issued, the corporation exists in perpetuity. As long as it pays its fees to the state and pays its taxes, the corporation will continue until someone takes the affirmative step of liquidating the corporation.

Who Is What in a Corporation?

What would you rather be, the president of ExxonMobil or a shareholder of ExxonMobil? Most people would opt for the former, because being the president of one of the 30 Dow Jones industrial average companies means you are highly compensated, while being a shareholder means maybe getting a dividend every three months.

People are often confused as to who is what in a corporation, and as we shall see shortly, the confusion can be costly when creditors come calling. There are three principal roles in every corporation, whether the corporation is ExxonMobil or Three J's, Inc: the shareholders (often referred to as the stockholders), the directors, and the officers. These three roles can be diagrammed as shown in Figure 7-1.

It's no coincidence that the shareholders are at the top of the pyramid. The shareholders are the owners. If the corporation has only one class of stock—common stock—and you own two-thirds of the shares, you are entitled to receive two-thirds of the annual profits; profits that are distributed are

Figure 7-1

dividends. If the business is sold, you are entitled to receive two-thirds of the sales proceeds. Most small businesses do not pay dividends because it results in double taxation: a tax of the profits at the corporate level and a tax to the shareholders when the dividends are distributed. Because dividends are not eligible for a tax deduction when they are paid, most small businesses avoid the problem of double taxation by distributing their earnings as deductible compensation or qualifying as an S Corporation (see page 90).

The shareholders are in the driver's seat because the shareholders elect the directors. The directors are the people who have the legal responsibility to operate the business. Most significant corporate actions cannot happen without the approval of the board of directors, acting as a board. If Joe, Jimmy, and Jane comprise the board of directors of Three J's, Inc., and they wish to authorize a corporate loan, it's not sufficient for Joe to vote yes while at the beach on Monday and Jimmy to vote yes while driving home from the ball game on Wednesday. They must vote at a board meeting. An exception to this under the corporate laws of every state is that unanimous consent may be provided in writing, without the necessity of a meeting.

Directors' approval is required to sell the business, take on a new business, borrow funds, liquidate, and perform a myriad of other acts outside the day-to-day operation of the business.

If you own a majority of the shares of a business, you control the business, since you will have the ability to control the election of the board of directors. Depending on state law, you may have the right to fire the directors the minute you obtain control, or you may have to wait until the next annual meeting of the board to replace the board with directors who are friendly to you. That fact hides a fact that is often lost on the owners of small businesses, which is that in a corporation that doesn't pay dividends, there is no difference between owning 51 percent and 99 percent of the shares, and no difference between owning 1 percent and 49 percent of the shares, other than in the event of the sale of the corporation. Owning 51 percent gives you as much control as owning 99 percent. Owning 49 percent means you will lose every time an election is held to the board of directors, just as if you owned only 1 percent.

This result can be mitigated by cumulative voting. Here's how it works: Let's assume that Able, Baker, Charley, and David each own 25 percent (250 shares) of the stock of ABCD, Inc. The board of directors has four members. David has very different (and unwelcome) ideas about how the corporation is spending its money. Able, Baker, and Charley would like to keep David off the board of directors. When their terms expire, Able, Baker, and Charley each cast their 250 votes in favor of their respective re-election. When the election for David's seat on the board comes up, Able, Baker, and Charley vote for Able's girlfriend, Lulu, who doesn't know a corporation from a kumquat, but who will do anything Able requests. Under cumulative voting, however, they could not do this; each shareholder would get 1,000 votes for the four directorships, which he could cast in any way he chose. David could cast 1,000 votes for himself, not vote in any of the other elections, and be assured a seat on the board even though he was a minority shareholder. Some states, such as California, require cumulative voting (*California Corporations Code* §2115). Others, such as New York and Illinois, permit cumulative voting, but also permit a majority of the shareholders to dispense with it (*New York Business Corporation Law* §803 and *Illinois Compiled Statutes* ch. 32 §740[b]).

The directors appoint the officers. The officers are the president, chief executive officer, vice presidents, corporate secretary, treasurer, and any other offices the board of directors wishes to create. The officers are charged with the day-to-day management of the business, always under the direction of the board; they are employees of the corporation, albeit often very highly compensated.

Public Corporations and Closely Held Corporations

ExxonMobil and Three J's, Inc. have many things in common. Both came into existence when the state in which they were incorporated granted them a charter. Both have a set of bylaws that were initially adopted by the board of directors. Both have shareholders who elect the board and a board that appoints the officers.

The difference, of course, is that ExxonMobil is a public corporation. All that means is that at least some of its shares have been registered by the Securities and Exchange Commission, and that ExxonMobil periodically reports its activities and the results of its operations to the SEC. Three J's, having only three shareholders, is a closely held or "close" corporation. It certainly does not report to the SEC, and except for reporting its earnings to the IRS and the state taxing authorities, reports to no one.

The biggest difference between public corporations and close corporations is that in a public corporation, the shareholders (investors) are not directors and are not officers. Most of the directors are not officers, and the officers are not controlling shareholders. In Three J's, Inc., Joe, Jimmy, and Jane are most likely all of the shareholders, all of the directors, and all of the officers.

We began this chapter by noting that corporations exist to afford limited liability to the investors. That makes sense in the case of ExxonMobil. If you buy a few shares of ExxonMobil, you will take the risk of the stock price declining, but if the company settles an antitrust suit for a few billion dollars, you would prefer not to be liable to pay it. That rationale is strained somewhat in the case of Three J's, where there are no "investors" in the traditional sense. Nevertheless, Joe, Jimmy, and Jane enjoy the same limitations of liability as do

ExxonMobil's shareholders. The unfairness of this result to legitimate creditors of Three J's is the cause of most of the limitations and exceptions to the general rule of limited liability.

S Corporations and C Corporations

Another significant difference between corporations like ExxonMobil and corporations like Three J's lies in how they are taxed. Every public corporation is subject to double taxation. First, the corporation's earnings are subject to corporate taxes, at corporate tax rates (currently a flat 28 percent). What's left over after the payment of the corporate tax is either reinvested by the corporation or distributed to the shareholders as dividends. The dividend distributions are not deductible, and the shareholders pay taxes on the dividends they receive, currently set at a flat 15 percent. The result is that the same earnings are taxed twice, first by the corporation and then by the shareholders.

Joe, Jimmy, and Jane could avoid this problem by not incorporating and conducting their business as a general partnership. However, as we shall see in Chapter 8, from an asset protection standpoint, operating as a general partnership is the absolute worst way to conduct business, since it increases everyone's liability. Joe, Jimmy, and Jane could incorporate and eliminate their corporate tax liability by paying themselves salaries and bonuses. But the IRS frowns on this technique, and often seeks to recharacterize the salaries and bonuses as what they often are—disguised dividends.

In 1962, Congress gave millions of small businesses a way of out of this conundrum with the enactment of Subchapter S of the Internal Revenue Code. Under "sub-S," a qualifying corporation (an "S Corporation") may elect to simply not be taxed. The corporation is ignored, and the shareholders are automatically taxed on their proportionate shares of the corporation's net income, in the same way that the earnings of a general partnership are taxed. There is something of a trap in subchapter S, however. Let's assume that Joe, Jimmy, and Jane elect sub-S status for Three J's. Let's also assume that Three J's has $300,000 in net income in 2008. But Joe, Jimmy, and Jane decide that it would be prudent to keep the $300,000 in the bank for some planned future expansion. Are Joe, Jimmy, and Jane taxed on the $300,000 that has not been distributed to them? Absolutely. Of course, they don't have the cash to pay their taxes, since no cash has been distributed to them. They are the not-so-proud owners of "phantom income," a common byproduct of S corporation status.

Most small businesses qualify for S corporation status. But any corporation that has more than 75 shareholders, or even one shareholder that is not an individual (e.g., another corporation, limited liability company, or partnership), or even one shareholder that is a foreigner not subject to U.S. taxation, may not elect S corporation status. In addition, in order to qualify, you must be an operating business. Businesses who do nothing but clip coupons from passive investments don't qualify. Corporations that don't qualify are often called "regular" corporations or "C" corporations, from subchapter C of the tax code governing such corporations.

There is a common misconception that S corporations do not provide their shareholders with the same asset protection that C corporations do. It's nothing more than a misconception. The only difference between S corporations and C corporations is in how they are taxed. S corporations and C corporations are formed in the same manner and are subject to the same rules with respect to how they are governed and the relations between their shareholders, directors, officers, and creditors. An S corporation's existence is ignored for tax purposes, but only for tax purposes.

Respondeat Superior ("Let the Master Answer")

An important legal doctrine not only does not limit the liability of a corporation, but expands it.

Let's assume that Three J's employs a file clerk. One day, Joe asks Jimmy to deliver an envelope filled with computer programs to a client. Jimmy sends the clerk. On the way to the client, the clerk is distracted by a woman in a short skirt, runs a stop sign, and rear-ends a motorcycle. The clerk is clearly negligent, and can be sued for his negligence. But the clerk's entire net worth consists of the $8.43 in his pocket, an MP3 player, and the clothes on his back. Suing him won't do the plaintiff much good. However, the plaintiff doesn't need to sue the clerk; he can sue Three J's.

A plaintiff's ability to sue the employer of a negligent employee isn't based on logic; it's based on public policy. Ages ago we decided that between the innocent plaintiff and the innocent employer, it was best to have the employer pay. For one, the employer hired the employee and gained the benefit of the employee's services. Secondly, the employer was in a better position than the victim to obtain insurance against the accident. In addition, making the employer liable will work to ensure that employers will be careful whom they send out into the streets. The victim has no control over that.

As a general rule, the employer will be liable for the employee's negligent acts only if the employee was acting "within the scope" of the employee's employment. The questions of what that "scope" is, what is "within" it, and what isn't have produced mountains of litigation over the years, with no clear-cut answers.

Let's go back to the file clerk. Clearly, he was acting "within the scope" of his employment, since he was running an errand for his employer. But as another example, let's assume that on his way to the client he passed the base-ball stadium and decided to take in the game before completing his mission. While at the game, the clerk got into a fistfight with another fan over who was the better center fielder, Willie Mays or Mickey Mantle. The clerk bloodied the nose of the fan, who sued not only the clerk but also Three J's. Was tak-ing in the ball game on the way to the client "within the scope" of the clerk's employment, or was the clerk, in the immortal words of Justice Benjamin Cardozo, on a "frolic of his own?"

Considering the public policy rationale for holding employers liable for the actions of employees, it should not be surprising that the ambit of "scope of employment" is very wide. Most often, if the actions of the employee are somehow tangentially related to the employee's duties, the employer will be held liable. That might include the baseball game that the employee takes in the way to the client.

Lately, there has been considerable publicity about sexual misconduct by priests involving parishioners and altar boys. The archdioceses and parishes who employ the priests have been held to account. Clearly, sexual misconduct

is not within the scope of a priest's employment. How can the parish that employed the priest be held to account? Because the contact that the priest had with the parishioner was within the scope of his duties, even if the priest acted outside of the scope of his employment by engaging in sexual relations with the parishioner.

Reducing Employer Liability

If you own a business, is there any way to insulate yourself from the actions of your employees? It's not easy. If your delivery driver runs over a pedestrian while making a delivery, the corporation will have to pay. But there is some liability you can avoid.

In recent years, we have seen a dramatic rise in workplace litigation involving sexual harassment and discrimination. The owners of a business cannot monitor every manager who decides it might be fun to grope a secretary. How can the owners avoid the huge liabilities that can result from a successful discrimination or harassment complaint? By establishing written policies that clearly describe exactly what conduct is prohibited, and by employing formal procedures that enable employees to confidentially air grievances before they become lawsuits. Attorneys who specialize in employment law can review or write an employment manual that will go a long way toward insulating you and your business from lawsuits arising from conduct you are not aware of.

Exceptions to Limited Liability

Forming a corporation doesn't mean that there are no circumstances under which you might be held personally liable for the debts of your corporation. This section lists the most important exceptions to the general rule.

Preincorporation Liabilities

I'm surprised by the number of people who believe that by incorporating their businesses, they can shield themselves from liabilities that arose prior to the date of incorporation. If the creation of a corporation is the creation of a separate legal person, then there was no such person prior to its creation. If the clerk who works for Joe, Jimmy, and Jane rear-ends a motorcycle prior to the date of incorporation of Three J's (i.e., if the clerk worked for a partnership comprised of Joe, Jimmy, and Jane prior to the formation of the corporation), then Joe, Jimmy, and Jane will all be liable for the clerk's torts before Three J's came into existence.

Personal Guarantees

Every banker is familiar with the concept of limited liability. Every banker knows that if a bank lends money to a corporation and the corporation goes out of business without repaying the loan, the bank is left holding the bag, because the shareholders and directors of the corporation are not liable for the debts and liabilities of the corporation. To avoid this trap, banks, land-lords, and others dealing with corporations require the individuals who con-trol the corporations to sign personal guarantees. A guarantee is exactly what it says: "If the corporation doesn't pay, I guarantee that I will." Not every cor-poration's officers and directors are required to offer their guarantees. When ExxonMobil borrows money, the directors don't have to guarantee the debt; ExxonMobil's credit is sufficient. But when Joe, Jimmy, and Jane wish to expand their fledgling business, their personal guarantees will likely be required.

It may not be possible to avoid a personal guarantee, but it is possible to mitigate the scope of a guarantee. The guarantee is part of the whole package of the loan, and it is negotiable to the same extent as the interest rate, the fees, and the security for the loan. For example, if Three J's borrows $600,000, the bank will likely ask Joe, Jimmy, and Jane to each guarantee the entire $600,000 debt, a concept often referred to as joint and several liability. That means that if Jimmy and Jane run off to Pago Pago and are never heard of again, Joe is stuck for the whole $600,000, something he may not have planned on when he went into business with the now-departed Jimmy and Jane. The way to avoid this trap is to insist that each of the guarantors will be liable only for his or her proportionate share of the debt.

A zinger that often appears in guarantees (always in the fine print) is the bank's option to accelerate the loan if one of the guarantors dies. You avoid this by informing the banker that this is not acceptable and needs to be deleted if they wish to make the loan. At that point, it's a simple matter of negotiation. If there are other banks who are hungrier for the business, they will delete the offending provision. Banks cannot make profits without making loans, and because banks compete against each other like competitors in any business, you might be successful in negotiating such a provision out of the guarantee.

As we saw in Chapter 6, if you live in a separate property state and only one of two spouses is the debtor, the creditors of the debtor-spouse can go after the property of only that debtor-spouse. The creditors of the debtor-spouse cannot go after the separate property of the other spouse. That advantage is eliminated if both spouses are debtors, which will happen if both spouses guarantee the debt. Married persons who are in business should be offended when their spouses who do not participate in the business are asked to join in the guarantees. This should be resisted.

Statutory Exceptions

In some cases, a statute imposes liability on corporate directors, shareholders, and officers for corporate liabilities.

The most common of these is the provision contained in the Internal Revenue Code that makes any "responsible" person liable for the taxes that are withheld from employees' wages but are not then turned over to the government. Why would anyone do this? If a business begins to fail, or if cash flow is tight, you cannot fail to pay the utilities or the rent. The employees need to be paid or they will leave, and if the suppliers aren't paid they stop shipping. Very often, the most expedient thing to do is make the IRS an unwilling, unsecured creditor by not paying over the employees' federal and state taxes or the required Social Security withholdings. Any controlling shareholder, and all directors and officers, are "responsible" persons for the purposes of this statute. A responsible person will be liable only if the failure to pay was "willful," but this is a very low standard, and usually translates into knowing that the tax withholdings weren't paid (26 U.S.C. §6672). Even if you didn't know that the IRS was not being paid, you might be held liable if you so completely delegated your responsibilities that you should have known. You might avoid liability if you can show you asked your corporate controller every week whether the IRS had been paid, and he assured you every week that he had personally made the payments, when in fact he had been using the money to buy baubles for his girlfriend. But aside from that, personal liability for the corporation's employment tax liabilities is a sure thing.

Let's change the facts. Let's assume that instead of failing to pay its employment taxes, the corporation doesn't pay its income taxes. This is far rarer, since corporations that have sufficient earnings to have a tax liability usually pay their taxes. Nonetheless, let's assume a corporation fails to pay. Can the IRS go after the shareholders or the directors for the corporation's income tax debt? Generally, no. The reason is that even the IRS must recognize the separateness of a corporation from its shareholders and directors, and absent a statute such as §6672 of the Internal Revenue Code, which authorizes the IRS to go after the responsible persons for the withholding taxes, the IRS can do nothing.

Let's change the facts again. Let's assume that a corporation pays its taxes, but fails to pay the employees' wages. Are the shareholders and directors liable? The answer is—maybe. Under the Fair Labor Standards Act, a federal statute, the United States Department of Labor may bring suit against the "employer" to collect the unpaid wages. The "employer" is anyone who directly controls the conditions of employment of the employees. That's a far narrower standard than the broad liability that all "responsible" persons have for the payment of employment taxes. In a large, diversified corporation, it may include none of the directors or executive officers.

One state—New York—makes certain shareholders liable for the unpaid wages of a corporation. Only the ten largest shareholders are liable, and only for six months' wages. That's because an employee must bring suit for the recovery of the wages within six months. But if such a suit is timely brought, each of the ten shareholders may be liable for all of the unpaid wages, overtime, severance pay, and unpaid vacation time (see *New York Business Corporations Law* §630).

"Piercing the Corporate Veil" and the "Alter Ego" Theory

Two closely related legal doctrines operate to ignore the very existence of the corporation, so as to permit a creditor to go after the shareholders as fully as if the corporation had never been formed.

"Piercing the Corporate Veil"

The underlying rationale that permits a court to "pierce the veil," i.e., to ignore the corporation, is that the shareholders themselves disregarded the corporation. If the shareholders disregarded the separate nature of the corporation, what's wrong with allowing a creditor of the corporation to do the same?

Here's a typical example: Nine years ago, Dr. Black, at the advice of this attorney, formed "Dr. Black, Inc., a Medical Corporation." In a little ceremony in the attorney's office, Dr. Black adopted the corporate bylaws and signed the stock certificates. Everyone was very pleased. Nine years later, the corporation has conducted no meetings. The corporation has no bank account. If you were to look at Dr. Brown's checkbook, you would see that purchases for medical equipment appear side by side with purchases at Toys-R-Us. In all these years, Dr. Black, Inc., a Medical Corporation has not yet gotten around to filing a corporate tax return. Dr. Black, Inc. is sued by a patient who trips on the carpet leaving the office. The complaint asks the court to pierce the corporate veil and hold the controlling shareholder—Dr. Black—personally liable for the corporation's judgment.

Based on these egregious facts, courts in most states would "pierce the veil" and hold Dr. Brown liable. Courts differ in their approach, but a shareholder's disregard of his or her own corporation is the surest way to have the corporation pierced. Corporations are ignored if their shareholders don't maintain corporate records, fail to sign contracts in the name of the corporation, and don't maintain separate financial records. See a checklist on the next page.

In many states, commingling is not the only criterion. Often, undercapitalization will result in piercing the veil, especially if it is coupled with commingling. Generally, undercapitalization is measured only when the

---

Avoiding the Piercing of the Corporate Veil: The Dos and Don'ts

The Dos

- Keep your own funds and the funds of your corporation separate.
- Maintain corporate minutes and other corporate records.
- Keep separate records for all of your corporations and other entities.
- Maintain separate officers and directors for each entity.
- Adhere to legal formalities when signing contracts, leases, etc.
- Obtain board of directors' approval for major corporate actions.

The Don'ts

- Do not divert corporate assets for personal uses.
- Never assert that a shareholder is liable for a corporate debt.
- Avoid identical ownership of more than one entity.
- Do not use the corporation as a shield for your or someone else's personal liability.

---

corporation is formed, not when it later begins to lose money and cannot pay its creditors. A corporation is undercapitalized if it is not likely to be able to pay the debts that naturally arise as it engages in business.

Even if commingling and undercapitalization exist, the veil will not be pierced in many states unless failure to pierce the veil would result in an "inequitable" outcome. This is a fairly high standard, since it is understood that limited liability is the reason corporations are formed in the first place. In order for this standard to be met, there must be some showing that the corporation was formed or availed of for some fraudulent purpose.

One state, Texas, severely limits the ability of a creditor to use the piercing doctrine. Under a Texas statute, a shareholder will not be held liable for the debts of a corporation unless the creditor can show that the shareholder caused the corporation to be used for the purpose of committing fraud, the corporation did commit the fraud, and the fraud was committed for the shareholder's personal benefit (see *Texas Business Corporations Act* Art. 2.21). That means that the maintenance of corporate formalities, the commingling of corporate and shareholder funds, and undercapitalization are all irrelevant in Texas. It means that the chances of a court piercing the veil in Texas are slim.

The Alter Ego Theory

A court may ignore the separate existence of a corporation if it finds that the corporation was the "alter ego" of another person or, more often, of another corporation. If one corporation is the alter ego of another, the assets of the second corporation can be reached to answer for the liabilities of the first. The alter ego theory is very close to the piercing of the corporate veil. Courts often state that the veil is being pierced because another corporation, or an individual in control of one or more corporations, is the alter ego of the disregarded corporation.

The alter ego theory is most often applied to disregard an undercapitalized or insolvent debtor corporation in order to reach the assets of a related and financially healthier corporation. Here is a typical example: Real Dirt, Inc. is a corporation owned by Mr. Bigg. Snow White, Inc. is also owned by Mr. Bigg. Neither is a subsidiary of the other; they are "brother-sister" corporations in that they have common ownership: Mr. Bigg. Real Dirt, Inc. operates a paint factory, and it has been cited by the Environmental Protection Agency for numerous violations and required to perform a cleanup far in excess of its assets. When it comes to enforcing the cleanup order, the EPA would like to go after Snow White's assets. Of course, Snow White, Inc. is a separate corporation, and it was not involved in the toxic spill that caused Real Dirt, Inc. to be cited. The EPA would like to prove that Real Dirt, Inc. and Snow White, Inc. are so close that their separate corporate identities should be ignored, i.e., that each is the alter ego of the other.

What it takes to prove that one corporation is the alter ego of the other is similar to what it takes to pierce the corporate veil. Failing to maintain the corporate formalities (no board meetings, no minutes, etc.) will usually result in one corporation being deemed the alter ego of the other. In one case, there were numerous corporate entities all under one corporate umbrella. An executive was called to testify, and he said that he was a "vice president." But as the attorney for the plaintiff began to reel off the names of the various corporations, the executive was forced to admit that even though he held the title of "vice president," he wasn't quite sure which corporations he was the "vice president" of. Needless to say, it wasn't too much of a stretch to find that each of these corporations was the alter ego of the other.

In addition to failure to maintain the corporate formalities, three other criteria are generally employed to determine alter ego liability:

- Dominance of one entity over another
- Economic dependency of one entity upon another
- Administrative dependency of one entity upon another

One entity can be said to dominate another if the same persons comprise the board of directors of both corporations. It's even worse if two or more corporations have the same people filling the same executive offices. In the previous example, there is no escaping the fact that Mr. Bigg is the sole shareholder of both Real Dirt, Inc. and Snow White, Inc., but these two entities would not be hurt if they had different people on their boards of directors.

Economic dependence exists when one corporation cannot stand on its own two feet and relies upon another corporation to exist. If Real Dirt, Inc. is insolvent, has never turned a profit, and relies upon Snow White, Inc. for capital infusions and loans, it might be fair to infer that Real Dirt, Inc. never had a bona fide separate existence, and was only split off from Snow White, Inc. to shield Snow White's assets from Real Dirt's liabilities.

Administrative dependence occurs when one corporation relies upon another for its day-to-day operations. If one corporation relies upon another for its accounting, bookkeeping, and legal functions, it may not really be a separate entity. It may be nothing more than the adjunct of another corporation.

The Limits of Limited Liability

We noted in Chapter 4 that before we can craft an asset protection plan, one of the questions we must ask is "Who is the defendant?" If the defendant is the corporation itself, a plaintiff armed with a judgment against the corporation will be able to seize the corporation's assets, but will be unable to go after the shareholders' assets—unless, of course, the plaintiff is successful in piercing the corporate veil or in proving that another corporation is the alter ego of the defendant. Planning for that day is sometimes called "inside-out" asset protection, i.e., the plaintiff has a judgment against the corporation ("inside") and now seeks to go "outside" the corporation to the shareholders or to another corporation in order to satisfy the judgment.

The situation is completely different if the defendant is the shareholder. If the plaintiff has a judgment against the shareholder but not against the corporation, the plaintiff will not likely be able to satisfy the judgment against the corporation, unless the corporation is the alter ego of the shareholder, a process sometimes referred to as "reverse piercing." But there may be an indirect way for the plaintiff to get at the corporation's assets. One of the shareholder's assets is that stock certificate that represents the shareholder's ownership interest in the corporation. If the shareholder is a majority owner of the corporation, the plaintiff who is able to seize the stock certificate has a road map to the corporation's assets, because majority ownership means control of the corporation. Once the plaintiff seizes the corporation, the corporation's assets will fall into the plaintiff's lap. Of course, if the shareholder does not own a majority interest in the corporation, the plaintiff, now armed with a minority stake in the corporation, may become a nuisance, but will not be able to liquidate the corporation for the plaintiff's own benefit.

We shall see in the following chapter that one of the advantages of limited partnerships and limited liability companies over corporations is that partners in limited partnerships and members of LLCs generally do not have stock certificates that can be seized. Creditors of partners in partnerships and creditors of members of LLCs generally have a difficult time going "outside-in", i.e., satisfying a judgment against an individual owner by going against the assets of the entity. This is the principal advantage that these entities have over corporations, and why the corporate form is becoming an increasingly disfavored form of ownership.

Planning Tips for Corporations

Here are a couple of planning tips to consider that might help keep your corporation in your hands and out of the hands of creditors.

Asset Protection Using Buy-Sell Agreements

One of the most common planning tools owners of closely held businesses employ is the buy-sell agreement, often referred to as shareholders' agreement. The planning it is used for is generally not for asset protection, but it can be.

Buy-sell agreements are invaluable tools for ensuring that a corporation survives the death, retirement, or disability of a shareholder. Let's take a typical example: Ellen, Sharon, and Daisy are equal shareholders in West Coast Wholesale Produce, Inc. Each of them is married, but none of their husbands works in the business. They have been advised that if the corporation were sold, it could fetch $6 million. Ellen, Sharon and Daisy each take $500,000 out of the business annually in salary, bonuses, and perks. Let's assume that Ellen were to die. Under Ellen's estate plan, her stock in the corporation goes to her husband. That presents a problem for Ellen's surviving husband, Eli, and for Sharon and Daisy. The last thing that Sharon and Daisy wish to do is take Eli into the business, considering his work habits (none) and his drinking habits (substantial). Eli doesn't wish to work in the business. The stock certificate he inherited from Ellen is worthless in his hands until the business is sold.

The solution for both Eli and the remaining shareholders is a buy-sell agreement saying that Eli must sell his stock to Sharon and Daisy (or back to the corporation) and the corporation must buy the stock from Eli. Technically, Eli has a "put" in the inherited stock and the corporation has a "call" on the stock. At what price should the stock be sold? The best way to establish the price is to have an independent, qualified appraiser determine the price, which, under the agreement, is binding on the buyer and the seller. The effect of the agreement is to provide a market for Eli to sell the stock and to provide a mechanism for Sharon and Daisy to avoid dealing with an unwanted business associate.

How do Sharon and Daisy raise the money to buy Eli out? The easiest way is to buy a life insurance policy on the lives of each of the shareholders. The death benefit should be reviewed annually to assure that it is sufficient to cover the likely buyout price. In our example, Eli gets the death benefit and Sharon and Daisy get his stock, without Sharon and Daisy having to dig into their pockets or to break the cash register to fund the buyout of Eli.

The tax code even provides Eli with a benefit, by making the purchase of the inherited stock nontaxable. This is as a result of the "step up in basis" rule. Generally, capital gains (and the taxes on the capital gains) are measured by the difference between your tax basis in the asset and the sales price of the asset. If I bought ExxonMobil stock for $40 per share, that's my tax basis. If I sell the stock for $100 per share, my capital gain is $60 per share. Let's assume that Ellen contributed $10,000 to the corporation when it was formed. That's her tax basis. If her stock was worth $2 million when she died, the gain inherent in the stock is a whopping $1,990,000. But wait! Eli inherited the stock. That means that the tax basis is "stepped up" to the $2 million date-of-death value, so that when he sells the stock back to Sharon and Daisy, his tax basis equals the amount he receives for the stock, resulting in no capital gain! (See 26 U.S.C. §1014.)

All that is fine for buying out the estate of a deceased shareholder, but what does it have to do with asset protection? The same buy-sell agreement can be used to assure that no creditor of any shareholder can ever get his or her hands on a shareholder's stock by including a "poison pill" in the buy-sell agreement. A typical poison pill says, "If anyone other than the original shareholders obtains control of any shareholder's shares, the corporation has the right to buy those shares for xxxx dollars."

Needless to say, the "xxxx" is a formula so low as to inhibit any creditor from going after the shares. Obtaining the shares becomes a fruitless exercise, since the corporation will take the shares back and give a very small check in return.

The poison pill is one of the few opportunities we have to do some predivorce asset protection planning. Let's assume that Ellen, Sharon, and Daisy have determined that the last thing they want to happen is for the stock in their corporation to become the subject of the divorce proceeding. They don't want to run the risk that one of their husbands might threaten to take a portion of their stock in the divorce, knowing that the result would be so horrible that they would pay a premium to avoid it from happening. So, the poison pill says that if any shareholder files a divorce petition, or has a divorce petition filed against her, the remaining shareholders have the right to buy out that share-holder's stock. They might sell her stock back after the divorce is final, but at least the stock will not be part of the division of assets in the divorce.

A Final Tip

Here is a tip easily stated:

> **Klueger's Rule of Corporate Ownership:** The corporation that provides the services should not be the same corporation that owns the assets.

Here's an example: Dr. Brown is a family practitioner, operating as "Arnold Brown, M.D., a Professional Corporation." Patients and insurance providers pay their bills to the corporation, and the corporation provides the medical services. Of course, Dr. Brown's corporation will not shield him from malpractice claims. Dr. Brown owns the building in which his medical clinic is housed. He also owns medical equipment that could fetch $250,000.

Should "Arnold Brown, M.D., a Professional Corporation" own these valuable assets? Of course not. Nor should Dr. Brown himself, because in the event of a malpractice action, he will be sued in his individual capacity. The real estate and the equipment should be owned by a separate entity—prefer-ably a limited liability company—that performs no medical services and that leases the equipment to the medical corporation. The medical corporation should enter into a premises lease with the LLC, and the rent should be a fair market rental. The result is that if creditors come calling, the corporation liable for the malpractice has no assets worth seizing, and the entity with the assets has provided no services.

Is it possible for a plaintiff to allege that the medical corporation and the limited liability company that owns the assets are really alter egos of each other, and should be collapsed into one entity? Not if we plan carefully. Each entity should be sufficiently capitalized, and all of the corporate formalities should be met. It would be great if the leasing entity would also lease space to a tenant other than the medical corporation, and even better if it leased med-ical equipment to another doctor.

Asset Protection Using Domestic Trusts

It is a rare asset protection plan that does not involve some form of a trust. If the trust is governed by the laws of one of the 50 states or the District of Columbia with a U.S. trustee, it's a domestic trust. If the trust is governed by the laws of a foreign country with a foreign trustee, it is, of course, a foreign trust. More on that in Chapter 10.

Trusts are favored asset protection devices for one basic, fundamental reason: with a trust, a person may transfer the title to an asset to someone else (the trustee of the trust) without losing the enjoyment of the asset or the income from the asset.

Who Is Who in a Trust

Let's take some of the mystery out of trusts. Let's see who the "players" are.

Every trust has at least three "players," the settlor, the trustee, and the beneficiary. The settlor is usually the person who creates the trust. In some states, the settlor is referred to as the trustor, the grantor, or the creator of the trust. The settlor is the person who deposits assets into the trust. The assets of the trust are the principal, or, for those of us who love the Latin, the trust *corpus.*

The settlor deposits the corpus with the trustee. The trustee is the most important—and active—player in a trust. The trustee holds and distributes the assets in accordance with the wishes of the settlor. The trustee is a fiduciary, acting for the benefit of the beneficiaries. The trustee cannot use the trust corpus for the trustee's personal benefit unless specifically authorized by the settlor. The trustee is legally obligated to use the trust corpus in a manner requiring at least as much (and often more) care as the trustee's own property. If the trustee messes up, the trustee can be sued by the settlor, the beneficiaries, or both. If the trustee really messes up, it's a crime.

Settlors sometimes create trusts and deposit assets with a trustee under the misimpression that the trustee acts as a fiduciary for the settlor. The trustee's fiduciary duty of care runs to beneficiaries, not the settlor.

The beneficiaries are the people for whom the trust is created by the settlor, and for whom the trustee manages the assets. They have the most passive roles in a trust, with nothing to do but wait for the trustee to do whatever the trustee is required to do under the trust. It comes as a sad surprise to many people who are the beneficiaries of trusts that they have no say in the operation of a trust. Of course, if the trustee breaches his or her fiduciary duty, the beneficiaries can sue to enforce the terms of the trust or ask a judge to toss out the trustee and appoint someone else.

Most states have no requirement that a trust be in writing, but most trusts are written because it's extremely foolish to create an oral trust. Anyone who wants to assure that the trustee does what the trustee is supposed to do, and that the beneficiaries receive what is intended for them, will create a written trust. Every trust created for asset protection purposes will be in writing. The document embodying the settlor's desires (and the trustee's instructions) is often referred to in the United States as the declaration of trust, the trust agreement, or simply the trust. Trusts created in foreign countries are often referred to as deeds of settlement.

Once the trust document is written and signed, the settlor will transfer assets to the trustee, and those assets become the trust corpus.

What tends to confuse many people about trusts is that the settlor, the trustee, and the beneficiaries often are the same people. Nothing prevents the settlor from naming himself or herself as the trustee, although, as we shall shortly see, to be both the settlor and the trustee may have negative asset protection and tax consequences. The trustee may also be a beneficiary of a trust. Indeed, a person may be a settlor, trustee, and a beneficiary of a trust at once.

Here's a common example. Let's assume Mr. and Mrs. Brown create a trust for their children. They are both the settlors and the trustees. When they transfer their residence to the trust, the deed will include a provision stating, "John Brown and June Brown, grantors, hereby transfer to John Brown and June Brown, as trustees of The Brown Family Trust, under instrument dated January 2, 2008."

If the trust also provides that Mr. and Mrs. Brown will receive the income from the trust during their lives, then the Browns are the settlors, the trustees, and the beneficiaries of the trust.

Living Trusts and Testamentary Trusts

A trust that comes into being during the settlor's lifetime is often called a living trust, or, for the lovers of Latin, an *inter vivos* trust. In the previous example, when Mr. and Mrs. Brown created the trust and signed over the ownership to themselves as trustees during their lifetime, they created an inter vivos trust.

A trust is sometimes created only when the settlor dies. The trust, created by the settlor's will, is called a testamentary trust. Let us assume that Mr. and Mrs. Brown have two young children. During their joint lifetimes, and during the lifetime of the survivor of them, they will care for their children. But if they both should die while their children are minors, they're not likely to want their children to receive their estate outright; they'll want someone to retain the estate for the children, distributing the assets to them only when the children are adults or otherwise competent to handle the assets. That's where the testamentary trust comes in. A trustee is named in the decedent's will who takes control of the assets on the decedent's death and administers the trust in accordance with the settlor's wishes.

Clients often ask me what they can say in a trust. The answer is almost anything. If you want to leave $10,000 to your cousin Sally provided she becomes an Eagle Scout, that's your prerogative. It's your money, and you're limited only by your imagination. The only things you cannot do with your money are a small class of bequests prohibited by public policy. For example, if you write a trust that leaves "Ten thousand dollars to my cousin Sally, provided she divorces her husband Joe," you can rest assured Sally will get the money if she stays married to Joe or not. Similarly, "Ten thousand dollars to cousin Sally, provided she is not married to a black man" will go to Sally, regardless of whom she marries.

Are living trusts better than testamentary trusts? In a few key aspects, they are. First, because a testamentary trust comes into being only at the settlor's death, it can provide no asset protection for the settlor. Depending on how the trust is worded, it might well provide a great deal of asset protection for the beneficiaries after the settlor dies.

A second advantage of the living trust over the testamentary trust (and the reason most living trusts are created) is that a living trust enables the settlor's estate to avoid probate when the settlor dies; a testamentary trust does not.

Little creates more confusion in the minds of nonlawyers than the whole probate process. Many people are aware that probate is something that needs to be avoided, but they aren't sure why. And if they know why they need to avoid it (because they went through it with a relative), they usually don't know how a living trust helps them avoid it.

Here's how. Let's assume that Mr. and Mrs. Brown own a home titled in joint tenancy. Mr. Brown owns a stock investment account and a certificate of deposit. Mrs. Brown owns a certificate of deposit. Mr. Brown owns a life insurance policy that pays $100,000 on his death to his designated beneficiary, Mrs. Brown. Mr. Brown has a one-page will that leaves everything to Mrs. Brown on his death, but no trust.

What happens when Mr. Brown dies? Mrs. Brown will have no problem getting the $100,000 death benefit from the insurance company. Because the life insurance policy is a contract Mr. Brown signed with the insurance carrier, all Mrs. Brown needs to do is present the insurance carrier with a certified copy of a death certificate, and a few days later she'll receive the money. The same is true of the home in joint tenancy. Because the essence of joint tenancy is that the survivor, who has the right of survivorship, gets to keep the property when the first joint tenant dies, all Mrs. Brown will need to do is present an affidavit and a certified copy of the death certificate to the county recorder to have the property titled in her name alone. The life insurance and the joint tenancy property pass to the survivor automatically; they're not part of the probate estate.

But what of the stock portfolio? Let's assume that Mrs. Brown visits the stockbroker, armed with a copy of Mr. Brown's will (which clearly and unambiguously leaves everything to her) and a copy of the death certificate. Will the stockbroker transfer the stock fund into Mrs. Brown's name? Not likely. The stockbroker will most likely inform Mrs. Brown that he can transfer title to the assets only if Mrs. Brown first obtains letters testamentary or letters of administration. Where do you get these? The probate court.

Probate is the process of physically transferring the title to assets from a deceased person to living persons. Note that the fact that Mr. Brown had a will that clearly left everything to Mrs. Brown doesn't avoid probate. Mr. Brown's will is a directive; it informs the probate court of where the assets are supposed to go. But because Mr. Brown can't reach up out of the grave to sign over the title to the stock certificates from himself to Mrs. Brown, Mrs. Brown needs the probate court to get the titles transferred to her.

Why is all of this so awful? If you've had a relative whose estate needed to be probated, you know. Depending on the state in which the estate is probated, the process will range from the merely inconvenient, if you're lucky, to the downright Dickensian, if you're not. You will spend anywhere from six months to two years in the clutches of lawyers. You will need to have the assets appraised, even if you have no intention of selling them. If you want to sell an asset, you'll need the probate judge's consent. You will get writer's cramp signing motions, petitions, and waivers. And the entire process will be completely open to public inspection. So you needn't be surprised if you're inundated by calls and letters from real estate appraisers, liquidators, and financial planners soliciting their services.

It's not only time-consuming and annoying, it's also expensive. Some states, like California, fix the amount the administrator and the lawyer may charge to probate the estate. In other states, it's whatever you can bargain for. But don't be surprised if the probate fees consume 5 to 8 percent of the estate. For what? For the little piece of paper, the letters testamentary, that you need to transfer the assets in accordance with the decedent's expressed will.

That's the bad news. The good news is that it's all completely avoidable with a living trust to which you have transferred your assets. Review the transfer of the residence from Mr. and Mrs. Brown to Mr. and Mrs. Brown as trustees of The Brown Family Trust. When Mr. Brown dies, the property is already in the trust, and Mrs. Brown, as cotrustee, already owns it. When Mrs. Brown dies, a successor trustee steps in and takes control of the trust. What is there for the probate court to do? Absolutely nothing. If Mr. and Mrs. Brown make sure that The Brown Family Trust, not either of them, has title to the stock certificates, the bank accounts, the certificates of deposit, and the real estate, there will be nothing for the probate court to do when either of them dies, and probate is avoided.

Some of my clients often express a concern that the probate court judges might frown on this obvious avoidance of the judicial system. Do they? No, they don't, for the same reason that criminal court judges aren't put off by people not committing crimes.

Living Trusts and Asset Protection

Dying is, for most people, too extreme a method to avoid one's creditors. We don't recommend death as a planning tool to most of our clients. But while we're on the subject, can you avoid your creditors by dying? If you set up a living trust, the answer is maybe. Here's why.

Let's assume that Debbie Debtor died owing $30,000 on six credit cards. She also signed a $10,000 promissory note, owed $1,200 to Dr. Smiles, her dentist, and owed $50,000 on a student loan. Further assume that Debbie didn't have a living trust, so that her estate had to be probated. One of the many things that her executor is required to do is publish a notice in a local newspaper stating that Debbie has died, and anyone who was owed money by Debbie should submit a claim to the executor. In most states, a creditor has a very limited time (anywhere from 30 days to six months) to file a claim. If you don't file a claim in that period of time, the executor may distribute the estate's assets to the beneficiaries, and you're out of luck.

Not only that, but 39 states also have a self-executing statute of limitations. If a creditor doesn't sue the estate for payment within a certain period of time, the creditor is out of luck. Moreover, these statutes of limitations start to run when the decedent dies, and they're not dependent on the executor ever starting a probate proceeding. The statute of limitations in California, Massachusetts, and Ohio is one year. It's two years in Florida and Illinois, and three years in Michigan (New York, New Jersey, and Pennsylvania, among others, have no such statute). If Debbie had died a resident of California, her creditors would have one year to sue to recover their debts. If they didn't, they could give up their claims.

Note that the executor needs only publish a notice that Debbie died and that her probate has been opened. There's usually little chance that her creditors will see the notice. If they don't see the notice, they won't know that Debbie died, and the self-executing statute of limitations will run out before they ever find out that she died! Is this too good to be true?

Yes, it is. In 1988, the Supreme Court ruled that if you start a probate and you know a creditor has a claim, telling him about the probate through a published notice isn't enough; it's a denial of the creditor's rights under the Due Process clause of the Fourteenth Amendment of the U.S. Constitution. If you know of a creditor's claim, you have to give the creditor actual notice, by sending a letter or by picking up the phone.

But here's where things get technical. The Due Process clause is violated only where there is some state action—that is, where the government somehow is involved in due process being denied. And there's nothing that involves the government more intimately than a probate proceeding.

But what if there is no probate, as in a case where the decedent had a living trust? Let's assume Debbie died on January 15, 2008. If all her assets were in a living trust, there would be no need to inform her creditors, because there would be no need ever to start a probate. If Debbie was a California resident, the clock would start to tick on January 15, 2008 and time would run out on January 15, 2009. If the creditors didn't learn of Debbie's death until more than a year later, they'd be out of luck.

Isn't this a denial of due process? No, it isn't, because there was no "state action." The Supreme Court specifically ruled that the mere running of a general statute of limitations is generally not sufficient to implicate due process.

Does that mean that Debbie's creditors are completely out of luck? Not necessarily. How did the executor keep the credit card companies from finding out that Debbie had died? Did he make the monthly interest payments on the credit cards, counting the days until the statute of limitations ran? Perhaps the executor himself committed fraud. Even if he didn't, there may be a state law that makes a trust liable for the debts of the settlor.

What about that student loan that Debbie owed? Can her estate use the state's self-executing statute of limitations to beat the U.S. Department of Education out of their debt? Probably not. The reason stems from yet another provision of the Constitution, the Supremacy clause, which makes federal laws superior to state laws where they conflict. It isn't likely that a federal debt will ever be barred by a state statute of limitations.

Revocable Trusts and Irrevocable Trusts

The most important thing you need to know about any trust is whether the trust is revocable or irrevocable by the settlor. The asset protection consequences are substantial.

If a trust is revocable, it will provide absolutely no asset protection to the settlor. That makes sense. If the settlor has the power to tear up the trust and retrieve all the assets given to the trustee, nothing should prevent a court from ordering the settlor to exercise that power in favor of a creditor.

For a trust to afford any asset protection for the settlor, it must, therefore, be totally irrevocable. That means that, at least technically, once you give the assets to the trustee, you cannot get them back. We say technically because, even though the language of the trust cannot require a trustee to return assets to the settlor, there is nothing to prevent a friendly trustee from voluntarily returning assets to the settlor should the settlor so request.

May the settlor of an irrevocable trust also be the trustee? Yes, but from an asset protection standpoint, it's not advisable. If the settlor is also the trustee, a court might order the trustee to exercise a power vested in the trustee in favor of a creditor. A court might do that whether or not the settlor is also the trustee. But if the trustee is independent of the settlor, it makes the argument that the trustee is acting only for the benefit of the beneficiaries more believable.

It isn't always easy to determine whether a trust is irrevocable. Often the trust will specify that the settlor reserves the right to amend or alter it at any time, or that the settlor may not ever alter or amend it. But often the trust is silent. In that case, it's necessary to check the powers the trust reserves to the settlor, and state law to determine if it creates a presumption in favor of revocability or irrevocability if the document is silent.

Is the Transfer a Fraudulent Conveyance?

The creation of a revocable trust isn't a fraudulent conveyance, because it isn't a conveyance. In the eyes of the law, the settlor armed with the power to retrieve the assets hasn't really transferred them. Because the settlor started out owning the assets and ends up owning them, he or she cannot be said to have made a transfer. That doesn't mean that revocable trusts don't serve useful purposes. As we have already seen, they avoid probate on the settlor's death. They can also serve to care for the settlor and the settlor's children or other loved ones during the settlor's disability.

If a trust is irrevocable, however, it is very definitely subject to the law of fraudulent conveyances. It is so for the simple reason that whenever the settlor transfers assets to a trustee, the settlor receives nothing in return. And as we saw in Chapter 4, one of the badges of fraud is the transferor not receiving anything in return.

That is not to say, however, that the creation of every irrevocable trust is a fraudulent conveyance. It just means that when we create an irrevocable trust, we need to "jump through the hoops." We need to assure that the settlor isn't rendered insolvent by the transfer, and that the transfer is done openly. And most important (you've heard this before), we need to create the trust and transfer assets to it before creditors come calling. Once again, an irrevocable trust works a lot better to defeat the claims of creditors if it's established before you develop creditors rather than after.

If the transfer of the assets to the trustee is not a fraudulent conveyance, an irrevocable trust serves very well to shield the assets from the settlor's creditors, because an irrevocable trust is, in the eyes of the law, a legal "person," separate and distinct from the settlor.

Self-Settled Trusts

A self-settled trust is a trust in which the settlor names himself or herself as a beneficiary. Even if the trust is truly irrevocable, in most states such a trust will not afford the settlor much asset protection. The settlor's creditors will be able to reach the trust's assets, irrespective of the irrevocable nature of the trust. This holds true whether or not the settlor is also the trustee of the trust. Of course, a trust in which the settlor is not a named beneficiary cannot be a self-settled trust.

Exceptions to the Rule

Recently, a number of states, notably Alaska, Delaware, and Nevada, have amended their laws to permit self-settled trusts. If you come within the narrow parameters of these statutes, you may be both the settlor and the beneficiary—even the sole beneficiary—and still shield the trust's assets from the claims of creditors (see *Delaware Code Ann.* tit. 12 §§3570-3576 and *Alaska Stat.* §34.40.110). These statutes are modeled after a number of the popular offshore asset protection countries, all of whom permit self-settled trusts.

To comply with the Alaska statute, the trustee must be an Alaska resident, an Alaska trust company, or a bank having its principal place of business in Alaska. Some of the trust's assets must be deposited in Alaska, and the trust must be irrevocable. However, an Alaska self-settled trust will provide the settlor with no asset protection if all or part of the trust's income or principal must be distributed to the settlor. In other words, if the settlor is a beneficiary, the trust must be discretionary to the trustee. Nor will the trust shield the settlor from child support arrearages. Finally, the trust will not trump fraudulent conveyance considerations. If the trust is created to hinder, delay, or defraud a creditor, it won't work.

Delaware and Nevada's statutes are similar to the Alaska statute in that they require the trustee to be an individual or trust company resident in their state. The trust must be discretionary as to the beneficiary's interest, and the trust must not have been created for the purpose of delaying, hindering, or defrauding creditors (see *Nevada Revised Stats.* §166.040).

Although these statutes are modeled after the asset protection features of some foreign jurisdictions, they suffer from limitations and uncertainties that foreign asset protection trusts do not suffer from. Let us assume that Mr. Green resides in California, a state that does not permit self-settled trusts. Mr. Green creates a trust in Alaska, naming an Alaska trustee. He deposits all of his assets into a bank located in Alaska. Mr. Green is sued in California, and a California court awards a judgment against Mr. Green. The plaintiff shows up in Alaska and registers his California judgment in Alaska, effectively making it an Alaska judgment. The plaintiff then shows up at the bank, seeking to levy upon the trust's assets. Must the Alaska bank honor the California judgment? The Full Faith and Credit clause of the Constitution would seem to require the bank—and the Alaska courts—to honor the California judgment. Alaska and Delaware enacted their statutes in 1997 (Nevada came along in 1999) and to this day, no one is sure how this issue will shake out, but it certainly calls the efficacy of Alaska, Delaware, and Nevada self-settled trusts into question. Needless to say, the courts of the Cook Islands, Nevis, Saint Vincent and the Grenadines, and a host of other offshore jurisdictions don't suffer from this problem.

Nor does the Full Faith and Credit clause pose the only constitutional limitation. If the creditor is the federal government, the Supremacy clause of the Constitution will trump the state law of Alaska, Delaware, or Nevada. Once again, however, the Supremacy clause has no bearing on the laws or procedures of a foreign country.

Discretionary Trusts

Transferring assets to the trustee of an irrevocable trust doesn't mean that the benefit of the assets is lost to you. Far from it. For example, if you transfer $1 million to an irrevocable trust and name yourself as an income beneficiary of the trust, there is nothing that prevents the trustee from distributing all or a portion of the annual income from the trust to you.

To keep your creditors' grasping hands off the annual income, you will need to create a discretionary trust, which is a type of irrevocable trust that gives the trustee the complete discretion to decide which of two or more beneficiaries gets paid and when. Here's an example of a clause that makes a trust a discretionary trust: "The trustees, in their sole and absolute discretion, may apply the whole, any portion, or none of the net income of the trust to one, some, or all of the beneficiaries of the trust, to the complete exclusion of one or some of the beneficiaries."

If the trust contains this or similar language, and there are in fact two or more beneficiaries, there's little chance a creditor could ever get at the income. Here's why: first, under the technical terms of the trust, no one beneficiary—including the settlor in the settlor's capacity as beneficiary—has the right to demand any income from the trustee; the trustee could cut the settlor out entirely. Second, there is an ancient principle that a creditor doesn't get an interest in a trust greater than the interest of the beneficiary. If a particular beneficiary cannot force the trustee to distribute any income to him or her, the beneficiary's creditors also cannot force a distribution. (See, for example, *California Probate Code* §15303.) Of course, should the trustee actually distribute trust income to a beneficiary, the beneficiary's creditors can go after that income. But if the beneficiary has creditor problems, and the trustee is friendly to the beneficiary, a distribution isn't likely to occur.

If you are the settlor of a trust and also a mandatory beneficiary of the trust, the trust will not afford you any asset protection (at least in most states) because the trust will be deemed to be a self-settled trust. The laws of most states simply provide that a creditor of a beneficiary of a trust can reach the assets of the trust if the beneficiary is also the settlor.

Spendthrift Trusts

When we considered assets placed into a retirement plan governed by ERISA, we noted that these assets are exempt from the claims of creditors due to the mandatory antialienation clause that is contained in each plan.

For a similar reason, the creditors of beneficiaries of a trust that contains a spendthrift clause will not be able to reach the assets of the trust. Such a trust is commonly known as a spendthrift trust. Every trust created for asset protection purposes is a spendthrift trust. Here's an example of a spendthrift clause: "No interest in the principal or income of any trust created under this instrument shall be anticipated, assigned, encumbered, or subjected to a creditor's claim or legal process before actual receipt by the beneficiary."

Now, let's see how this provision works in real life. Let's assume that your nephew is a beneficiary of a trust you set up that contains spendthrift language as in the previous quote. Your nephew becomes a stock market addict, throwing all his cash at his brokers. One day, after he's run out of money, he cajoles his broker into lending him more money to buy stocks, based on the fact that in a few years the trustee will be required to make a distribution of trust assets to him. So the nephew signs an irrevocable assignment, assigning his interest in the trust to the broker. When the entire brokerage account is frittered away, the broker knocks on the trustee's door, demanding payment.

Is the assignment enforceable? No, it isn't, due to the language of the spendthrift clause. Read it again. It says that a beneficiary's interest in a trust may not be anticipated, which is what the nephew did, or assigned or encumbered (i.e., made subject to a security interest or lien), which is also what the nephew did.

It sounds too easy to exempt a trust from a beneficiary's creditors merely by adding one paragraph, but that's pretty much how it works. The reason it's so easy is that no one forces anyone to put money into a trust, and if you do transfer your money into a trust, you should be able to do it on your own terms. After all, if you had never established a trust for your nephew (which is your right), your nephew's creditors could never have attached your assets.

Some state laws limit the efficacy of a spendthrift clause. Creditors who provide "necessities" to a beneficiary, such as health care and food, are not subject to the spendthrift limitation. Also, since the spendthrift limitation is a creature of state law, it is probably not binding on a federal agency.

Irrevocable Trusts and Gift Taxes

Most Americans have a pretty good sense of the income tax, because most Americans have a good percentage of their paychecks withheld to pay income taxes, and those who aren't subject to withholding must still file an annual income tax return. Most people have an even closer appreciation of sales taxes, because they pay sales taxes almost every day.

It's the gift tax that remains a stranger to most people. A gift tax is due on the value of any gift. Not only that, it is the donor, the person who makes the gift, not the recipient (the donee), who is principally liable for the gift tax. So why don't I have to pay gift taxes every time I buy a bicycle for my son or a Barbie doll for my daughter? Because every person is allowed a $12,000 per calendar year exemption from gift taxes, per donee. For example, if I give $12,000 in cash to my son on December 31, and stocks and bonds worth $12,000 to my son on the next day, January 1, I pay no gift taxes. But if I give my son $4,000 on May 1 and $9,000 on June 1, $1,000 of the June 1 gift, being the amount in excess of $12,000 for that calendar year, is subject to gift taxes. And I get to pay it, not my son.

Most of my clients are incredulous when they learn about the gift tax. They cannot understand why the government gets involved in this transaction. After all, if I want to give my assets to my children, my nephews, or the Los Angeles Dodgers, that should be no one's business, least of all the U.S. Treasury. And if anyone should be liable for the gift tax, it should be the person receiving the windfall, not the person giving it. What's going on here?

Here's what. The gift tax is a necessary backstop to the estate tax. It prevents people from eliminating their exposure to estate taxes by giving everything away before they die. For example, if Uncle Irving, knowing he is about to depart this mortal coil, calls his relatives to his deathbed and parcels out all the assets, the relatives get everything and the tax collector is left holding the bag. If there's no gift tax, there's no estate tax. That's why there's a gift tax.

If an irrevocable trust really is a separate legal person, we run the risk that a transfer to the trustee of the irrevocable trust will result in an immediate gift tax. Protecting ourselves from the claims of future creditors is one thing. Doing it at the price of an immediate gift tax is something else again.

Fortunately, there is a way out. For gift tax purposes, only completed gifts are subject to gift tax. If we purposefully structure the trust so that the gift is incomplete, there is no gift to tax. We can make a gift incomplete by giving the settlor the power to shift distributions among certain classes of beneficiaries. Making a gift incomplete for gift tax purposes should not mean that the trust is revocable, resulting in the continued shielding of the trust's assets from the claims of creditors.

Irrevocable Trusts and Income Taxes

Even though we want the trust to be the owner of the assets for asset protection purposes, there are a number of reasons we'll want the settlor of the trust to be the one who is taxed on the annual income from the trust. First, the settlor may need the annual income to maintain his or her lifestyle. Second, the settlor may need the income tax deductions that the assets yield (such as depreciation deductions) to be included in his or her own tax return, rather than the trust's.

There is a simple way to accomplish this end. The trust has to be designed for income tax purposes as a "grantor" trust. We can accomplish this in a number of ways, the simplest being merely to state that the trust's income and deductions go to the settlor. If the settlor doesn't want the income, knowing there is a good chance creditors will get the income if it is distributed to him or her, but wants the trust's deductions, there are other ways we can wire the trust so that it qualifies as a grantor trust. For example, we can give the sett-lor the power to distribute trust income among a class of beneficiaries other than himself or herself. That should be sufficient.

Life Insurance and Life Insurance Trusts

Millions of people own life insurance. Considering that fact, it's astounding how little people know about their own life insurance. The reason isn't a mystery. Most people find the charts and projections that insurance agents foist on us to be absolutely incomprehensible and mind-numbing.

Let's review the basics. Every life insurance policy has three "players," the policy owner, the insured, and the beneficiary. Most people understand that the insured is the person whose life is covered by the insurance. If the insured dies, the insurance company pays the beneficiary. The role that throws many people is that of the owner. As you might suspect, the owner is the person who owns the policy. The owner is usually the insured, but not always. I can own a life insurance policy on the life of someone else, provided I have an insurable interest in his or her life. The concept of the insurable interest is what prevents me from taking out a $1 million policy on the life of a Bowery bum and then lacing his next martini with poison. I have an insurable interest in my family members and my key employees, but not in strangers.

If I'm the owner of a life insurance policy, I'm responsible for the premiums. But I also get to make all the decisions. If I wake up one morning and decide I no longer love the named beneficiaries, I'm free to change them. If I decide the policy has become too expensive, I can cancel it.

In spite of the insane complexity of many insurance products, there are basically only two types of life insurance. The oldest type, usually called term insurance, has nothing but a death benefit. If the death benefit is $1 million and the insured dies, the beneficiaries get $1 million. The second and more modern type of insurance has not only a death benefit, but also an investment feature. The premiums are often far higher than the premiums for term insurance, because the premiums go to buy an investment portfolio for the owner. As with any investment portfolio, the invested capital can do well or do poorly.

Depending on the type of coverage you buy, however, the success of the investment portfolio may affect the death benefit or it may not. It may affect your premiums or it may not. Life insurance that has an investment element as well as a death benefit is often called whole life insurance.

From an asset protection standpoint, who the owner is and the type of insurance she or he owns is vitally important. If you're not the owner, then neither the policy itself nor the investment portfolio can be attached by your creditors. If you are the owner, the amount available to your creditors depends on the type of policy it is. If you own a whole life policy, it's likely that your creditors will be able to get at the investment portfolio, commonly known as the cash value or the cash surrender value of the policy, just as they could with any investment portfolio you might own. But if the policy you own is a pure term policy with nothing but a death benefit when the insured dies, the creditor has nothing to attach until the insured dies.

Even if you own a whole life policy, you may be protected by a state exemption. A number of states, including Florida, Colorado, Illinois, Iowa, Kansas, Michigan, Texas, Ohio, Minnesota, and Wisconsin, exempt either the death benefit or the cash value of a life insurance policy from the clutches of creditors. However, it is vital to check the state exemption. Most states shield the recipient of the death benefit (i.e., the policy beneficiary) from the owner's creditors, but only if the beneficiary is the spouse or dependent of the deceased insured. Other states, including California, Florida, Arizona, and Iowa, also exempt a portion of the cash surrender value. Anyone with creditor difficulties needs to know what the applicable state exemption is, because that's the amount you can safely keep in the policy without worrying about your creditors.

Irrevocable Life Insurance Trusts

Little in the world of estate planning and asset protection is more insanely complex than life insurance trusts. If you can't handle too much complexity, all you need to know is that life insurance wrapped inside an irrevocable trust is a very good way to both lower your estate taxes (and the estate taxes of the beneficiary of the insurance) and keep the death benefit and the cash value out of the grasp of your creditors as well as the beneficiaries' creditors. Armed with that, you can skip to the next chapter. If you want to know how irrevocable life insurance trusts (ILITs) work, stick around.

Most people know that the proceeds of life insurance aren't subject to income taxes. What many people don't know (because insurance agents don't tell them) is that if you own a life insurance policy, or are the beneficiary of one, the death benefit is included in your estate for the purposes of calculating your estate tax, even if the insurance is payable to someone else. Here's an example: Mr. Brown has assets other than life insurance worth $1.2 million. He is also the owner of a life insurance policy that pays $500,000 to his daughter, Anna, on his death. When Mr. Brown dies, Anna gets the $500,000 free of income taxes, but Mr. Brown's estate is considered to be worth $1.7 million. If Anna is Mr. Brown's only heir, the estate taxes on the $500,000 worth of insurance mean that she gets about $150,000 less than she would have, because the estate tax must be paid before she can get anything. Now you know why many life insurance agents don't like to discuss estate taxes.

Is all this avoidable? Happily, it is, with an ILIT. If Mr. Brown were to create an ILIT and transfer the life insurance policy to his ILIT, it wouldn't be subject to estate taxes, because he wouldn't be the owner, his ILIT would be. The asset protection benefit should also be apparent. The life insurance (and its cash value) isn't subject to the claims of his creditors, because the ILIT owns the policy and the cash value, not Mr. Brown.

At this point, your reaction should be: "Wait a minute! This is too easy! If I can avoid estate taxes and creditors by simply creating an irrevocable trust and transferring the life insurance to the trust, why can't I do it with all my assets?"

The answer lies not in the vagaries of the estate tax, but in the gift tax. Let's assume that Mr. Brown's home was worth $500,000, and that he transferred his home to an irrevocable trust. If the transfer were a completed gift, there would be an immediate gift tax based on the value of the home. The gift tax rates are (not coincidentally) the same as the estate tax rates. The result would be that Mr. Brown would be inducing a present tax in order to avoid a future one, which is usually very poor tax planning.

So why is life insurance different? The answer lies in a quirk of the gift tax law. Let's assume that Mr. Brown were to buy a life insurance policy insuring his life that has a $500,000 death benefit. Mr. Brown is the owner and the insured, and he designates his daughter Anna as the beneficiary of the policy. After paying the first year's premium, most of which goes to pay the agent's commission, the cash surrender value of the $500,000 policy is $1,000. Let's assume that the day after he buys the policy, he transfers it to an ILIT. That's when Mr. Brown finds, much to his surprise, that the gift tax isn't based on the $500,000 death benefit, but on the $1,000 cash value. If Mr. Brown had bought a term policy, one having no cash value, the gift tax would be based roughly (but not exactly) on one year's premium.

The result is that life insurance is usually the one asset we can strip out of an estate, avoiding estate taxes, without getting hit with a huge gift tax. As a bonus, the policy is out of the hands of the owner and free from the clutches of the owner's creditors.

Fine. But where's all the complexity? The complexity results from the fact that we don't want to pay the gift tax either, no matter how small.

Most people know that you can make a gift of money or property valued at $12,000 to any person during the year, and not pay gift taxes. Couples can make $24,000 gifts to any person and still pay no gift taxes. For example, if Mr. and Mrs. Brown have three children and six grandchildren, they can give away $216,000 ($24,000 to each of them) on December 29, 2008, and another $216,000 on January 1, 2009, and pay no gift taxes.

What most people don't know is that the $12,000 gift tax exclusions apply only to present gifts. If I hand you $12,000, it's a present gift, but a gift to a trust doesn't qualify as a present gift. In order for an ILIT to work, we will be making gifts to the trust. If there's an existing insurance policy, we'll be transferring that policy to the trust. Even if we create the trust and then have the trust buy the policy, we'll still be making annual gifts to the trust; the trust, which doesn't have any income, will need cash to pay the premiums on the insurance policies it owns. It can get that cash only if someone makes a gift of the premiums to it.

So how do we avoid paying the gift tax when we transfer the policy itself or the annual premiums to the trust? The answer comes courtesy of one D. Clifford Crummey, who in 1968 convinced the Ninth Circuit Court of

Appeals that if you write a trust that gives the beneficiaries the right to withdraw money from the trust (regardless of whether they exercise that right) in the same year that you contribute to the trust, it qualifies as a present interest. And because it qualifies as a present interest, the gifts to the trust are tax-free, provided you don't contribute more than $12,000 per year per donee.

Since 1968, ILITs have come to be known as Crummey trusts, and the beneficiaries' annual withdrawal rights have become known as Crummey powers. All this is just paperwork, because Crummey beneficiaries never exercise their withdrawal rights.

Another bit of complexity pushes all this over the edge of insanity. The IRS, which generally acquiesces to this scheme, has ruled that you can't draft the beneficiaries' withdrawal rights in the fine print on page 158 of the trust and assume they'll never learn of their withdrawal rights. You must tell the beneficiaries that they have withdrawal rights. Not only that, the IRS has ruled that it isn't exactly cricket to inform them of their annual withdrawal rights around 10:00 P.M. on New Year's Eve. You must give them adequate notice.

The result is a Crummey letter that we need to send to every beneficiary every year. These Crummey letters are crazy, because very often the trustees who write the letters are also beneficiaries, which means that they write letters to themselves! Also note that our Crummey letters have a space on the bottom for the beneficiary to formally waive his or her withdrawal rights. Because the beneficiaries are often small children, their guardian, who may also be the trustee, signs the waiver for them. It's all crazy, but it's an essential part of the game if you want to avoid the gift taxes. Don't thank me; thank Crummey.

The Three-Year Rule

There's one final point regarding life insurance and ILITs. A provision in the tax code says that if the owner of the insurance dies within three years of the transfer of the policy to the ILIT, the value of the policy is included in the estate for the purpose of computing the estate taxes. In other words, if you outlive the transfer by three years, the value of the insurance isn't included in your estate. If you don't, it is. For those persons contemplating the transfer of an existing policy to an ILIT, our considered legal advice is to drive safely and wear your galoshes in the snow.

A Typical Crummey Letter

Mr. Wallace Brown
1111 Santa Monica Blvd. #300
Santa Monica, CA 90321

RE: Gift to The Brown Irrevocable

Dear Wallace:

Please be advised that I have received a gift from Sandra Brown to the Brown Irrevocable Trust. This gift is an amount of cash in the sum of $30,000.00.

You are a beneficiary of this trust. Under the provisions of this trust, you are allowed to withdraw funds equal to all or a portion of the value of this gift. You have the privilege of exercising or not exercising your power to withdraw the funds.

If you choose to exercise your power to withdraw funds, you must do so in writing delivered to the undersigned within 60 days of this notice. If you choose not to exercise your power, this gift will be held in trust, which trust will be for your benefit in accordance with the terms of the trust.

If you choose to exercise your withdrawal rights, please notify me. If you choose to waive your withdrawal rights, please indicate by executing this letter in the space provided below and returning this letter to me.

Very truly yours,

John Smith
Trustee, The Brown Irrevocable Trust

I hereby elect not to withdraw any part of the aforementioned gift.
Wallace Brown

Asset Protection Using Limited Partnerships and Limited Liability Companies

For people who own investment real estate, such as multifamily apartment buildings, office buildings, or shopping centers, nothing beats holding the property in some form of entity such as a limited partnership (LP) or limited liability company (LLC). These entities provide their owners with the maximum flexibility to structure their business relationship as they (and not some government regulator) wish to, provide the most tax-efficient form of ownership, and most importantly, provide the owners with the maximum asset protection one can get for real estate. LPs and LLCs can provide asset protection for non-real-estate assets as well, but our choices are greater with respect to liquid assets. A foreign trust will always provide greater asset protection for liquid assets than an LP or an LLC; there is no point in using these entities for liquid assets.

A Brief Review of Corporations

Let's review some important concepts we learned about corporations in Chapter 7. We noted that the hallmark of the corporate form of doing business is the limited liability of the shareholders. If a corporation owes money to trade creditors, or commits a tort, or loses a business lawsuit, the judgment is against the corporation. The shareholders may lose their investment if the corporation goes bankrupt, but that's all they can lose. The notable exceptions are if a creditor of the corporation is able to pierce the corporate veil, or if the corporation is the alter ego of the shareholders or another corporation.

A creditor seeking to satisfy a judgment against the corporation by going after the shareholders is going "inside-out," i.e., going from within the corporation out to the shareholders. The protection the corporate form provides against this is often referred to as inside-out asset protection.

If a creditor already has a judgment against a shareholder and seeks to satisfy the judgment against the assets of the corporation, the creditor is going "outside-in." This is the context where the asset protection limitations inherent in the corporate form become manifest: the creditor seeking to go "outside-in" may do so by attaching the corporate stock owned by the debtor-shareholder, and if the debtor-shareholder owns a controlling interest in the corporation, the creditor now controls the corporation. As we shall see shortly, it is in the "outside-in" context that LPs and LLCs are vastly superior to corporations.

The Asset Protection Booby Prize Goes to ... General Partnerships!

Most nonlawyers have a general idea of what it means to be a "partner" in a "partnership." That idea is usually pretty close to the legal definition of a partnership: "two or more persons in business as co-owners for profit." On numerous occasions, I've had clients who are shareholders in corporations introduce their fellow shareholders to me as their "partners." Even though a corporation has no "partners," we all understand what was meant; they're partners in the business.

When most people think of a "partnership," they think of a general partnership, as opposed to its cousin, the limited partnership. General partnerships are easily formed; no document needs to be filed with the state or the county. If no particular business license is required, you can form a general partnership and go into business on a handshake; no written partnership agreement is required.

It's so easy to form a general partnership that you can be a partner in a general partnership without knowing it. Here's an example: Bob Smith and Cindy Jones own a duplex. Cindy lives in one half, and they lease the other half to tenants. One day, they agree over lunch that if Bob pays the remodeling costs, Cindy will handle the trash collection, sweep the sidewalk, and deal with the tenants. They agree to split the rent. Even though they may never have thought of themselves as such, Bob and Cindy are partners in a general partnership, because they're in business together as co-owners for profit. It's as simple as that.

It's simple, but it's crazy. And as we shall see, being a general partner in a general partnership can be an asset protection nightmare.

It's crazy because, as a general rule, each partner in a general partnership is the agent of the partnership, with the authority to legally bind the partnership. And that is an open invitation for trouble.

Let's assume that Bob Smith, Cindy Jones, and eight other people form a general partnership named "Real Estate Associates" to own and operate a high-rise apartment building. One day, Bob wakes up and decides he's going to install new carpeting in the entire building. Never mind that the expense will bankrupt the partnership, or that he forgets to inform his nine other partners of the purchase. The purchase order, made out to "Real Estate Associates," is signed by "Bob Smith, General Partner." The carpet is installed, and the bill comes. Is Real Estate Associates obligated to pay it? Absolutely. That's because each partner in a general partnership is an agent of the partnership, with the authority to bind the partnership on contracts, debts, and almost any other legal document.

Let's assume that the ten partners in Real Estate Associates had signed a partnership agreement. The agreement appoints Cindy Jones as the

Managing General Partner, giving her the sole authority to make purchases and sign legal documents on behalf of the partnership. Let's further assume that Bob, flying in the face of the restriction in the partnership agreement, goes ahead and orders new carpeting, again signing the purchase order as "General Partner." Is Real Estate Associates still bound by what Bob has done? Yes! That's because as a general partner in a general partnership, Bob has the "apparent authority" to legally bind the partnership, and anyone supplying goods or services to the partnership isn't obligated to inquire into Bob's authority. Of course, Cindy and her eight other partners might well have a claim against Bob for violating the partnership agreement, but that doesn't affect the partnership's liability on the debt.

And that's not nearly the worst of it. Let's assume that Real Estate Associates doesn't have the money to pay the debt. In fact, Real Estate Associates is in bankruptcy, and its building is about to be sold to pay its mortgages. Can the carpet supplier sue Bob on the debt? Absolutely. Can the carpet supplier (and all of the partnership's other creditors, for that matter) sue the nine other partners? Yes! That's because in a general partnership, each partner is liable for all of the debts of the partnership. That means that the partnership's creditors can attach the personal nonbusiness assets of every general partner, even general partners who didn't participate in or have knowledge of the creation of the debt.

Consider what happened to two of my clients a few years ago. They were duped by two con men into investing in a hotel in Idaho. The deal was that my clients would be passive investors who wouldn't participate in the management of the hotel, which would be entirely in the hands of the con men. They formed a general partnership to operate the hotel. Years went by, and my clients received no distributions from the partnership. They had been allocated some tax write-offs, so they didn't grieve too badly over the loss of their investment. Years passed, and they heard nothing. But one fine day they were contacted by everyone's least favorite creditor, the Internal Revenue Service (IRS). It seems that the con men not only stole the money my clients had invested, but also failed to pay the withholding taxes and Social Security taxes for the hotel's employees, which, with interest and penalties, now amounted to hundreds of thousands of dollars. Because the con men had long disappeared, the IRS decided to collect the money from my clients. Impossible? Not at all. The IRS reminded them that they had been general partners with the con men in the hotel business, and as general partners they were each liable for all of the partnership's debts, regardless of whether they knew of the debts.

It should be obvious by now that being a general partner in a general partnership can be the very worst form of asset protection. Why, then, do people do it? As we've seen, it's easy and cheap to go into business as general partners. Many people also feel that there are tax advantages, because a general partnership pays no income taxes; the profits of the partnership are passed through to the partners, who pick up their share of partnership profits (and losses) on their individual tax returns.

As we shall see, all the advantages of a general partnership are preserved in a limited liability company with none of the disadvantages. People who have not been advised or who have been poorly advised of the alternatives form general partnerships. All of which brings us to Klueger's Rule of General Partnerships.

> **Klueger's Rule of General Partnerships:** Anyone who becomes a general partner in a general partnership is crazy.

All about Limited Partnerships

A general partnership is a disaster in both the "inside-out" and the "outside-in" contexts. A creditor of a general partner can get at the assets of the partnership, and a creditor of the partnership can get at the assets of all the partners. Things are very different if the partnership is a limited partnership.

Who's Who in a Limited Partnership

A general partnership can be formed on a handshake, and you can be a general partner without even knowing it. Not so with a limited partnership. Limited partnerships are entirely creatures of state law, and you cannot form one without complying with the requirements of the state's version of the Revised Uniform Limited Partnership Act (RULPA), enacted by every state except Louisiana. That usually means filing a limited partnership certificate with the secretary of state of the state in which the partnership will conduct its business, paying the appropriate fees, and naming someone as the agent for service of process in case the limited partnership is sued. The filing requirements and the fees are minimal, but you can't be a partner in a limited partnership until you comply.

Every limited partnership has at least two partners, one of whom must be a general partner, and the other of whom must be a limited partner. There is no limit on the number of general or limited partners a limited partnership can have, and many limited partnerships have hundreds or thousands of limited partners. Nor is there any limit on who may be a limited partner. A corporation, a trust, or even another partnership may be a general or limited partner, as may a noncitizen or nonresident of the state or even of the United States.

Limited partnerships are often called "family limited partnerships," or FLPs. There really is no such thing as a "family" limited partnership, and no state recognizes a distinction between "family" limited partnerships and limited partnerships. That's why we don't use the term here.

The general partner in a limited partnership is no different than the general partner in a general partnership. He or she (or it) is an agent of the partnership, with the apparent authority to bind the partnership legally by his or her (or its) acts. The general partner is also personally liable for all of the partnership's debts, and a creditor can go after a general partner's personal assets to satisfy a partnership's debts ("inside-out" debt collection).

What makes limited partnerships so radically different from general partnerships is how the limited partners are treated. A limited partner has almost no right to manage the affairs of the partnership. Every state gives a limited partner some rights necessary to protect his or her (or its) interest, such as the right to inspect partnership books and the right to vote on the replacement of a general partner, but these rights are very limited. Nowhere may a limited partner sign a contract or incur a debt legally binding the partnership. Any limited partner who tries to assert such authority becomes a general partner, with all the legal liability that that entails.

In return for not having any right to manage the partnership, the limited partners have no personal liability for the partnership's debts, other than the possibility of losing their investment. Thus, for the limited partners, the "inside-out" aspect of debt collection is eliminated. Here's a typical example.

Sue Jackson wants to open a restaurant and catering business. She needs approximately $200,000. Sue forms a limited partnership, "Quick Eats, Ltd." She sells subscriptions to 20 friends at $5,000 per subscription, and invests the remaining $100,000 herself. She will act as the general partner, and her investors will be the limited partners, each with the right to receive 2.5 percent of the annual profits of the business. If there are no profits, each will be allocated 2.5 percent of the annual losses.

Let's assume that things don't go too well for Sue's business. Not only does the business lose money, but one of Sue's truck drivers injures a pedestrian just before Sue remembers she didn't have insurance. The pedestrian sues for $10 million, as do many vendors. Quick Eats, Ltd. files for bankruptcy. Can the pedestrian and the other creditors pursue Sue's personal assets? Absolutely, because she was the general partner, personally liable for all of the partnership's debts.

That fact often confuses my clients. Let's assume that the limited partnership agreement makes Sue the 50 percent general partner. It says that she gets 50 percent of the limited partnership profits, and is liable for 50 percent of the partnership's debts. But that doesn't mean that a creditor of the partnership is limited by the terms of the partnership agreement. Because she is the general partner, Sue has unlimited liability.

There is one exception to the general rule of limited liability of the limited partners, and it's the same exception that we saw in the corporate context. If a creditor of the partnership can pierce the corporate veil (yes, that's what it's called, even when referring to partnerships), by proving that the partners ignored their own partnership, a creditor will be able to do so as well.

Absent the very rare piercing of the corporate veil, the limited partners are insulated from the debts of the partnership. All that they stand to lose is their investment when the partnership goes under. In short, there is no "inside-out" debt collection against limited partners.

The ability to shield one's assets from the partnership's creditors is not an insignificant advantage, but it is far from the principal reason that limited partnerships are effective asset protection devices. A limited partnership can be used as a refuge from one's personal creditors, because all that the creditors can do is obtain a charging order, which, as we shall soon see, isn't much.

All about Charging Orders

We saw in Chapter 3 that if your assets are titled in your own name, your creditors will have no difficulty finding them (by asking you, under oath, where they're located) and attaching them. Keeping your valuable assets in your own name makes life too easy for your creditors.

Let's assume that before Sue Jackson started her catering business, she set up a limited partnership, "The Jackson Family, Ltd." She wants to keep all her assets under her control, but she needs to have at least one general partner and at least one limited partner. Sue names her husband, Charlie, as the general partner, with the right to receive 1 percent of the partnership's profits and losses. Sue is the principal limited partner, retaining the right to receive 97 percent of the partnership's profits and losses. She names her children, Adam and Becky, as 1 percent limited partners. She accomplishes all this by filing a certificate with the secretary of state and drawing up a partnership agreement (often called "articles of limited partnership") that pays particular attention to asset protection.

The next and most important thing that Sue does is transfer her assets to the partnership, so that the partnership, not she, owns them. That means that if she owns a few parcels of real estate, she must change all the titles to the real estate. If she owns a stock portfolio, all the stock certificates bearing her name must be torn up and new certificates must be issued showing that the limited partnership owns the stock. Ditto for bank accounts, certificates of deposit, and even other partnership interests. It's work, but it's essential.

Sue won't need to worry about incurring any capital gains taxes by transferring appreciated assets into the partnership. With minor exceptions, the tax code exempts from taxation the transfer of appreciated assets to the partnership. The only notable exception to the rule is if the partnership relieves Sue of debts in excess of her tax "basis" in any of the assets. For example, if Sue transfers a building that she bought for $1 million that she depreciated down to $600,000 and that has a mortgage on it of $800,000 to the partnership, the $200,000 difference between the $800,000 debt and the $600,000 "basis" represents a gain. However, if she's a 97 percent partner, she needs to report only 3 percent of that $200,000 gain.

Let's assume again that Sue's restaurant business goes under, leaving all sorts of creditors holding the bag. Because she was the general partner in Quick Eats, Ltd., she's personally liable for all of its debts. The creditors obtain judgments against her and then issue a subpoena to her, demanding that she appear and answer questions under oath regarding the whereabouts of her assets.

Sue can't lie under oath, but she doesn't need to. They ask her if she owns any real estate, and the answer is no (the partnership does). Ditto for any cash, stocks, and bonds. Near the end of the inquiry, one of the creditors' attorneys asks her if she owns any partnership interests. Because she's under oath, she must tell the truth. She responds by telling the creditors that, yes, she does indeed own an interest in a partnership: a 97 percent limited partnership interest in "The Jackson Family, Ltd." Sue has been thoughtful enough to bring a copy of the partnership agreement with her.

They ask her about the partnership's assets, and again, she tells them everything. What can the creditors do to get at the partnership's assets? Not much. That's where the charging order limitation comes in. At first blush, the charging order sounds like a weapon in the hands of the creditors, and it is. The problem is that it's a popgun where a cannon is needed, but it's the only weapon the creditors have.

What is a charging order? Section 703 of RULPA ("Rights of Creditors") states: "On application to a court of competent jurisdiction by any judgment creditor of a partner, the court may charge the partnership interest of the partner with payment of the unsatisfied amount of the judgment with interest. To the extent so charged, the judgment creditor has only the rights of an assignee of the partnership interest. This Act does not deprive any partner of the benefit of any exemption laws applicable to his or her partnership interest."

In plain English, the charging order makes a creditor of the debtor-partner the assignee of the debtor-partner's right to receive distributions of partnership income. Assume that next year, The Jackson Family, Ltd. decides to distribute $1,000 to its partners. As a 97 percent partner, Sue would be entitled to receive $970. Armed with a charging order, the partnership would be required to pay the $970 to Sue's creditors, rather than to Sue. But that's all the creditors get. They don't get the right to dissolve the partnership, and they certainly don't get the right to any partnership assets. Because Sue was a limited partner, they don't obtain any right to manage the partnership, which remains exclusively in Charlie's hands, and Charlie has a vested interest in seeing that Sue's creditors get nothing.

In some states, such as Arizona and Florida, state law makes it clear that the charging order is the only remedy that the creditor has. Arizona's statute says, "This section provides the exclusive remedy by which a judgment creditor of a partner may satisfy a judgment out of the judgment debtor's interest in the partnership" (*Arizona Statutes Ann.* §29-341; see also *Florida Statutes Ann* ch. 620.153). In other states, such as Minnesota and Virginia, the courts have ruled that the charging order is the only remedy that a creditor has.

Why would a state legislature or a court be so restrictive to creditors? The theory is that permitting a creditor to bust up a partnership in order to seize the assets of one of the partners would be unfair to the other partners. And so, to avoid the disruption of a partnership's business, a compromise of sorts is struck. The creditor gets whatever the debtor-partner gets whenever the debtor-partner would get it, but that's it.

The effect of the charging order in the context of a family limited partnership should, by now, be obvious. Nothing requires Charlie to distribute any money to anyone. The creditors will probably have to wait forever to get anything. Rather than wait forever, they might elect to settle the debt for pennies on the dollar.

The charging order concept isn't limited to limited partnerships; it applies to general partnerships as well. But the Uniform Partnership Act (UPA), which covers general partnerships (and limited partnerships unless RULPA has a contrary provision), provides creditors with a far more powerful weapon than does RULPA. Under UPA, a creditor may, in an appropriate circumstance, get a judge to order the sale of partnership assets if the mere assignment of the right to partnership distributions yields the creditor nothing. The inability of the charging order to provide the debtor with any real protection in the "outside-in" debt collection context is another reason limited partnerships are favored over general partnerships.

How powerful a charging order might be depends upon the relationship between the debtor-partner and the general partner. If the debtor is one of thousands of limited partners in a vast real estate syndicate, a charging order delivered to the general partner will likely result in the distributions that would have gone to the debtor-partner going instead to the creditor. If the limited partner controls or has influence over the general partner, the charging order may be a truly toothless weapon.

Planning to Mitigate the Charging Order

As ineffective as a charging order might be, we can plan ahead to make a charging order completely toothless. Let's return to Sue Jackson, the 97 percent limited partner in The Jackson Family, Ltd. Let's assume that Sue is involved in a car accident, and as a result a multimillion-dollar judgment is entered against her. The plaintiff conducts a debtor's exam and discovers that Sue is a 97 percent limited partner in The Jackson Family, Ltd. Of course, the next thing that happens is that a charging order is served on the general partner of The Jackson Family, Ltd., ordering him to pay to the creditor any distributions that would have gone to Sue. If Sue and the general partner are friendly, the partnership can stop all distributions; this means that the creditor gets nothing, but Sue gets nothing as well. A waiting game ensues. If the creditor is willing to outwait Sue, the creditor will win, because Sue cannot stay in business forever without getting paid. If the creditor is impatient, Sue might be able to settle the claim for pennies on the dollar. Once again, we return to our mantra from Chapter 3: know your creditor.

But let's change the facts. Let's assume that Sue isn't a 97 percent partner. Rather, the 97 percent partner is "The Sue Children's Trust," of which Sue is the trustee. The Sue Children's Trust is an irrevocable trust, making it a separate legal entity. When the charging order directed against Sue is delivered to the general partner, he reads it carefully and says, "No such partner here," and neatly deposits the charging order in the trash. The 97 percent partner—the trust—receives the distributions unaffected by the charging order. Can a charging order be directed against The Sue Children's Trust? Not a chance. It didn't cause the automobile accident that resulted in the debt, and there is no judgment against it.

Could the creditor allege that the creation of The Sue Children's Trust was some sort of fraudulent conveyance? Possibly. If Sue was the original partner, and she transferred her interest in the partnership to the newly created trust only after the accident, the creditor might be able charge the interest of the trust. At the risk of being repetitious, it all comes back to Klueger's Shortest Rule: plan early.

A Few Words about Phantom Income

There is a particularly delicious quirk with respect to charging orders that may require the creditor to pay money to the IRS without getting anything in return. To understand this little gem, one needs to understand some basics of partnership taxation.

It is a basic principle of tax law that partners are taxed on their proportionate shares of partnership income, regardless of whether that income is distributed to them. For example, if I am a 10 percent partner in a real estate partnership, and the partnership has $100,000 in net income during the year, I'm subject to tax on 10 percent of the $100,000, or $10,000. If the general partners decide that they can't distribute the income to partners because they need $100,000 to install a new roof, it's too bad for me. I'm still liable for the taxes on $10,000, even though I didn't receive any cash from the partnership to help pay the tax. This little problem is known as "phantom income."

Now let's assume that I'm no longer a partner, because my creditors obtained a charging order. Are my creditors subject to the phantom income? Must they pay taxes on the pro rata share of partnership income that wasn't distributed to them? The law isn't clear on this point. The IRS, in Revenue

Ruling 77-137, made it clear that if you are the "assignee" of a partner's interest in a partnership, you're liable for the assignor's share of the partnership's taxes. In our previous example, Charlie will certainly send IRS Form K-1 to the creditors around tax time, indicating that they are liable for their share of the partnership's income, even though he distributed nothing to them. It'll make them squirm, and that may be all we need to get the creditors to settle on our terms.

But that's still not all. Depending on how aggressive you want to be, it may be possible to get cash to the debtor-partner, even though the creditor, armed with the charging order, gets nothing. That's because the charging order attaches the partner's right to distributions from the partnership in his or her capacity as a partner. But partners often deal with their partnerships in capacities other than as partners, and are compensated as such. For example, a partner in a real estate partnership may also act as the partnership's broker or property manager. Could Sue Jackson get paid as a consultant to the partnership? Perhaps. The creditors will scream to the judge that the whole thing is a sham. But it's something worth considering.

Fraudulent Conveyance?

If you transfer all your assets to a limited partnership, is it a fraudulent conveyance? It shouldn't be. As we saw in Chapter 4, the sine qua non of fraudulent conveyances is the transfer of property without equivalent value in return—that is, a gratuitous transfer. But whenever you transfer assets to a partnership, you do get something in return: a partnership interest. That partnership interest may not be worth much to a creditor due to the charging order concept, but that doesn't make it a fraudulent conveyance.

All about Limited Liability Companies

Consider all of the possible ways to own a business. You can conduct the business in your own name as a sole proprietor, which is the worst form of ownership from an asset protection standpoint. If there are two or more owners, you have a number of choices. You can form a general partnership. The partnership's income will not be subject to double taxation, because the partnership itself doesn't pay taxes. A general partnership affords its owners a great deal of flexibility, because we can write the partnership agreement to allocate certain accounting items to one or more partners and exclude others. For example, if one partner contributes a building to the partnership, it might be fair to allocate all the depreciation deductions attributable to the building to just that partner. We can't do that in a corporation, where every shareholder gets his or her share of partnership profits and losses, period. But, as we have seen, a general partnership is an asset protection disaster.

A limited partnership affords us the same flexibility as a general partnership. Within limits imposed by the tax code, we can allocate certain tax deductions and credits only to certain partners or classes of partners. If it's properly formed and operated, a limited partnership will also be subject to only one level of taxation. It represents a good asset protection vehicle, but only for the limited partners. The general partners are still personally liable for all of the partnership's debts.

If we want to limit the liability of all the owners, we might consider forming a corporation. We'll obtain a certain degree of asset protection, but at a price. Corporations don't provide us with the flexibility that partnerships do. We also run the risk of double taxation. If we're not careful (and even if we are and the corporation is very profitable), we'll wind up paying corporate income taxes on the corporation's profits, and a second round of taxes when those profits are distributed to shareholders in the form of dividends. We can avoid double taxation by filing an election with the IRS to be taxed as an S corporation. The result of this election is that our corporation is taxed like a partnership, which means that the corporation isn't taxed at all. The shareholders are taxed on their proportionate share of corporate earnings, regardless of whether those earnings are distributed to them. But not every corporation qualifies to make the election. There may not be more than 75 shareholders, or if just one of those shareholders isn't an individual (no corporate or partnership shareholders, please!), or if just one of those individuals is a nonresident alien (no foreigners, please!), it destroys the S corporation election for everyone.

Take a look at Table 9-1. As you can see, there is something wrong with each form of doing business, even though the limited partnership comes closest to satisfying all our needs. The notable limitation of the limited partnership is that it provides absolutely no protection to that unfortunate soul who becomes the general partner. Prior to the adoption of LLCs in California in 1994, I often sat in meetings with business owners who wished to form a limited partnership to either run a business or acquire a parcel of real estate. When the discussion turned to who would be the general partner, they suddenly developed hearing problems or other maladies that required them to quickly repair to the restroom.

	General Partnership	Limited Partnership	Regular Corporation	S Corporation	Limited Company
Formation formalities	No	Yes	Yes	Yes	Yes
Flexibility	Yes	Yes	No	No	Yes
Avoid double taxation	Yes	Yes	No	Yes	Yes
Restrictions on ownership	No	No	No	Yes	No
Asset protection	No	No	Yes	Yes	Yes

Table 9-1. Analysis of different forms of ownership

Is there a form of ownership that combines all the advantages of each of these forms of ownership with none of the disadvantages and limitations? Now there is.

The limited liability company (LLC) gained rapid acceptance in the late 1980s and early 1990s, and every state now has legislation permitting LLCs. However, state laws regarding LLCs vary to a greater degree than do state laws regulating limited partnerships.

All state LLC laws strive to do the same thing, which is to keep all of the best features of corporations and partnerships while shedding all the disadvantages. In large part, these laws achieve that goal. If there is any disadvantage to the LLC as a form for holding assets and doing business, it is that LLCs are newer than limited partnerships. Consequently, many attorneys shy away from recommending them to clients, and many clients fear to form LLCs. But that disadvantage has receded over the years. There is no reason today not to form an LLC.

Clients often ask: "Is an LLC a kind of partnership?" or "Is an LLC a form of corporation?" The answer is that an LLC is neither a partnership nor a corporation, but a new form combining the best of both.

An LLC doesn't have shareholders or partners, but "members," who are like shareholders in a corporation and partners in a partnership in that it is the members who own the LLC. There are no restrictions on who may be a member; this is a big advantage over the S corporation, which places numerous restrictions on who may be a shareholder, with potentially catastrophic results if those restrictions are violated. Unlike the limited partners in a limited partnership, the members may fully participate in the management of the LLC without losing their limited liability.

An LLC may (but isn't required to) have one or more "managers" who manage the affairs of the business, much like the officers of a corporation or the general partner of a partnership. Unlike the general partner of a limited partnership, no one in an LLC is personally liable for the debts of the LLC; there is no "inside-out" debt collection, with the sole exception of piercing the corporate veil, which is present here as it was for corporations and LPs. If the members of an LLC ignore its existence, it is very likely that a court will also ignore its existence and permit the LLC's creditors to go after the members.

An LLC also preserves the tax advantages of a general or limited partnership. If the members so elect, an LLC in most states is not a taxpayer, but instead passes its profits and losses through to its members (an LLC may, for whatever reason, structure itself so that it is subject to taxation). LLCs afford their members the same flexibility to allocate LLC deductions, credits, and items of income among the members as do partnerships. Depending on the state in which the LLC is formed, the operating agreement, or, as it's termed in Texas, the LLC regulations, will spell out who gets what income, tax advantages, compensation, and so on.

Single-Member LLCs

One significant difference between a limited partnership and an LLC is that a limited partnership must have at least two partners, including at least one general partner and at least one limited partner. In contrast, every state permits you to form an LLC that has only one member. There are tax advantages inherent in single-member LLCs, but they pose an asset protection trap.

The tax advantage of a single-member LLC is that if the LLC has only one member, the LLC will be a disregarded entity for tax purposes. There is a difference between being a pass-through entity for tax purposes, which every S corporation and every electing limited partnership and LLC is, and a disregarded entity. If a single-member LLC is disregarded, it's as if the LLC does not exist. We noted earlier that an S corporation may have only individual shareholders; it may not have another corporation, partnership, or LLC as a shareholder. But it may have a single-member LLC as a shareholder, since that LLC is disregarded. We noted earlier that if an asset is transferred into a partnership, and the transferor is relieved of debt in the course of the transfer, the transferor will be taxed on the "cancellation of indebtedness" income. But that doesn't happen if the LLC—the transferee—is a disregarded entity.

But single-member LLCs are not a good idea from an asset protection standpoint. No state LLC makes any distinction in its charging order statutes between single-member and multimember LLCs. Let's review why states limit a creditor of a member to the charging order: It's to prevent the operations of the entity from being disrupted as a result of the debts of one of the members. In other words, the charging order limitation exists not to give the debtor-member a break, but to protect the interests of the other members. That rationale disappears if there are no other members.

Moreover, we noted that a creditor could always get at the assets of a member if the creditor could pierce the corporate veil or prove that the entity is the mere alter ego of the member. It is inherently easier to prove alter ego if the LLC has only one owner.

We sometimes need to scurry about to try to find other owners, so as to avoid single-member status. In a pinch, the business owner's spouse should be a co-member. If the spouses reside in a community property state, they should enter into a transmutation agreement to make it clear that each spouse has a separate property interest in their own membership interest. If the business owner's children are adults, it does not hurt to make them members as well. If we have multiple members, and one of the members becomes subject to creditors, we then have people other than the debtor-member who have an economic stake in the entity available to stand before the judge and argue that the liquidation of the entity would harm their interests, and they are not debtors.

The Diminution of the Charging Order Limitation

As we have seen, the best part of LLCs is that they are governed by the same charging order concept as limited partnerships. Thus, all that a creditor of an LLC member could get is an assignment of the member's interest in LLC distributions; the creditor couldn't force the sale of LLC assets or participate in the management of the LLC.

In recent years, a growing number of states, including California, Colorado, and Illinois, have sought to mitigate the charging order limitation by giving a creditor the right to foreclose on a member's interest in the LLC. Note that this does not give the creditor the right to foreclose on the LLC's assets or liquidate the assets, and it's not clear just what rights the "foreclosure" of a membership interest gives the creditor that a charging order does not (see *Colorado Revised Stats.* §7-80-703, *Illinois Comp. Stats.* §180/30-20, and *California Corporations Code* §17302).

Both the California and the Colorado statutes provide a mechanism for pulling the rug out from under a creditor. Both states allow the membership interest of a debtor-member to be redeemed before the foreclosure sale takes place. Let's return to Sue Johnson. Let's assume that she owns a 97 percent interest in "The Jackson Family LLC." Let's assume that the operating agreement of the LLC provides that if one member's interest is subject to any charging order, seizure, or other similar event, the other members can buy out the interest of the debtor-member. The California statute does not specify how much the purchaser must pay for the debtor-member's interest. Could her children buy Sue's interest for $1? The statute doesn't prohibit it, but that's too risky for me. It's better to have a formula that provides a low but reasonable buyout amount.

Series LLCs: The New Kid on the Block

We have observed that an LLC (or, for that matter, an LP) will, by means of the charging order limitation, afford "outside-in" asset protection. But let's assume that the debtor is not a member of the LLC, but the LLC itself. Here's an example: an LLC owns an apartment building. A tenant falls on a stairwell that he alleges was negligently maintained. The defendant becomes the LLC itself. Nothing shields the liability of the LLC from creditors. If the LLC's insurance coverage is insufficient, or if the LLC has no insurance, this creditor could seize the apartment building. But let's assume that the LLC owns two apartment buildings, and after the creditor seizes the apartment building, the judgment remains unsatisfied. Can the creditor seize the other apartment building, the one that had nothing to do with the accident? Absolutely, since it is an asset of the debtor, the LLC.

One way to avoid this result is to have each apartment building owned by a different LLC. In most states, that's the only way to shield the assets of one LLC from the liabilities of another. But this solution presents its own problems. First, it's expensive, since each LLC must obtain its own charter from the state and pay annual filing fees to maintain the charter. Second, it might not work. If you own ten LLCs, each owning one apartment building, it's possible that each LLC would be considered the alter ego of the others, especially if each LLC has the same owner, is operated from the same address, and has the same employees.

Five states—Delaware, Nevada, Illinois, Oklahoma, and Iowa—have a solution to this problem: the "series LLC." Pioneered by Delaware, this gives the owners of an LLC the option to create an unlimited number of "series" or "cells" within the LLC. Each series can contain one or more assets. As long as the owner of the LLC maintains separate books of account for the respective series, the assets of each series are walled off from the liabilities of the other. If you own a fleet of taxicabs in Illinois, each series in your LLC can own just one taxicab. If one taxicab injures a pedestrian, the creditor can seize only that taxicab; he or she cannot touch the other taxicabs in the different series. What holds true for taxicabs applies for apartment buildings or any other assets you might decide to stuff into the various series.

Assume that you don't own apartment buildings in Illinois or Delaware, but you do in California. Can you import the Delaware law by forming a Delaware LLC and registering it as a foreign LLC authorized to do business in California? You should. After all, that's what a state says when it allows you to register a foreign LLC: it says that even though the LLC wasn't formed under the home state's laws, the foreign state will follow the home state's laws. Unfortunately, series LLCs are so new that no case has tested this proposition.

Will an LLC or an LP Shield the Family Residence?

The asset that is nearest and dearest to most people is the family residence. It may also be the most difficult to protect.

The reason is as follows: We began by saying that a partnership is an association of two or more persons engaged in business as co-owners for profit. Similarly, a limited liability company is just that, a company. You can always make the case that managing your stock portfolio or investment real estate is a business; it's all that some people do. But what's your home doing in a limited partnership? What does that have to do with any business? That's the argument creditors will make to the judge to prove that a limited partnership was nothing but a sham that should be ignored. If at all possible, employ some other asset protection device to protect your home; keep it out of the limited partnership or the LLC. In Chapter 11 we will explore a better means to protect the family residence—the Qualified Personal Residence Trust.

Foreign Asset Protection Trusts

A foreign trust is a trust governed by the laws of a foreign country. How does a trust become governed by a foreign country's laws? By the trust saying so, as follows: "This trust shall be governed, in all respects, by the laws of the Cook Islands. The courts of the Cook Islands shall have exclusive jurisdiction to determine any matter arising out of the execution, interpretation, or enforcement of any provision of this trust or the effect of any provision of this trust or of the laws of the Cook Islands."

After the trust is signed, it should be registered with the Registrar of Trusts or whatever other government agency is charged with administering trusts. This is all that's required. A foreign trust does not need to be written in a foreign language, nor does it need to be signed in a foreign country. The assets that the trust owns do not need to be located in that

> country. In fact, the trustee does not need to be located in the country by whose laws the trust is governed, but it would be an odd trust that did this.
>
> We saw in Chapter 8 that every trust has three "players": the settlor, who creates the trust, the trustee, who holds legal title to the assets of the trust, and one or more beneficiaries. The same holds true of a foreign trust. But that's where the similarities end.

How Do Foreign Trusts Work (so Well)?

Let's return to some fundamental principles. We saw in Chapter 2 that a creditor armed with a judgment has the right to haul the judgment debtor into court for a debtor's exam. At the debtor's exam, the debtor is placed under oath and required to spill the beans. That puts the debtor in the uncomfortable position of telling the truth or committing a crime—perjury—to avoid disclosing the assets. Since most people are unwilling to commit a crime to save an asset, a smart lawyer will learn everything about the debtor's assets. It boils down to this: asset protection isn't about hiding assets. It's about structuring assets so creditors cannot get at them, even if the creditors learn of their existence and their whereabouts.

We saw in Chapter 4 that a creditor's principal remedy if a transfer has been deemed to be a fraudulent conveyance is to ignore the transfer and proceed against the transferee to obtain the asset. If I live in California and I transfer my stock portfolio to my nephew Irving to avoid the hot breath of my creditors, and Irving gives me nothing in return, my creditors, who previously had no claim against Irving, now have the right to sue Irving to recover the transferred assets. The creditor might have to hire a lawyer in Maine (where Irving lives), which might be somewhat expensive, but it's not prohibitive. They have courts in Maine, and lawyers in Maine, and the laws of Maine are subject to the Full Faith and Credit clause of the Constitution, which requires the courts of Maine to honor the judgment that the creditors obtained in California.

But life becomes far more complicated if the transferee of the asset is located in the Cook Islands, which are located in the Pacific Ocean, or in Saint Vincent and the Grenadines, which is located in the Caribbean, or on the Isle of Man, which is located in the Irish Sea between Scotland and Ireland. Unlike the state of Maine, these countries are not governed by the Full Faith and Credit clause. If the creditor shows up in the Cook Islands alleging that the transfer of the assets to the Cook Islands trustee was a fraudulent conveyance, a court in the Cook Islands will decide that issue based upon the laws of the Cook Islands, not the laws of Maine. As we shall see shortly, that's only the beginning of the difficulties facing a creditor seeking to enforce a judgment in one of these countries.

Why Not a Swiss Bank Account?

Clients often ask me why they need to form a foreign trust. Why not simply place the money in a Swiss bank account? After all, everyone has heard about Swiss bank secrecy laws. Don't they even have numbered accounts, so that not even your name appears on the account?

Everything you've heard about Swiss bank secrecy is true. Debtor's exams in Switzerland are not only not countenanced, they're illegal! If you went to Switzerland in an attempt to conduct a debtor's exam on a Swiss banker, you could be arrested. The problem is that the Swiss bank secrecy laws focus on the banker, not the debtor. If you are the debtor and you live in California, there is nothing preventing the creditor's attorney from asking you the whereabouts of all of your bank accounts. At that point, you have to spill the beans, because you're under oath. You also control the Swiss bank account, even if it is a numbered account. What is worse, you are also under the jurisdiction of California courts. If a judge orders you to turn the money in your Swiss bank account over to the creditor, there is no way to prevent it. The fact that the banker would not have to disclose anything about the account to anyone is completely irrelevant.

We might well include a Swiss bank account as part of our foreign trust planning, but there is very little asset protection in a foreign bank account standing alone.

What about a Foreign Corporation?

We spilled a lot of ink in Chapter 7 discussing the asset protection benefits of corporations. Rather than deal with a foreign trustee, why not just form a foreign corporation and stuff the assets into the corporation? Won't that work? It might, but if it fails it will fail for the same reason that a foreign bank account won't work. Just as you control a foreign bank account, you also control the foreign corporation. If you own a majority interest in the stock, an aggressive creditor will learn of the existence of that controlling interest at the debtor's exam. The creditor will then apply for a turnover order from the local judge. Because the judge has jurisdiction over you, you will be required to turn over the stock. Armed with the controlling interest in the company, the creditor will be able to get at the assets.

Once again, we might use a foreign corporation or foreign limited liability company as part of our foreign asset protection planning, but a foreign corporation by itself will not provide very much asset protection.

How It Plays Out

Using a foreign trust differs from using a foreign bank account or foreign controlled entity in this fundamental respect: a foreign trust interposes another party—the foreign trustee—between the debtor and the creditor. When the creditor applies to the judge for an order requiring the debtor to turn over the assets, the debtor, through the debtor's attorney, responds, "Your Honor, I cannot turn over the assets, because I don't own them. The assets are owned by Aegis Trust Services Ltd., a trust company located in Saint Vincent and the Grenadines. They own the assets under the terms of an irrevocable trust established for my spouse and children. I would be happy to show you a copy of the trust, but I am powerless to turn over the assets."

The judge cannot compel the person who owns the assets—Aegis Trust Services Ltd.—to turn over the assets, because the judge has no jurisdiction over Aegis. Aegis, through its attorneys, might make a special appearance before the judge. A special appearance is an appearance you make for the purpose of telling a judge that the judge has no jurisdiction. Showing up does not give the court jurisdiction. At the special appearance, Aegis' attorneys would say, "Your Honor, we cannot comply with your order to turn over the trust's assets to Mr. Brown's creditors. As the trustee, we owe a fiduciary duty to preserve the asset for the trust's beneficiaries, who are Mr. Brown's spouse and children. Under the terms of the trust, a copy of which you have before you, we are charged with providing for their health, support, and educational needs. We cannot dissipate the trust's assets for Mr. Brown's creditors. To do so would expose us to a lawsuit from Mr. Brown's children and would also imperil our license to act as a trust company. We respectfully decline to comply."

The avoidance of turnover orders and the irrelevance of fraudulent conveyance statutes is how foreign trusts provide asset protection in the United States. We shall see shortly how they provide asset protection in the foreign country, should an aggressive creditor seek to enforce the judgment in that foreign country.

Why Foreign Trusts Don't Work as Well for Real Estate

We noted in Chapter 3 that before we can craft an asset protection plan, we need to focus on the most important criterion: the assets we are seeking to protect. A debtor with a $5 million stock portfolio can make perfect use of a foreign trust; a debtor with domestic real estate valued at $5 million, less so. Here's why.

Firstly, the laws of most states require a court to use the law of the *situs* of the trust with respect to personal property. If the trust says it's governed by the laws of the Cook Islands and the trustee is located in the Cook Islands, then the situs is the Cook Islands. If the trust holds cash or other liquid assets, a U.S. judge should (but might not) apply the laws of the Cook Islands, which in all respects will be more favorable to the debtor than the laws of any state in the United States. However, if the asset is real estate, the judge is generally not required to apply the law of the situs of the trust, but the law of the situs of the real estate, which if located in any state will be more favorable to the creditor.

Secondly, and more fundamentally, foreign trusts work less well for real estate for the simple reason that real estate is the one asset you cannot move. All the niceties of the choice of law aside, at the end of the day, the real estate is still right under the nose of a local judge. If a judge doesn't have jurisdiction over a person, but has jurisdiction over an asset, it's called *in rem* jurisdiction, and it works just as well. The judge might say, "Mr. Brown, I realize I don't have personal jurisdiction over the trust or the trustee, but I certainly have in rem jurisdiction over the parcel of real estate located right here in Los Angeles County. Will someone kindly hand me a blank deed, and I will sign a judicial deed turning the real estate over to the creditor."

Of course, when that happens, the creditor wins.

Is It Possible to Convert Real Property to Personal Property?

Personal property is governed by the law of the situs of the trust. Real property is governed by where the real estate is located. Can we ensure that the trust directly owns no real estate, so as to avoid the application of U.S. law? Perhaps. Let's assume that the foreign trust directly owns no real estate. Instead, it owns an interest in a foreign partnership or limited liability company. The partnership interest in the partnership or the membership interest in the LLC is, under the laws of every state, personal property. Thus, it might be possible to convince a U.S. judge to use the laws of the situs of the trust, rather than local state law.

Drafting the Trust

In most respects, a foreign trust is like any domestic trust we discussed in Chapter 8. Needless to say, a foreign trust must be in writing. Although most states permit oral trusts (at least for non-real-estate assets) anyone seeking to avoid creditors with an oral trust is truly crazy. The trust will designate the beneficiaries, either by name or by class ("My children, in equal shares . . ."), and will instruct the trustee as to how the trust's assets are to be managed for the beneficiaries. Sometimes the foreign trust will dovetail with the settlor's domestic living trust, requiring or authorizing the trustee of the foreign trust to transfer the assets of the foreign trust to the trustee of the domestic trust in the event of the settlor's death. Requiring the cessation of the foreign trust is not a good idea. If one of the settlor's beneficiaries is fighting creditors at the time of the settlor's death, and the living trust requires a distribution to that beneficiary, it would result in the beneficiary's creditors grabbing the distribution. It's best to have the transfer to the living trust be discretionary, rather than mandatory.

Here are some of the features of a typical foreign trust.

A Foreign Trust Is an Irrevocable Trust

A trust may be revocable or irrevocable by the settlor. If the trust is created for asset protection purposes, the trust must, by its express terms, be irrevocable. If the trust is revocable, and the settlor resides in the United States, a local judge may order the settlor to exercise his or her power to revoke the trust. Once the trust is revoked, all the assets come back to the settlor and are subject to attachment by the settlor's creditors. If the settlor refuses to exercise his or her power to revoke the trust, a judge could hold the settlor in contempt.

The fact that a foreign trust is irrevocable does not mean that the settlor is locked into the trust forever. The fact that the trust is irrevocable means only that no one can force the settlor to revoke or amend it. If the settlor later wishes to revoke or amend it, the settlor merely needs to give notice to the trustee. If the trustee is careful, however, the trustee will first assure itself that the request to terminate the trust is not really an order from a court to turn over the trust's assets to creditors. A careful trustee will require the settlor to sign an affidavit to the effect that the request is not really the product of duress. More on that later when we discuss the role of the trust protector.

A Foreign Trust Is a Grantor Trust

I am frequently asked if a foreign trust can be used to reduce or defer the settlor's taxes, as well as to provide asset protection. Generally, the answer is no. A foreign trust created by a U.S. settlor will usually be at best tax-neutral: it will neither increase nor decrease a settlor's taxes. The reason is that a foreign trust is a grantor trust for U.S. tax purposes, which means that the trust's income (and losses, if any) flow back to the settlor and are reported by the settlor on his or her personal tax return. A foreign trust is a grantor trust because the Internal Revenue Code says so: any trust governed by the laws of a foreign country that has at least one U.S. beneficiary (which every asset protection trust will have) is, by definition, a grantor trust (26 U.S.C. §679).

A Foreign Trust Is a Discretionary Trust

A foreign asset protection trust should never require a trustee to make a distribution of income or trust principal to any beneficiary. A trustee who is required to distribute cash to a beneficiary will do just that, and when the money is distributed, nothing will shield the distributed funds from the beneficiary's creditors. The trust should instead give the trustee the authority to withhold distributions from a beneficiary for any reason the trustee deems advisable, which means, of course, that the trustee will withhold distributions in the event that the beneficiary's interest in the trust is subject to attachment.

Not all settlors can afford to part with the income from the trust's assets for an extended period of time; many require a distribution. To the extent that a distribution is made, the asset protection benefits of the trust are minimized. It's possible to mitigate the effects of this by creating a foreign bank account. The bank account might be used to directly pay the settlor's expenses, avoiding any direct transfer to the settlor. But as we have seen, assets in a foreign bank account controlled by the settlor are subject to attachment.

May the Settlor also Be a Beneficiary?

We saw in Chapter 8 that there is no asset protection in a domestic "self-settled" trust, i.e., a trust in which the settlor is also a beneficiary. A number of states, including Delaware, Alaska, and Nevada, have abolished the prohibition against self-settled trusts, but in doing so they were mimicking the rule that exists in any country we choose for a foreign trust.

Not only may the settlor be a beneficiary of a foreign trust, but the settlor may be the sole beneficiary. However, this is not a good idea. We saw earlier that the day might come when the trustee will have to look the judge squarely in the eye and tell the judge that the trustee is a fiduciary for the trust's beneficiaries, such as the settlor's spouse and children. That argument has less force if there is no beneficiary other than the settlor. If the settlor is married and the marriage is solid, I would prefer that the settlor not be a beneficiary at all.

If we have multiple beneficiaries, the trust should provide the trustee with the discretion to pick and choose among beneficiaries. This is especially true if the settlor is one of the beneficiaries. If making a distribution to one beneficiary will result in the beneficiary's creditors attaching the distribution, I would prefer the trustee to make the distribution to another beneficiary.

A Foreign Trust Will Contain a Spendthrift Clause

We also saw in Chapter 8 that a domestic trust will contain a spendthrift clause, which is a prohibition on a beneficiary of a trust from "assigning or anticipating" the beneficiary's interest in the trust. It is the provision that prevents a creditor of a beneficiary from attaching the beneficiary's interest. A spendthrift clause is of less importance in a foreign trust, but we will include such a provision anyway. It is less important due to the other provisions of the trust that make the distributions inherently more difficult to attach than distributions from a domestic trust.

The Antiduress Clause

Foreign trusts are heavily marketed by financial planners, banks, and trust companies, and this marketing has increased with the advent of the Internet. One of the features of foreign trusts that are driven by the marketing is the antiduress clause that appears in many foreign trusts.

Here is a typical antiduress clause: "The Trustee is directed: (1) to recognize and accept instructions or advice, or to exercise any power, only which are given by or are the result of persons acting of their own free will and not under compulsion of any legal authority or legal process; and (2) to ignore any advice or any directive, veto, order, or like decree of any court or administrative body, where such has been instigated by directive, order, or like decree of any court or administrative body."

In other words, if the trustee receives any order from any court that the trustee believes is the result of duress, such as a court order, a turnover order, an attachment, or a levy, the trustee is instructed by the terms of the trust to ignore it. Some people believe that the antiduress clause is the very heart and soul of a foreign asset protection trust.

The antiduress clause is designed to obviate a U.S. settlor from appearing to be in contempt of a judge's order. Let's assume that Mr. Brown has a judgment entered against him. The creditors conduct a debtor's exam and learn that Mr. Brown created a foreign trust. They learn who the trustee is, and they discover the whereabouts of the assets. Mr. Brown appears before the judge, and the judge says something like this: "Mr. Brown, I realize that I do not have jurisdiction over the trustee, who is located in the Cook Islands, or over the assets, which are located in a Swiss bank account of which the trustee is the signatory. But I do have jurisdiction over you. I hereby order you—under penalty of contempt—to request the trustee to repatriate the funds in the trust and turn them over to the creditors."

What does Mr. Brown do? He complies, because it's a court order. And what does the trustee do when it receives the settlor's request? It deposits the request in the trash, because the request is the result of duress, which the trustee is specifically prohibited from honoring. Is Mr. Brown in contempt? Not at all; he complied with the judge's order. The fact that Mr. Brown is powerless to compel the trustee to remit the trust's assets is not Mr. Brown's fault; he did everything he could. It is an ancient principle that you can never be held in contempt if you are powerless to do what a judge orders. As we shall see later in this chapter, however, a judge is not always convinced that a settlor is as powerless to control the trustee as the settlor would have the judge believe.

I don't think that the antiduress clause is as important as some people think it is. If you trust your trustee, and if the trustee is true to his, her, or its fiduciary obligation to the beneficiaries, there is no need for an antiduress clause. The trustee should not turn trust assets over to creditors, whether an antiduress clause exists or not. An antiduress clause might be particularly useful if the trust has no beneficiaries other than the settlor. In all other instances, the antiduress clause is a little bit like chicken soup: it can't hurt, but it's questionable how much it can help.

The Flight Clause

A flight clause, sometimes known as a "flee" clause, authorizes a trustee who believes that creditors might succeed in obtaining trust assets to relocate the trust to another country with another trustee. Generally, foreign trusts work so well that removing the trust's assets to another country is not needed. To be honest, I've never seen a flight clause in operation.

The Trust Protector

As we have seen, trusts created under U.S. law have settlors, trustees, and beneficiaries. Trusts created in jurisdictions that have their origin in British law include a fourth player: the trust protector. Most of the countries we use for foreign trusts are indeed founded on British law. The protector is a person who sort of sits on a cloud high above the trust, making sure that everything goes according to plan. He or she doesn't do anything unless something goes wrong, or is about to. The protector usually has the power to fire the trustee if the protector feels that the trustee is not sufficiently guarding the trust's assets, has itself become subject to the jurisdiction of a U.S. court, or is in danger of giving up the trust's assets for any other reason. The protector may also have the power to name a successor trustee, move the trust to another country, or delete a named beneficiary if the protector feels that a distribution to the beneficiary will be subject to attachment.

We do not use protectors very often, for a simple reason. If the protector is himself or herself a U.S. citizen or otherwise subject to personal jurisdiction in the United States, having a protector may result in more harm than good, if the protector can be ordered to exercise his or her powers. Most of our clients do not have a relative or friend located in foreign country whom they trust to serve as a protector. Needless to say, the settlor should never be named as the protector.

The Letter of Wishes

Another feature of British trust law that has no counterpart in the United States is the letter of wishes. The letter of wishes is just what it sounds like: a letter that the settlor sends to the trustee indicating what the settlor's desires are. Because the letter exists only in the files of the foreign trustee, it cannot be disclosed on a debtor's exam. The letter of wishes is not contractually binding on the trustee, but everyone understands that the trustee will honor the settlor's express wishes unless the trustee feels that it will result in assets going to a creditor.

A letter of wishes can say almost anything. Usually, the letter expresses an instruction to deliver trust assets from time to time to the settlor or to another person the settlor does not wish to mention in the written trust. A settlor may revoke a letter of wishes by simply sending another letter to the trustee.

Selecting the Trustee

It should be readily apparent by now that the person doing the heavy lifting is the trustee, especially if creditors come calling. Selecting the right trustee can be the most important asset protection decision a person can make. Let's consider some of the variables.

May You Be a Co-Trustee of Your Own Foreign Trust?

We used to think that a U.S. settlor could be a co-trustee of his or her foreign trust, understanding that if there was a problem with creditors, the U.S.-based trustee would resign, leaving only the foreign trust company to act as the sole trustee. We also preferred to have a U.S.-based trustee as a convenience; it meant not have to ship documents to the foreign trustee for signature every time we wished to buy or sell trust assets. But ever since the Ninth Circuit Court of Appeals' decision in *Federal Trade Commission v. Affordable Media* (more on that shortly), we have shied away from U.S. co-trustees. Some practitioners still name their U.S.-based settlers as co-trustees, but in light of this case, it's dangerous. Don't do it.

May the Trustee Have a Presence in the United States?

I once had a representative of a foreign trust company pitch his company's services to me. He told me how old they were, how careful, how discreet, and how skilled they were in handling their clients' money. I then asked the representative if the trust company had any offices in the United States. "Oh yes," he replied, "we have offices all over the United States. Very convenient." That was the end of the interview. If you select a trust company solely to manage your money, it doesn't matter where the trust company is located. But if you select a trust company with asset protection in mind, the trust company cannot have any presence whatever in the United States. If it does, the trustee could become subject to court orders issued by a U.S. judge and could be liable for contempt if it ignores the judge's order. In fact, if you have a trustee that is subject to U.S. court orders, you don't have a foreign trust at all: you have a domestic trust.

It is not even a good idea to select a trust company that has no presence in the United States but is a subsidiary of a bank or trust company that does have a U.S. presence. The parent company could be made subject to a court order, with the subsidiary deemed to be the mere agent of the parent.

Which Trust Companies Are Best?

You shouldn't be a co-trustee, and the trust company shouldn't have an office in the United States, but that hardly solves the problem of selecting the right trustee. Selecting a trustee is very much like selecting a roof contractor: they all talk the talk, but not all of them deliver.

We work with two or three foreign trust companies to the exclusion of all others. We have found that these trust companies are knowledgeable and responsive, and that they place their clients' needs before their own. Over the years, we've had some bitter experiences with a few foreign trust companies who lost interest once the fees were paid. Just as when you're engaging a roofing contractor, it's best to get recommendations from people who have had a relationship with a particular trust company for years.

Selecting the Foreign Jurisdiction

There are more countries in this big world that want your trust business than deserve to get it. Every now and then, a new country pops up trying to horn in on the foreign trust business. After it becomes apparent that it does not have an international trust law or an infrastructure capable of supporting foreign trusts, it fades away, to be later replaced by another upstart.

Approximately ten foreign countries are fairly good candidates as jurisdictions for foreign trusts. I believe that the hands-down best is the Cook Islands. In recent years, Nevis (in the Caribbean) and Saint Vincent and the

Grenadines (also in the Caribbean) have cloned the Cook Islands trust law, putting them on a par with the Cook Islands. Turks & Caicos, the Isle of Man, and the Cayman Islands are also pretty good, but if you can just as easily go to the best, why go somewhere not as good? Let's examine the criteria for a good jurisdiction for a foreign asset protection trust.

The Jurisdiction Must Not Recognize Foreign Judgments

The heart and soul of the foreign asset protection trust is that the country in which the trust is formed, i.e., the situs of the trust, will not enforce a judgment rendered by a U.S. court.

Let's do a little review. We have already seen that if a California jury renders a verdict in favor of a plaintiff, and if the plaintiff tries to enforce that judgment in Maine, Maine will be required to give credence to that judgment, per the Full Faith and Credit clause of the Constitution. The Full Faith and Credit clause is the provision that calls into question the efficacy of such debtor-friendly states as Alaska, Delaware, and Nevada for asset protection. Also, if the creditor is an arm of the United States government, such as the Internal Revenue Service or the Federal Trade Commission, the Supremacy clause of the Constitution will likely trump any state statute, no matter how debtor-friendly it is.

But assume that a creditor obtains a judgment, but the debtor's assets are located in France. When the creditor goes to France and seeks to register the California judgment, will the court in France go along? It will not because the Full Faith and Credit clause binds France, but because a treaty between the United States and France requires France to recognize U.S. judgments and requires the United States to recognize the judgments of French courts. The United States has treaties with scores of countries to this effect. Nor does it end there. In addition to these bilateral treaties, the United States and many other countries are signatories to numerous multinational treaties dealing with reciprocity of information, service of summons, and the taking of depositions, all designed to assist foreign creditors in the enforcement of foreign judgments.

Even if a foreign country does not have a formal treaty with the United States, it might still elect to give credence to a foreign judgment, under the doctrine of "comity." Under this doctrine, a court in one country will honor a judgment of the court of another if the court is convinced that doing so will further the commercial relations between the two countries, that the country in which the judgment was granted conducts its judicial system fairly, and that enforcing the judgment does not violate some public policy of the country being asked to enforce the judgment.

Needless to say, any country that is a candidate for a foreign trust will not have a treaty with the United States to enforce a foreign judgment, nor will it grant comity to a foreign judgment.

Consider section 13D of the Cook Islands International Trusts Act of 1984. It provides: "Foreign judgments not enforceable. Notwithstanding the provisions of any treaty or statute, or any rule of law or equity to the contrary, no proceedings for or in relation to the enforcement or recognition of a judgment obtained in a jurisdiction other than the Cook Islands against any interested party shall be in any way entertained, recognized or enforced by any Court in the Cook Islands to the extent that the judgement is based upon the application of any law inconsistent with the provisions of this Act or the Trustee Companies Act 1981-2."

In other words, if anything in the judgment is inconsistent with Cook Islands law, the Cook Islands won't enforce the judgment. Plenty of Cook Islands law is inconsistent with the trust laws of any state in the United States, so the practical result is that no judgment rendered by a U.S. court will be enforced in the Cook Islands. The same applies in Nevis and Saint Vincent and the Grenadines, both of which have adopted the Cook Islands trust act.

It should be noted that the refusal of the Cook Islands to give credence to a foreign judgment is contained only in its trust law. If a foreign creditor sought to enforce a foreign judgment involving a corporation, a partnership, or any asset not owned by a Cook Islands trust, a court in the Cook Islands might have an easier time giving credence to the foreign judgment.

If a jurisdiction will not enforce a foreign judgment, what does that mean? Let's assume that a judgment was entered by a Massachusetts court against Dr. White. The claim arose as a result of an automobile accident. Because the Cook Islands will not enforce the Massachusetts judgment, does it mean that the plaintiff has to start all over again? Does it mean that the plaintiff must bring the investigating police officer, the witnesses, the examining physician, and all the evidence to the Cook Islands—an obviously impossible task? It might, except for one crucial fact: Dr. White doesn't live in the Cook Islands! In other words, even if the plaintiff were willing to relitigate the lawsuit in the Cook Islands, no jurisdiction against the defendant in the Cook Islands exits. No case against Dr. White of any kind can be brought under the Cook Islands International Trusts Act.

As we shall see shortly, one action could be brought in the Cook Islands. The plaintiff might sue the Cook Islands trustee, alleging that the transfer of assets into the Cook Islands trust was a fraudulent conveyance, based on Cook Islands law. That's no easy task.

The Foreign Trust Must Be a Trust under United States Law

One thing you will notice about all of the preferred foreign trust jurisdictions is that they are all either former British colonies or protectorates, or like the Isle of Man, have a centuries-old tradition of British law. This is no coincidence. All of these countries have trust laws whose trusts closely resemble trusts formed in the United States: they all have settlors, trustees who hold legal title to the assets, and beneficiaries who hold beneficial title to the assets.

If the United States cannot recognize the thing we're dealing with as a trust, the United States might not tax the thing as a trust. Worse, it might tax it as a corporation. As we saw in Chapter 7, a corporation that does not make an election under Subchapter S to be ignored as a taxpayer will be subject to a second round of taxation. The distributions from the trust—if the trust is taxed like a corporation—will be subject to tax.

If you're dealing with a document that comes out of a non-British country, you cannot be sure how the U.S. will treat it. It comes as a surprise to many of my clients that Switzerland has no law of trusts. The closest thing to a trust in Switzerland is a *Stiftung*. Under the U.S.-Switzerland Income Tax Convention, a Stiftung is indeed taxed as a corporation. Switzerland may be a great country for bank secrecy, but not for trusts.

The Foreign Jurisdiction Must Not Subject the Trust to Taxation

Most people would agree that subjecting ourselves to present taxes in order to avoid a future creditor is poor planning. As a result, any country that is friendly to foreign trusts must also be a tax haven, i.e., it must not subject the trust, or any of the assets of the trust, to income taxes. All of the countries we have considered are tax havens.

The Foreign Jurisdiction Must Permit Self-Settled Trusts

In most cases, the settlor of the trust will also want to be a beneficiary of the trust. We saw in Chapter 8 that in most U.S. states—Alaska, Nevada, and Delaware are the notable exceptions—a "self-settled" trust will afford no asset protection to the settlor. Any country wanting to attract foreign trusts will permit self-settled trusts. Indeed, a trust formed in the Cook Islands may have only one beneficiary: the settlor. It's not a good idea, but the Cook Islands and all the other jurisdictions previously mentioned will permit it.

The Foreign Jurisdiction Must Be Strict on Fraudulent Conveyances

We noted earlier that foreign trusts are often oversold. Part of the sales pitch is to convince the prospective client that places like the Cook Islands, Nevis, and Saint Vincent and the Grenadines have laws designed to make it impossible for creditors to win in those countries, and that the judges and legislators there have engaged in a vast conspiracy to stiff the creditors. It's simply not true. The judges are every bit as impartial in these countries as they are in the United States. The laws are not all written to tip the scales in favor of the debtors; only one is—the law dealing with international trusts.

We saw that a creditor cannot enforce a U.S. judgment in the Cook Islands, and as a practical matter, cannot litigate a claim in the Cook Islands. But a creditor can bring an action alleging that the transfer of the assets to the Cook Islands trustee was a fraudulent conveyance. That case will be determined under Cook Islands law, and in this context Cook Islands law is very tough.

We saw in Chapter 4 that if a creditor alleges a fraudulent conveyance in the United States, the creditor may prove that the conveyance was fraudulent due to actual fraud or constructive fraud. A creditor can prove constructive fraud if the transfer rendered the transferor insolvent. Under Cook Islands law, the creditor must prove that the transfer was made with the "principal intent" to defraud the transferor's creditors, and that the transferor was insolvent following the transfer. If the fair market value of the transferor's assets after the transfer exceeds the value of the creditor's claim, it's conclusive proof that the transfer was not fraudulent. Moreover, the burden of proof is on the creditor, and the creditor must prove that the transfer was fraudulent beyond a reasonable doubt.

It doesn't stop there. The Cook Islands statute of limitations for bringing such a claim is so short that even if the transfer was fraudulent under Cook Islands law, it's not likely a creditor will make it to the Cook Islands in time. Assume that the automobile accident that resulted in the lawsuit against Dr. White occurred on January 1, 2008. The plaintiff must bring an action against Dr. White in a court in Massachusetts before January 1, 2009. If not, the plaintiff cannot ever bring a claim in the Cook Islands alleging that a transfer to a Cook Islands trustee was fraudulent. Assume that the plaintiff does bring an action against Dr. White in Massachusetts by January 1, 2009, but on February 1, 2008, Dr. White signed a Cook Islands trust and transferred his assets to the Cook Islands trustee on that date. If the plaintiff does not bring an action in the Cook islands alleging a fraudulent conveyance by February 1, 2010—two years from the date of transfer into the trust—then the plaintiff can never bring the action. Of course, if Dr. White transferred the assets to a Cook Islands trust on January 1, 2006, then the plaintiff's case in the Cook Islands was too late on the date of the accident. We'll invoke Klueger's Shortest Rule one more time: *plan early*.

All about Mareva Injunctions

As tough as the Cook Islands (and those other countries following British law) can be on claimants who arrive too late, the Cook Islands can be tough on people who don't create a Cook Islands trust early enough.

Let's assume that Dr. White, who was involved in an automobile accident on January 1, 2008, created and transferred assets into a Cook Islands trust on June 1, 2008. The plaintiff brought a negligence case against Dr. White on March 1, 2008, and was awarded a judgment on December 1, 2008. Let's further assume that the plaintiff conducted a debtor's exam and discovered the existence of the Cook Islands trust on January 15, 2009. What can the plaintiff do? We have seen that the plaintiff cannot enforce the judgment in the Cook Islands and cannot bring an action alleging negligence in the Cook Islands, because there is no jurisdiction there against Dr. White. But if the plaintiff brings an action against the Cook Islands trustee alleging that the transfer to the trustee was a fraudulent conveyance under Cook Islands law prior to June 1, 2010—two years from the day the assets were transferred to the trust—a Cook Islands court will hear the case.

Here's where things get really nasty. If the plaintiff hires a Cook Islands attorney, that attorney will waltz into a court in the Cook Islands and apply for a Mareva injunction. He won't tell the trustee that he's doing it; the trustee will learn of it only after the Mareva injunction has been granted. The Mareva injunction is an order directed at the trustee, ordering the trustee to freeze the assets. The Mareva injunction will instruct the trustee not to take any action that would impair the plaintiff's right to ultimately get at the assets. That could include not resigning as the trustee (so much for the flight clause in the trust), not acting as a director or manager of any company owned by the trust, or not acting as a signatory of any trust bank account. The trustee will undoubtedly obey the Mareva injunction. A trust company could lose its license to act as a trust company if it violated a court order.

Mareva injunctions got their start in 1975 in a British case, *Mareva Compania Naviera S.A. v. International Bulkcarriers, S.A.* Since then, Mareva injunctions have been granted in the Cook Islands, Australia, and Singapore, and there is no reason to believe that a Mareva injunction would not be granted in any country governed by British common law. A Mareva injunction will not be granted in the United States, at least not in a federal court. The Supreme Court ruled in *Grupo Mexicano de Desarrollo S.A. v. Alliance Bond Fund, Inc.*, 527 U.S. 308 (1999), that Mareva injunctions are such a radical departure from American principles of equity that they will not be granted by U.S. courts.

The grant of a Mareva injunction does not mean that the plaintiff wins; it just freezes the assets temporarily. If the trustee can convince the court that the transfer to the trustee was not a fraudulent conveyance, the Mareva injunction will be lifted. Remember, the plaintiff must convince the court that the transfer was a fraudulent conveyance "beyond a reasonable doubt," which is a difficult burden. Of course, a Mareva injunction will always be lifted if the trustee convinces the court that the plaintiff was late in bringing the case.

We have seen some of the features that every foreign trust jurisdiction must have. Let's review some of the additional beneficial features of some of the better asset protection jurisdictions.

Abolition of Forced Heirship

Here's a real horror story, one that is absolutely true. Two elderly people married in Florida. Each owned substantial assets prior to their marriage. Each had grown children and grandchildren. They did not have a prenuptial agreement. They both wrote wills giving all of their separate property to their respective children and grandchildren. The wife died first, and after she died a dispute broke out between the wife's children and the surviving husband over the ownership of a small item of personal property. He claimed it was his, but the children wouldn't give it up.

The husband got his revenge—big-time. He exercised his "spousal right of election," a right that every surviving spouse has in Florida and in almost every state that does not recognize community property. The spousal right of election gave the husband half of the wife's estate, even though she didn't leave him anything in her will! The right of election allows a surviving spouse to call back into the estate all assets that the deceased spouse purported to give to anyone else.

Avoidable? Absolutely, with a foreign trust in the right jurisdiction such as the Cook Islands, Nevis, or Saint Vincent and the Grenadines. These countries have eliminated forced heirship, which is what the spousal right of election is. Had the wife transferred her assets into a foreign trust, the husband could have done nothing to recover the assets.

Abolition of the Rule against Perpetuities

There was a time in ancient England when lords would place their estates in trust forever, with the result that the king's treasury lost out on the death taxes that would have been due every time an owner died. The result was the enactment of the Rule against Perpetuities, which placed a limit on the amount of time that assets can be held in trust.

Whole generations of law students have cracked their heads on this rule, trying to decipher its meaning and its ramifications. I was one of them. At the risk of oversimplifying, here is the rule: If someone places property into a trust, the trust must end no later than the death date of the last grandchild living at the time of the creation of the trust, plus 21 years.

To see why this matters, we must consider the Generation Skipping Transfer Tax, or GST, as it is now officially known in the tax code. The GST is designed to prevent you from giving your assets to your grandchildren. It's not because the IRS hates your grandchildren: it's because if you "skip" a generation (if you give assets to your grandchildren, you've skipped your children), the IRS loses the estate tax it would have collected on the assets your children would have given to their children, i.e., your grandchildren. A person may give up to $2 million to grandchildren without incurring the GST, but above that, the GST is confiscatory; it's Congress' way of telling you not to skip a generation.

If you place assets into a U.S. trust for the benefit of your grandchildren, those assets will eventually pop out of the trust because the Rule against Perpetuities will one day bring the trust to an end. When that day arrives, someone will pay the GST. But not if the assets are placed in a foreign trust in a country that has abolished the Rule against Perpetuities, which every jurisdiction seeking to attract foreign asset protection trusts will have done.

How Not to Do It: All about *FTC v. Affordable Media*

In 1998, the Federal Trade Commission brought a civil lawsuit against Denyse and Michael Anderson. They had been selling investment interests in partnerships that in turn would sell such items as the "Talking Pet Tag" and the "Aquabell," a water-filled barbell. The Andersons sold these investment interests between the hours of 11:00 P.M. and 4:00 A.M. on cable television. The revenues they received from later investors were used to pay dividends to the earlier investors—a classic Ponzi scheme. The court referred to the Andersons as "a modern-day telephonic Bonnie and Clyde." The suit sought an injunction against them, asking that they be prohibited from any further telemarketing activities.

In 1995, the Andersons had created a Cook Islands trust, using a Cook Islands trustee. Significantly, however, the Andersons were themselves co-trustees of the trust. They were also the beneficiaries of the trust and the protectors of the trust.

The FTC not only asked the court to order the Andersons to stop the infomercials, but under its very broad powers, it asked the court to order the Andersons to repatriate the assets they had sent to the Cook Islands. The court granted the order.

In response to the court's order, the Andersons sent a letter to the Cook Islands trustee asking that the trustee repatriate the funds. The trustee not only refused, but terminated the Andersons as co-trustees, pursuant to the broad antiduress powers contained in the trust. The Andersons also attempted to resign as protectors of the trust. The Andersons then claimed that complying with the court's order was impossible, i.e., they had done everything that the court had ordered them to do.

The court disagreed and held the Andersons in contempt, and the Ninth Circuit Court of Appeals upheld their contempt conviction. In *FTC v. Affordable Media, LLC*, 179 F.3d 1228 (1999), the court accepted the proposition that impossibility is a defense to civil contempt, but rejected their claim that compliance with the repatriation order was in fact impossible, since they remained in control of the trust. The principal reason was that the Andersons remained the protectors of the trust. Under the trust, a protector had the power to appoint new trustees. The court also found that the antiduress provisions of the trust were subject to the protector's power to amend, veto, or ignore. In short, their continued control over the trust vitiated the defense of impossibility.

The court also found that the Andersons had used the trust as a private piggy bank, drawing on the trust's assets for such purposes as payment of their personal taxes; this was more evidence of their control of the trust.

The Anderson case, as *FTC v. Affordable Media* has come to be known, has taught us a number of things. For one, you should never be a co-trustee of your foreign trust. Resigning as the co-trustee when things get hot under the collar simply won't do. Secondly, you cannot be a protector of your trust. If anyone is the protector (and if you trust your trustee, it's an open question if anyone needs to be the protector), that person should not be subject to U.S. jurisdiction and should have only negative powers over the trustee; the protector should not have the power to appoint a new trustee.

It's important to remember what the Anderson case is not: it's not about fraudulent conveyances. If the FTC had alleged a fraudulent conveyance, the FTC would have had to bring the case in the Cook Islands. It turns out that the FTC actually did try to bring a case against the Cook Islands trustee in the Cook Islands, but was completely unsuccessful in the effort.

Where Are the Assets in a Foreign Trust Actually Located?

If you create a trust in the Cook Islands with a trustee located in the Cook Islands, are the assets themselves in the Cook Islands? They need not be, and should not be.

Where, then, are they? The assets can be anywhere in the world, provided that they are titled in the Cook Islands trust. That means that if you want to sell assets titled in the trust, the trustee will need to sign whatever paperwork is required to sell the assets. When replacement assets are purchased, the trustee will be required to sign the applications, purchase orders, or whatever other documentation is required to purchase the assets.

The assets should not be located in the Cook Islands. If a creditor is motivated enough to bring an action in the Cook Islands seeking a Mareva injunction, the Mareva injunction will freeze the assets if that's where they are. The Mareva injunction will be ineffective if the assets are located elsewhere.

Can the assets be located in the United States? Perhaps, but it's a bad idea. Here's why. Let's assume that a court in Massachusetts enters a judgment against Dr. White. Long before the judgment was entered, Dr. White created a Cook Islands trust and transferred title to all his assets to the "White Irrevocable Foreign Assets Trust." The brokerage firm of Dale and Hoar, 1 Beacon Street, Boston, MA, opened an account for "Southern Pacific Trust Company, Trustee, White Irrevocable Foreign Assets Trust." All of the account opening forms and applications were duly signed by Southern Pacific Trust Company; Dr. White's name appeared on nothing. Then, one fine day, a court in Boston issued an attachment order directed to Dale and Hoar, ordering them to turn over to Dr. White's creditor all the assets in their possession belonging to Dr. White. Should Dale and Hoar take the position that they hold no assets belonging to Dr. White, neatly depositing the turnover order in the circular file? They should. Can you be certain that they will do this? I can't. If Dale and Hoar decide that their 200-year-old reputation is best served by complying with the court's order, the creation of the foreign trust has done Dr. White absolutely no good. That's why foreign trusts should own foreign assets, not domestic assets.

What foreign assets? There are as many choices for foreign investments as there are domestic investments. The investments can be held in dollars, in euros, or in a wide variety of foreign currencies. Foreign investments can be safe and liquid (e.g., a foreign bank account or foreign money market fund), or they can be more risky and offer a better rate of return, such as foreign securities and mutual funds.

Disadvantages?

What are the downsides to a foreign trust? Not many, but there are a few.

Lack of Control

If all of your assets are in a local bank, you can access your account by walking into the bank. You might even be able to transfer them with little more than a few mouse clicks. If the assets are with a local broker, it won't take much more time to transfer the assets. But you won't be able to move assets in a foreign trust with anywhere near that kind of speed. If you're a day trader, foreign trusts aren't for you.

Costs

The creation of a foreign trust is generally the most expensive asset protection step you can take. In addition to the legal fees and establishment fees you will incur in the year the foreign trust is set up, the foreign trustee will charge annual fees to manage the trust and the trust's assets. Your accountant will love your foreign trust, because your accounting bills will also go up.

If you own U.S. appreciated securities and wish to sell those securities in order to acquire foreign assets, you will incur federal and state capital gains taxes on the sale.

Disclosure to the Internal Revenue Service

We have seen that a foreign trust is tax-neutral. As a grantor trust, it neither increases or decreases your federal or state income taxes. The income, profits, and losses of the investments will flow directly through to you as the settlor of the trust and be reported on your personal income tax return. Nevertheless, you will be required to file two annual reports to the IRS, Forms 3520 and 3520A, disclosing all of the transfers you have made to foreign trusts. These forms are "informational returns" and result in no additional tax. Form 3520 is the settlor's report, and Form 3520A is signed by the trustee. Despite the fact that these returns are not filed with the settlor's personal return (they don't even go to the same IRS Service Center), some people believe that filing them increases the settlor's audit risk. No evidence justifies this urban legend, and even though people may be chary of filing these returns, they must be filed. The penalties the IRS can assert if these forms are not filed can be draconian.

In addition, if the establishment of a foreign bank account is part of your asset protection plan, you must disclose to the IRS that you control a foreign bank account. That fact is disclosed every year on the settlor's personal return.

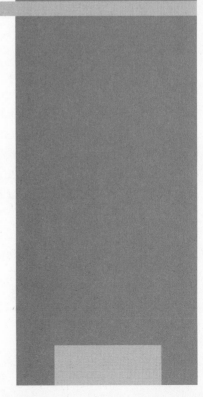

CHAPTER
11

Some Advanced Asset Protection Techniques (and One Simple One)

Advanced Technique #1: Equity Strips

Not everyone plans ahead. It often happens that the creditors come calling before the planning is done. This can be the result of sheer inertia, but just as often is the result of a lawsuit that comes as a bolt from the blue. Whatever the cause, the transfer of an asset after a claim has arisen (whether or not the lawsuit has actually been filed) will likely be deemed a fraudulent conveyance. As we have seen, the result will be that the creditor will be able to ignore the transfer and proceed directly against the transferee to recover the asset.

If the asset is cash, securities, or another liquid asset, that result may not be too troublesome, because the creditor, in order to proceed against the transferee, might have to proceed against a Cook Islands trustee—a lawsuit that will likely be decided under the laws of the Cook Islands, not a pleasant prospect to the creditor.

But if the asset is real estate, we have a problem. We cannot transfer the asset to the Cook Islands, and any domestic transfer may be subject to an attack as a fraudulent conveyance. Is it time to throw in the towel? Not necessarily.

Assume that Mr. Johnson owns an apartment building with a fair market value of $2 million, subject to a mortgage that has an outstanding principal balance of $400,000. He is the owner of the building. Last month Mr. Johnson was involved in an automobile accident, and this morning he received a notice that he is being sued for $10 million. At this point, any transfer of the building will likely be deemed a fraudulent conveyance. Of course, Mr. Johnson should never have owned a valuable parcel of real estate in his own name; it should have been owned by a limited liability company or a trust. But part of asset protection planning is playing the hand we're dealt, and the hand we're dealt here is that the building cannot be moved. If a judgment is entered against Mr. Johnson, the creditor will record the judgment against him. The result will be a lien against the building. The creditor could then commence an action to attach the building, similar to a foreclosure sale. The creditor might have to pay the $400,000 mortgage, which is a small price to pay to seize a building valued at $2 million; the creditor will net $1.6 million.

But assume that Mr. Johnson strips the equity out of the building by borrowing $1.6 million, or as close to $1.6 million as he can. There are now two mortgages on the building, not one. If the creditor forecloses on the building, he will receive nothing except the expense and trouble of the sale, which is a considerable disincentive to an attempt to seize the building in the first place. Very often, creditors will examine the mortgages encumbering a property, and if too much debt exists, they won't even try. The result is that we have shielded the property without transferring it.

Some think that equity strips are magic bullets, but they're not. Let's assume that the $1.6 million second mortgage is sufficient to dissuade the creditor from proceeding against the building. The judgment against Mr. Johnson isn't going away any time soon. Under the laws of most states, the creditor will be able to renew the judgment indefinitely; there is no statute of limitations on the ability to collect. As time goes by, two things will likely happen. The first is that the balances on the $400,000 first mortgage and the $1.6 million second mortgage will be reduced. The second is that the property will appreciate. The result of one or both of these occurrences is that, over time, equity in the building will be sufficient to motivate the creditor to seize it. In the interim, Mr. Johnson will have made monthly mortgage payments to maintain and enhance a property for his creditor. Could Mr. Johnson keep borrowing on the property so as to prevent the buildup of any equity? Not a chance. No one will lend anything on a property that has a $10 million judgment ahead of it. If equity stripping is to work, it must happen before the judgment is entered, not after.

Clients sometimes ask me if they cannot simply give a phony mortgage to their nephew Irving so as to clutter up the title, in order to dissuade a creditor from going after the property. That works only against stupid creditors. Smart creditors and their lawyers will want to see the proof that Irving actually loaned the $1.6 million to Mr. Johnson, and if there is no proof, the transaction will be ignored at the foreclosure sale.

All of this ignores the problem of what to do with the $1.6 million that was borrowed in order to effect the equity strip. It is undoubtedly an asset that Mr. Johnson's creditors could seize if they could find it. It might be possible to stuff it into a qualified plan or other exempt asset if Mr. Johnson has such a plan.

Equity Strips and Foreign Trusts

For some lucky people, the combination of an equity strip and a foreign trust may be just the thing the doctor ordered. Let's assume that Mr. Johnson not only owns the building, he also has another $1.6 million. When a judgment is entered against him, a creditor could seize not only the building, but also the $1.6 million in cash. Is there a way to shield both assets at once? There is, provided that Mr. Johnson had had the foresight to establish a foreign trust. Here's how it works:

Step 1: Mr. Johnson transfers $1.6 million to Southern Pacific Trust Company as trustee of The Johnson Foreign Assets Trust, a trust established in the Cook Islands.

Step 2: Southern Pacific Bank & Trust, a bank located in the Cook Islands and affiliated with Southern Pacific Trust Company, loans Mr. Johnson $1.6 million. The loan is evidenced by a promissory note and is secured by a $1.6 million mortgage. Southern Pacific Bank & Trust requires a compensating balance of $1.6 million in order to make the loan. But the mortgage is genuine; it is not a loan from nephew Irving.

Step 3: The $1.6 million that the Cook Islands bank has loaned to Mr. Johnson is deposited in The Johnson Foreign Assets Trust. Southern Pacific Bank & Trust takes possession of it, buying a certificate of deposit in favor of the trust.

The transaction can be diagrammed as follows:

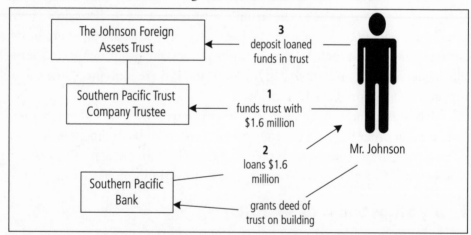

The result is, of course, that (1) the equity in the building has been stripped out in a real loan from a real bank, and (2) the $1.6 million has been shielded from creditors. This arrangement is not without cost. The Cook Islands bank will pay interest to Mr. Johnson on the CD, and Mr. Johnson will pay interest on the second mortgage, but Mr. Johnson will never receive more in interest than he pays. The spread is the cost.

Bottom Line

How well an equity strip will work depends in large part on the creditor. Equity strips work best if the creditor is in it for the quick kill. That is usually the case if the claim is a tort claim, such as an automobile accident or malpractice claim. The claim was brought to coerce a settlement, and if the plaintiff's attorney sees that the result of a trial is waiting around forever for equity to build up in the asset, it tends to soften him up. With equity strips, the debtors settle for less.

Advanced Technique #2: Private Annuities (and Self-Canceling Installment Notes)

A Short Primer on Annuities

If you buy a life insurance policy from an insurance company, you're essentially making a bet with the insurance company as to how long you will live. If you buy a policy that has a $1 million death benefit, and you're hit by a truck as you leave the insurance agent's office, the insurance company is the big loser and the beneficiaries of the insurance policy are the big winners—at least in terms of what they received ($1 million) and what was paid for the policy (one premium). If, on the other hand, you live to be 110, the insurance company will be the big winner, having collected premiums for decades while giving you nothing in return. Actuaries earn their living by making sure that insurance companies win the bet more often than they lose.

An annuity is the reverse. If you give $1 million to a life insurance company, they promise to give you a fixed dollar amount every year for as long as you live. You're the "annuitant." If the annuity is a joint and survivor annuity, the insurance company promises to pay a fixed amount for the joint lives of you and another person, usually your spouse. If the day after you hand the $1 million to the insurance company you and your wife are both hit by a truck, the insurance company is the big winner. If you or your wife live to be 110, the insurance company is the big loser.

There are, of course, as many variations on annuities as there are variations on life insurance policies, and most annuities written today bear little resemblance to the "straight" annuity described above. Most annuities (and life insurance products) have investment features and are not reduced to zero if the annuitant dies. Many annuities can be cashed in, and many offer fluctuating payments. By the time you're done, it may be an annuity in name only, and really more like a mutual fund.

If the payments don't begin the month after you buy the annuity contract, it's a deferred annuity. Many annuities don't begin to pay out until the annuitant reaches retirement age. If the insurance company doesn't have to begin making payments for many years, each payment will of course need to be much larger than it would have been had the payments begun much sooner. A deferred annuity can be a handy way to give a person nearing retirement an assured income stream upon retirement.

Most annuities are sold by insurance companies, but they need not be. A private annuity is an arrangement for a private buyer to acquire an asset from a seller (the annuitant) in exchange for a guaranteed stream of cash. The buyer can be a relative of the seller, or a trust or company established by the seller. As such, a private annuity can be an ideal asset protection device.

Private annuities have been used for decades to defer income taxes and to reduce or freeze estate taxes. They may still be used to reduce estate taxes, but as income tax deferrals, they're dead. The IRS amended its regulations regarding private annuities in October 2006; the sale of appreciated assets by means of a private annuity contract will now result in immediate taxation for the seller, even before the annuity payments are received.

Annuities still work to reduce estate taxes. Let's assume that Mrs. Jones, a widow, has an estate in excess of $7 million. If she dies in 2008, the first $2 million will be excluded from estate taxes and the rest will be taxed, which could result in a tax bill in excess of $2.5 million. Let's also assume that she owns a home that has a fair market value of $2 million. The home might contribute to upwards of $1 million in estate taxes. Let's assume that Mrs. Jones were to sell the home to her son for $2 million. Nothing is accomplished if she sells the home to her son for cash, because the cash will replace the home in her estate. If she sells the home to her son for a promissory note, the value of the note will also replace the home in her estate, resulting in no estate tax savings.

But if Mrs. Jones sells the home for a private annuity, and Mrs. Jones dies before she receives $2 million in annuity payments from her son, everything changes. If she dies after receiving only one payment of $10,000 from her son, and doesn't spend the $10,000, all that is included in her estate is the $10,000. The house is not included because she sold it. The income stream that she would have received is not included because of the very nature of the annuity contract: the payments cease upon her death.

The risk inherent in any private annuity is that the annuitant (Mrs. Jones) will outlive her life expectancy. In that case, the annuitant may have received more than the value of the property sold, increasing the estate taxes. That means that in our example, Mrs. Jones's son will have paid more for the residence than if he had bought it for cash.

Private Annuities and Asset Protection

A private annuity can be an ideal device to remove an asset from the clutches of creditors without violating the fraudulent conveyance rules. As such, a private annuity can be a particularly useful tool if the debtor has not planned early, so that any gratuitous transfer of the asset will likely be a fraudulent conveyance.

Let's return to Mrs. Jones. Unfortunately, while terrorizing Colorado Blvd. in Pasadena on her Harley, she cuts off a van filled with Girl Scouts, littering Colorado Blvd. with injured Girl Scouts and cookies. Litigation ensues, resulting in numerous judgments against her. The $2 million home is there for the taking. As we have seen, all the creditors need to do is record the judgment in the Pasadena courthouse, and eventually they will collect.

But things aren't as easy for the creditors if, before the judgments are entered, Mrs. Jones establishes an irrevocable trust of which her children are the beneficiaries. She sells the home to the trust, and in exchange receives the trust's promise to pay a semiannual annuity. Each annuity payment is based on the fair market value of the home (Mrs. Jones made sure to have it appraised), her life expectancy, and an interest rate provided by the IRS that changes monthly. After the sale, there is no real estate to attach, merely an income stream. Each payment that Mrs. Jones is scheduled to receive from the trust is subject to attachment, but that's not nearly as pleasant a prospect to a creditor as seizing the home.

Is this a fraudulent conveyance? Not likely. The transaction is, after all, a sale, and one at a demonstrable fair market value. If Mrs. Jones dies, there is nothing for the creditors to seize. Depending on where Mrs. Jones resides, there may be nothing to seize even during her lifetime. As we saw in Chapter 5, a number of states, notably Florida, exempt annuities from creditors' claims. Even if an annuitant does not live in a state that exempts annuities, creditors can be kept at bay by structuring the sale as a deferred annuity. If it is structured as such, the annuitant will have to wait to receive the first payment, but so will each creditor.

For added asset protection, it's possible to marry a foreign asset protection trust with a foreign annuity. The seller does not necessarily have to be the annuitant. The annuity can be paid to someone other than the seller, in which case the annuity is *pur autre vie*, i.e., "for the life of another." Let's assume that Mrs. Jones establishes The Jones Foreign Assets Trust and assigns $1 million in cash to the trustee. The trustee sells the $1 million to a Swiss annuity company in exchange for the Swiss company's promise to pay an annual annuity for the life of Mrs. Jones. The annuity payments are paid to the trustee. The trustee doles out the annuity payments in accordance with the terms of the trust, which may be to Mrs. Jones, or to her children, or to no one, depending on the state of Mrs. Jones's difficulties with her creditors. An asset that could easily have been attached has now disappeared into the coffers of a Swiss life insurance company, never to be seen again. It makes settlement negotiations that much easier. This can be diagrammed as shown on the next page.

Self-Canceling Installment Notes (SCINs)

We saw that one of the risks inherent in an annuity is that the annuitant might live "too long," in which case not only the estate planning aspects but also the asset protection benefits of the annuity might explode in our faces. This problem can be solved with a SCIN.

Let's return to Mrs. Jones. To remove a valuable piece of real estate from her estate—and from the clutches of her creditors—Mrs. Jones sells her $2 million home to her son, Irving. In return, she receives Irving's promissory note. The note is like any other note, except for one additional feature: Irving

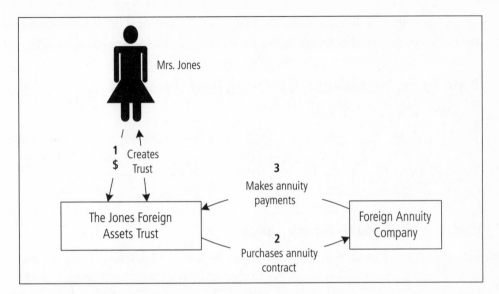

Mrs. Jones

1 Creates
$ Trust

3
Makes annuity
payments

The Jones Foreign
Assets Trust

Foreign Annuity
Company

2
Purchases annuity
contract

may cease making payments on the note on the first to occur of (1) the full payment of the note, or (2) Mrs. Jones's death. If Mrs. Jones lives to be 110, Irving will have to make payments only until the note is fully paid. If Mrs. Jones dies next year while turning wheelies on Colorado Blvd., the note is canceled. The result is that neither the house nor the note is included in her estate for estate tax purposes.

The IRS has some pretty stiff rules for SCINs, and if you don't follow the rules, the property that you "sold" will wind up back in your estate. For one, each SCIN payment will be greater than a note would otherwise have been if the note did not have the self-canceling feature. That makes sense. Any seller who knew that the note might end if he or she were to suddenly die would demand a premium on the note, and most buyers would be willing to pay it. Secondly, the IRS will not let the term of the note be longer than the seller's life expectancy. If Mrs. Jones is 75 years old, the IRS might countenance a 10-year note, but not a 30-year note.

SCINs have the same asset protection benefits as annuities. An asset that could easily have been attached by creditors is suddenly removed from their clutches. The transaction is impervious to attack as a fraudulent conveyance, since the transaction is a sale, at fair market value.

Bottom line: Both private annuities and SCINs are ideal for sheltering real estate if no other tool is available, i.e., if the debtor has not planned early.

Advanced Technique #3: Qualified Personal Residence Trusts (QPRTs)

The IRS allows us to employ a very nifty device to reduce estate taxes, the Qualified Personal Residence Trust. For some people, the QPRT is the closest thing to taking money from the IRS. But QPRTs have asset protection benefits as well.

How QPRTs Reduce Estate Taxes

Mr. Grand is 50 years old. He owns a home worth $1.1 million. His estate, including his business, his stock portfolio, and his vacation home in Jackson Hole, has a combined value of $6 million. If Mr. Grand, who is unmarried with two grown children, dies in 2008, the estate tax will top out at $1.6 million. Can we do anything to lower the estate tax? Yes, but first we need to review a little theory.

Let's assume that Mr. Grand were to make a gift of the home to his children today. The gift would be worth $1.1 million. Grantors, not grantees, are liable for the gift tax, but since Mr. Grand (and every other citizen) has a $1 million lifetime exclusion from gift taxes, Mr. Grand would pay gift tax only on the $100,000 that is not shielded from gift tax. Now assume that instead of making an immediate gift of the $1.1 million home to his children, Mr. Grand were to place the home into an irrevocable trust. The trust would hold the property for 10 years, at which time the house would pop out of the trust and be distributed to Mr. Grand's children. Would the gift still be $1.1 million? No way. It would be less, because making the children wait to get the property makes the property inherently less valuable. An IRS table might tell you that the value of a $1.1 million residence when you have to wait 10 years to get it is $464,352. The same table might tell you that if the term of the trust were 15 years, the gift would be worth $332,117, and if the term of the trust were 20 years, the gift would be $229,998. The longer the term of the trust, the smaller the gift, and the less of

Mr. Grand's $1,000,000 lifetime gift tax exclusion he needs to use.

In reality, the IRS table is valuing the present value of the "remainder interest" in the trust. Mr. Grand is keeping the possessory interest, i.e., the right to live in the house for the term of the trust, and is giving away the remainder interest.

If all that is true, why doesn't Mr. Grand select a 40-year term, so as to reduce even further the amount of the gift? He could, but here is the catch: to remove the house from the estate for estate tax purposes, Mr. Grand must out-live the term of the trust. If not, the whole thing unravels and the house comes back into the estate. Mr. Grand may select a 40-year term, but if he does, he's betting the IRS that he will live to be 90.

The IRS lets you do a QPRT not only for your residence, but also for a vacation home. The vacation home must truly be a vacation home, and not a rental. If you depreciate the home on your taxes, it won't qualify for a QPRT.

How QPRTs Provide Asset Protection

In case you missed it, a QPRT is an irrevocable trust. The residence goes out of the settlor's hands on day one. Is it a self-settled trust? Not really. The benefici-aries of the trust have to be people other than the settlor; if not, the residence is included in the estate. Fraudulent conveyance? Perhaps, but it's difficult to prove. Is a transfer done to reduce estate taxes, pursuant to rules promulgated by the IRS, a transfer designed to delay, defeat, or defraud a creditor?

For the very last time, we'll repeat the mantra: you have a better chance of avoiding a fraudulent conveyance challenge if you *plan early*.

A Simple Technique: Sell the Asset

At times, the most effective technique is also the simplest. We noted earlier that the most difficult asset protection is asset protection for real estate, for the simple reason that the real estate cannot be moved. If the asset protection is done late in the game, it is likely that anything we do will be branded as a fraudulent conveyance and the creditor will be able to follow the asset into the hands of the transferee.

But assume that the debtor who has substantial equity in the asset simply sells it for its fair market value. There is now no real estate to attach, and there cannot be an allegation that the transfer was a fraudulent conveyance, since the buyer paid a reasonably equivalent value for the residence. If the buyer paid cash, the seller now has a fistful of cash instead of real estate—cash that can be seized. But cash is infinitely more difficult to seize than real estate.

Now, assume further that the the real estate we want to protect is the debtor's primary residence. It's the asset closest to his heart, and he simply cannot contemplate selling the residence because he cannot abide the thought of moving. It's unlikely that we will find an investor willing to buy the residence and still allow our debtor to remain in the residence under a lease. Are we out of options?

Not necessarily. If the debtor is lucky, he or she will have children, parents, or siblings who are willing to buy the residence for fair market value. If we are really lucky, the buyers will be able to pay cash for the residence and give our debtor a fair market lease, permitting the debtor to remain in the residence. There are negative tax consequences in this: the buyer (who is now also the landlord) will have rental income to the extent of the rent that is received, without the tenant having an offsetting deduction for the rent that is paid. Depending on where the transaction takes place, the property taxes may increase as a result of the sale. But these are minor consequences compared to the loss of the residence.

Let's assume we're not lucky, and the children (or the parents) do not have the cash to buy the residence. That leaves us with either going to the bank to finance the sale, or having the seller finance the buyer.

This latter option is the most likely. Assume that the residence is worth $1 million, and already is burdened by a $200,000 mortgage. To sell the residence for its fair market value (thus avoiding a claim that the sale was a fraudulent conveyance), the seller would have to "carry" the buyer to the extent of $800,000. The $800,000 second mortgage would have to be paid. If not, the debtor's creditors could seize the debt and foreclose upon the residence, defeating the purpose of the entire transaction. But if the second mortgage is paid, the creditor has a problem. What was once easily attachable real estate with $800,000 in equity is now a promissory note that is perhaps payable over the next 30 years. For a creditor in a hurry to collect—which includes most creditors—this is not a pleasant prospect.

Safeguarding Your Business

Throughout this book, we have assumed that asset protection is what we do if and when there is a lawsuit. There may be a few things we can do to either prevent a lawsuit or enhance the chances of winning a lawsuit, especially in an employment context.

Mandatory Arbitration

We saw way back in Chapter 1 that Angela Venizelos sued Dr. Nguyen on a trumped-up charge of sexual discrimination. Fortunately, Dr. Nguyen had safely protected his assets before the lawsuit was brought, substantially decreasing the chances that Ms. Venizelos could get at the assets in the unlikely chance that she were to prevail. But lawsuits are expensive, and plaintiffs' lawyers working on a contingency fee basis bring frivolous lawsuits armed with the knowledge of how expensive they are. Is there a way to simply prohibit an employee or former employee from bringing a lawsuit?

Yes, there is—by requiring the the employee to bring a claim before an arbitrator rather than a court. Employees (and their attorneys) hate arbitration, and do whatever they can to avoid it. But a well-drafted arbitration agreement may be all you need to prevent an employee or former employee from bringing a lawsuit.

Arbitration has two principal advantages for the employer. Firstly, arbitration is far cheaper and faster than litigation in court. That means that the plaintiff's attorney, who is already on a contingency fee, cannot threaten bottomless attorney's fees for the defendant as a result of an endless lawsuit. Devoid of this threat, the plaintiff's attorney is far less likely to exact a quick and cheap settlement. The second advantage is that there are no juries in arbitration, which means that the plaintiff cannot hope to achieve a big score from a runaway jury. If the plaintiff prevails (and there is less chance of that in arbitration), the award will be based on a fair approximation of the plaintiff's damages and not on a jury's contempt for the wealthy. Now you see why employees and their attorneys hate arbitration.

A Primer on Arbitration

An arbitrator is like a judge, and often may be a retired judge, but isn't a judge. An arbitrator has many of the powers of a judge; the key power is the ability to decide a case and have that decision enforced upon the parties. Unlike a judge, an arbitrator is not an employee of the state. An arbitrator is a private person who is selected by the parties by means of an arbitration agreement.

The right to have the arbitrator's decisions enforced is also governed by the arbitration agreement and a state or federal statute that gives the winning party in an arbitration the right to go to court and have the arbitrator's decision confirmed by a judge. Once that happens, it's the same as if the judge had decided the case.

There can be no arbitration unless the parties have first agreed to it, either by signing a separate arbitration agreement or including an arbitration clause in another agreement (e.g., an employment agreement, a purchase and sale agreement between vendors and purchasers with respect to the sale of goods, or an agreement between professionals such as doctors and patients, lawyers and clients, stockbrokers and their customers, etc.). Indeed, the list of possible arbitration contexts is almost endless, but in no case can someone be forced into arbitration without first agreeing to it.

The arbitration agreement usually spells out who the arbitrator will be by naming the company employing the arbitrator, such as the American Arbitration Association. The agreement will usually specify the number of arbitrators, usually one or three. On occasion, the agreement will specify whether or not the parties, by submitting to arbitration, have waived the discovery rights they would have had if they had not chosen arbitration. As we saw in Chapter 2, discovery involves the right to ask the opposing party written questions ("interrogatories") or require the other party to appear at a depostion. If you don't agree that these rights are preserved in arbitration, they are waived.

A typical arbitration provision that appears in a limited liability company operating agreement is reproduced on the following page. It requires all the members of the LLC to arbitrate any claims any of them may have against each other or the LLC, obviating the expense of litigation.

A party usually begins arbitration by filing a Notice of Claim with the arbitrator. The Notice of Claim takes the place of the complaint in civil litigation: it sets forth the reason the claimant feels aggrieved and the amount that the claimant is seeking. The other party to the arbitration is named, and the arbitrator then gives the defendant the opportunity to answer. If the defendant fails to respond, a default can be taken against him or her, just as in civil litigation.

> ## A Typical Arbitration Clause
>
> **Arbitration:** Any action to enforce or interpret this Agreement or to resolve disputes between the Members or by or against any Member shall be settled by arbitration in accordance with Civil Code Section 1280 et seq., including the right to discovery as set forth therein.
>
> Arbitration shall be the exclusive dispute resolution process in the State of California, but arbitration shall be a nonexclusive process elsewhere.
>
> Any party may commence arbitration by sending a written demand for arbitration to the other parties.
>
> Such demand shall set forth the nature of the matter to be resolved by arbitration.
>
> Arbitration shall be conducted at a place mutually agreed upon by the Parties.
>
> The substantive law of the State of California shall be applied by the arbitrator to the resolution of the dispute.
>
> The parties shall share equally all initial costs of arbitration.
>
> The prevailing party shall be entitled to reimbursement of attorney fees, costs, and expenses incurred in connection with the arbitration.
>
> All decisions of the arbitrator shall be final, binding, and conclusive on all parties. Judgment may be entered upon any such decision in accordance with applicable law in any court having jurisdiction thereof.

That's where the similarities between civil litigation and arbitration end. The biggest difference is how quickly the case comes before the arbitrator. You don't wait months or years for the case to be heard; you usually wait only weeks. You usually don't spend tens of thousands of dollars on motions and court appearances before the case is ever heard, and when the case is heard, there is no jury and no courtroom. Both sides appear in an office—often the arbitrator's office—and very informally present their cases. Forget everything you ever saw watching Perry Mason. There are no histrionics, no orotund speeches, and no dramatic gestures, since there is no jury. It tends to go very fast.

Arbitration is something of a roll of the dice for both sides, since one generally cannot appeal the decision of an arbitrator. Only in the extremely rare instance where the arbitrator manifestly ignores the law will a court of appeals overturn an arbitrator's decision. If you win an arbitration, you won; if you lose, you lost. Generally, the decision of the arbitrator is final.

Arbitration and Mediation Compared

Arbitration is often confused with mediation, but they are worlds apart. A mediator's role is to attempt to facilitate the settlement of a case. A mediator has no power to force a settlement and certainly no power to decide a case. Parties will often attempt mediation, but only when the mediation has failed will the arbitrator be brought in.

Are Arbitration Agreements Enforceable?

Because arbtration is quick and cheap (or at least cheaper than litigation) and because arbitration does not involve juries, many plaintiffs' attorneys will try to move heaven and earth to avoid an arbitration agreement. Often, they are successful. That puts a premium on careful drafting of the arbitration agreement.

In 2001, the United States Supreme Court, in *Circuit City Stores v. Adams* 532 US 105, 149 L.Ed. 2d 234, 121 S. Ct. 1302, ruled that the Federal Arbitration Act did not preclude the enforceability of an arbitration clause requiring the arbitration of an employment agreement. Since the case emanated from the Supreme Court, whose decisions are the law of the land, you would think that that would be the end of it. Far from it, especially in the Ninth Circuit Court of Appeals, the federal circuit court that includes California.

Prior to *Circuit City Stores*, the California Supreme Court considered arbitration agreements in *Armendariz v. Foundation Health Psychcare Service*, 24 Cal. App. 4th 83 (2000). In *Armendariz*, two employees filed a complaint against their employer alleging that they had been terminated as a result of their sexual orientation. Both employees had signed employment agreements requiring them to arbitrate all employment disputes, but they refused to submit to arbitration, alleging that the agreements they had signed were unenforceable. The employer sued them to enforce the arbitration clause. The California Supreme Court ruled that employers could require their employees to arbitrate all employment claims, including sexual discrimination and harassment claims. Specifically, the Supreme Court ruled that there was nothing in the California Fair Employment Housing Act—the statute that bars discrimination—that prevents arbitration.

Whether the court would enforce this particular arbitration agreement was another matter, and this particular agreement was found wanting. Although *Armendariz* applies only to California agreements, the court's holding should guide the drafting of arbitration agreements everywhere.

For an arbitration agreement to be enforceable against an employee or former employee, it must contain the following:

- **A neutral arbitrator.** This may appear obvious, but you would be surprised how many employers try to foist obviously biased arbitrators on their employees. Many years ago, I read an arbitration clause in a bank's loan documents that named an arbitrator I had never heard of. It turned out that the company chosen as the independent arbitrator was in fact a creation of the bank.

- **Limitations on the costs of arbitration to employees.** We noted earlier that, in the long run, arbitration is cheaper than litigation. But the initial filing fee is usually greater to start an arbitration than it is to start a lawsuit. For an impecunious employee, it may be prohibitive. Consequently, the arbitration agreement should provide that the employee will not have to pay any more to start an arbitration than to start a lawsuit.

- **Adequate discovery.** We noted that the right to take depositions and submit written interrogatories can be waived in arbitration. The arbitration agreement should make it clear that these rights are preserved.

- **No limitations on remedies.** This is very important. In order to be enforceable (at least in California), the agreement cannot reduce what an employee could win if the employee were to sue in court. If a federal or state statute gives the employee the right to recover attorney's fees if he or she prevails in court, the arbitration agreement cannot provide for a waiver of attorney's fees.

- **Judicial review**. We have seen that an arbitrator's decision is generally not reviewable, except in the most egregious of cases where the arbitrator ignores the law. The *Armendariz* court seems to have wanted broader rights of appeal, but it is unclear what these rights would be.

- **Mutuality of claims.** If any claim an employee has against the employer must be brought before an arbitrator, any claim the employer has against the employee must also be brought before an arbitrator. Arbitration cannot be solely at the discretion of the employer.

If your arbitration agreement contains these features, you are a long way down the road to prohibiting your current or former employees from suing you. That won't prevent an occasional claim from being brought, but it will eliminate that form of armed robbery known as the frivolous lawsuit.

Are New Arbitration Agreements Enforceable against Existing Employees?

Let us assume that you do not have a mandatory arbitration agreement with your current employees. Can you give each of them a mandatory arbitration agreement and have them sign it? Will the agreements be enforceable?

Perhaps, but it is not certain. An arbitration agreement is a contract, and in basic contract law every contract must be supported by mutual consideration. If I promise everything, and you promise nothing, it's not an enforceable contract. If the employee signs the arbitration agreement, you have benefitted. But what has the employee gained?

It's possible that what the employee has gained is the employer's promise to also be bound by arbitration. Better yet, what the employee may be gaining by signing the arbitration agreement is continued employment. If you make it clear to the employee that signing the arbitration agreement is a condition of continued employment—that failing to sign means getting fired—then the arbitration agreement will be backed by mutual consideration, the key to enforcement.

Make Sure They Are Signed

Many employers have employment manuals that spell out the conditions of employment for all of the employees. Often, the employment manuals will make reference to mandatory arbitration. Many employers require every employee to sign a statement saying that the employee has read and understands the employee manual.

It is not sufficient to have the employees sign a statement saying they have read the employee manual. Because an arbitration agreement is a contract, it must be signed by the employee. If not, it will not be enforced.

Non-competition Agreements

If your business is like most, think of the "capital" that remains in the office at the end of the day—the computers, the furniture and fixtures, the inventory. Now think of the "capital" that leaves via the elevator every day: the experience, the know-how, the insights of the work force. The furniture and fixtures can be replaced. The work force can also be replaced, but at a much higher cost and over a longer period of time. What is worse, your furniture cannot start a competing business and telephone your customers offering them better service at lower prices. Your employees can.

Can employees be prevented from competing with your business? Unfortunately, the answer is "maybe." It depends on where you live.

One thing is certain: You can prevent an employee anywhere from competing with you while the employee is working for you. Any employment agreement that restricts the employee to working only for you will be enforced. The issue is whether you can prohibit an employee from competing with your business after the employee leaves. In the typical example, the employee will leave for the purpose of setting up a competing business. Where, and under what conditions, can you prevent it?

The most typical state statutes permit non-competition agreements if they are limited in terms of time and geographic area. For example, Texas will enforce a non-competition agreement if it is limited in terms of the time, area, and scope of activities and imposes no greater restraint on the employee than is necessary to protect the goodwill of the employer (see *Texas Business and Commerce Code* §15.51). For example, if a business is located in Houston and sells to customers only in Houston, it is pointless to prohibit the former employee from competing everywhere in Texas; no court will enforce it. What is more problematic is the permissible time limitation. I generally recommend to clients that they restrict the employee for no more than two years after the termination of employment, on the grounds that a longer limitation might risk not being enforceable at all.

Here is an example of how varied are the governing state statutes. Some states—Texas included—permit the courts to cut down a non-competition agreement that is overly broad in terms of geography or time without voiding the entire agreement. Wisconsin (*Wis. Stats.* §103.465) and Michigan (*Mich. Stats.* §445.774a) have statutes of this type. South Dakota's permitted period of non-competition is written right into the statute: two years (see *S. Dak. Codified Laws* §53-9-11).

On the other side of the spectrum, Colorado prohibits any non-competition agreement that restricts the employment of any employee, whether skilled or unskilled, but Colorado will permit non-competition agreements for executive and management personnel (see *Colo. Rev. Stats.* §8-2-113). Equally restrictive are Hawaii (*Haw. Rev. Stat.* §480-4) and Oklahoma (*Okla. Stat.* tit. 15 §217-219a). The most restrictive is California, which imposes a flat ban on non-competition agreements, rendering void any agreement that restrains anyone from engaging in any lawful profession (see *Cal. Business & Professions Code* §16600).

New York's law is a complete muddle. Non-competition agreements are upheld only if all three prongs of a three-pronged test are met: (1) the agreement must be no broader than what is necessary to protect the employer's "legitimate interest," (2) the agreement must not impose an "undue hardship on the employee," and (3) the agreement must not be "injurious to the public." The key is the first prong. An employer will have a "legitimate interest" in prohibiting a salesman who had direct contact with the employer's customers from setting up a competing business and contacting those customers. An agreement that prohibits the salesman from contacting any of the employer's customers, whether the salesman had ever contacted those customers or not, will not be upheld.

Every state statute that prohibits non-competition agreements—even California's—contains an exception for non-competition agreements that arise in the context of the sale of a business. If I sell my business to you, you can prohibit me from competing with the business that I just sold you.

Drafting the Non-Competition Agreement

Every non-competition agreement must be so tight that it will squeak. The reason is that every non-competition agreement arises in the very same context: the employee leaves his or her employer, either voluntarily or involuntarily, and then decides to compete with the former employer. The former employee then remembers the non-competition agreement he or she signed and takes it to a lawyer, who proceeds to place the agreement under a microscope in the hope of finding a hole in it. That's why these agreements have to be drafted as tightly as possible.

Here is part of a tight non-competition agreement:

NON-COMPETITION AGREEMENT

THIS AGREEMENT, made and entered into this 31st day of January, 2001, by and between DELBERT JONES (hereinafter referred to as "JONES") and SMITHTOWN ENTERPRISES, INC., a Texas Corporation (hereinafter referred to as "the Corporation")

RECITALS:

WHEREAS, the Corporation is engaged in the marketing of educational materials to schools, school districts, and other educators, and

WHEREAS, JONES is an independent contractor for the Corporation, engaged in the marketing of the Corporation's educational materials, and

WHEREAS, JONES has on this date entered into an extension of his independent contractor agreement with the Corporation, and

WHEREAS, during the course of his extended engagement as an independent contractor, JONES will gain access to substantial proprietary information of the Corporation relative to

---

its customers, marketing strategies, and educational materials, the unauthorized disclosure of which would be detrimental to the success of the Corporation and which could result in the failure of the Corporation's business prospects, and

WHEREAS, the Corporation is justified in seeking to prevent the unauthorized disclosure of any of its proprietary information and trade secrets, and

WHEREAS, as a result of JONES' engagement as an independent contractor, he has gained sufficient knowledge of the Corporation so as to successfully compete with the business of the Corporation, and

WHEREAS, the Corporation is justified in seeking to prevent JONES from competing with the business of the Corporation;

NOW, THEREFORE, in consideration of the premises, and of the mutual representations, covenants, warranties, and promises herein contained, the parties hereto stipulate and agree as follows:

1. <u>Agreement Not to Compete</u>. JONES hereby stipulates and agrees that during the term of this Agreement, he will not compete with the business of the Corporation in the City of Houston, Texas. All of the following shall be prohibited to JONES:

   a. Marketing, selling, distributing, or otherwise dealing in the educational materials of any publisher, author, or distributor of school books, computer software, or other educational materials;

   b. Acting as a compensated advisor or consultant to any school, school district, publisher, author, or distributor of educational materials, if such services are connected with the acquisition of educational materials;

   c. Owning an interest in any corporation, partnership, or other entity actively engaged in the marketing of educational materials; or

   d. Disclosing to any person any trade secret, proprietary information, customer list, account list, work in progress, research and development, or any other material not in the ordinary course of his engagement, which would harm the business of the Corporation;

   e. Being affiliated with, employing, or engaging any person to perform any act prohibited hereunder.

> 2. <u>Consideration</u>. As consideration for JONES' covenant not to compete, the Corporation hereby agrees to pay JONES a cash sum equal to One and One-Half Percent (1-1/2%) of its annual gross receipts from sales, for the four consecutive annual fiscal years of the Corporation, commencing with the fiscal year beginning on February 1, 2001.

Why is this non-competition agreement so tight? It doesn't only prohibit Delbert Jones from competing with Smithtown's business, but prohibits him from "employing or engaging any person to perform any act prohibited hereunder." That means that even if Jones tried to circumvent the agreement by working through his wife or his son, that ploy wouldn't work; Jones is also barred from working through anyone else.

Non-Competition and Arbitration

Can you make a non-competition agreement subject to arbitration? In other words, if you want to make sure a non-competition agreement that an employee signs must be interpreted—if at all—by an arbitrator and not by a jury, can you make the non-competition clause the subject of an arbitration clause? Absolutely. It will prevent the employee seeking to compete with you from going before a jury for sympathy.

Agreements Limiting Theft of Trade Secrets

It is difficult in many states to prevent an employee from competing with you. It is far easier to prevent an employee from walking out the door with your trade secrets and using them for his or her own benefit or the benefit of a competitor.

Forty-three states and the District of Columbia have enacted a version of the Uniform Trade Secrets Act (UTSA), which prohibits an employee from walking off with your trade secrets. If the statute is violated, the employer can not only sue the former employee for damages, but also get an injunction prohibiting the use of the stolen materials. The remaining seven states, including New York, New Jersey, and Pennsylvania, rely upon common law principles to prohibit the theft of trade secrets.

The UTSA defines a "trade secret" very broadly to include "information, including a formula, pattern, compilation, program, device, method, technique or process that (1) derives independent economic value, actual or potential, from not being generally known to, and not being readily ascertainable by proper means by other persons who can obtain economic value from its disclosure or use and (2) is the subject of efforts that are reasonable under the circumstances to maintain its secrecy."

Under this definition, not only will all of the computer programs you have developed constitute trade secrets, but so will the formulae you use to determine prices and markups, your internal profit margins on certain items you sell or service, and the methods you employ to manufacture goods or provide services. The identities of your customers may not be a trade secret, but if you have created a database of their names, addresses, and telephone numbers, that customer list is a trade secret; anyone walking out the door with a computer disk that contains that database is stealing a trade secret and is subject to an injunction.

It is not sufficient to rely upon the statute to protect your trade secrets. The employee manual should define, as broadly as possible, all the things you wish to protect. Each employee must sign an agreement acknowledging that he or she will receive trade secrets, will not disclose them to any person without authorization, and will return any materials containing trade secrets if and when the employee is terminated. Under the agreement, the employee must consent to the jurisdiction of the local court and agree that an injunction prohibiting the use of trade secrets is proper.

A typical agreement prohibiting the use of trade secrets appears on the following pages.

CONFIDENTIALITY AGREEMENT

THIS CONFIDENTIALITY AGREEMENT, made and entered into this _____ day of October, 2008, by and between CYBERSPACE BUSINESS, INC., (herein "Cyberspace") and [Name], [Address]

(herein "Employee").

RECITALS:

WHEREAS, Cyberspace desires to engage Employee as an employee of Cyberspace and Employee desires to be engaged as an employee on the terms and conditions described herein; and

WHEREAS, during the course of Employee's engagement with Cyberspace, Employee will come into possession of and information relating to Cyberspace's proposed business, marketing plans, procedures and pricing structures, target market, computer software, and operating manuals (herein collectively referred to as the "Materials"), all of which constitute proprietary information and trade secrets valuable to Cyberspace and which would be destructive to Cyberspace's business if disseminated to competitors; and

WHEREAS, the parties hereto stipulate and agree that Cyberspace has a right to protect the Materials and all of the proprietary information and trade secrets contained therein from unauthorized disclosure;

NOW, THEREFORE, in consideration of the foregoing premises, and of the mutual representations, promises, and warranties herein contained, the parties hereto stipulate and agree as follows:

1. <u>Confidential Nature of Proprietary Information</u>. Employee agrees that any of the Materials of Cyberspace received from Cyberspace or from any other person or entity shall be kept strictly confidential, and shall not be disclosed to any person or entity without the prior written consent of Cyberspace. Employee further agrees that only those persons within its organization that are approved by Cyberspace shall have the right to obtain any Materials or other proprietary information. Employee agrees that Cyberspace would not have hired Employee but for Employee's representation and warranty regarding Employee's continued safekeeping and non-disclosure of the Materials, and that Cyberspace's continued employment of Employee is expressly

contingent upon Employee's continuing duty to refrain from unwarranted disclosure of the Materials. Employee further represents and warrants unto Cyberspace that Cyberspace shall have the right to terminate Employee in the event of Employee's breach of this provision regarding confidentiality and non-disclosure.

2. <u>Return of Proprietary Information</u>. In the event that Employee voluntarily or involuntarily ceases his or her engagement, then Employee shall forthwith return to Cyberspace any and all Materials or other proprietary or confidential information obtained from Cyberspace during the course of Employee's engagement with Cyberspace.

3. <u>Remedies; Attorneys' Fees</u>. In the event that Cyberspace deems that Employee has breached any of the provisions of this Agreement, then Cyberspace shall have the right to bring suit against Employee seeking a temporary restraining order requiring Employee to cease and desist his or her breach of this Agreement. The right to bring an equitable action shall not be the exclusive remedy. In any such action, the prevailing party shall be entitled to an award of its attorneys' fees and costs of litigation. In addition to the foregoing, Cyberspace shall have the unrestricted right to access the work station, computer terminal, and any and all computer files, disks, and other peripherals located on Cyberspace's premises to determine if a breach of this Agreement shall have occurred or is occurring, and in so doing shall have the right to view and remove any files or programs.

4. <u>California Law; Personal Jurisdiction</u>. Each of the parties hereto submits to the personal jurisdiction of the Los Angeles Superior Court with respect to any litigation arising out of the interpretation or enforcement of this Agreement. This Agreement shall be governed by the laws of the State of California.

DONE AND DATED as of the date first set forth hereinabove.

Cyberspace Business, Inc.

By: _____
   Its President

   _____
   "Employee"

Asset Protection for the Disabled and Your Children

Parents or guardians who provide financial assistance to disabled children face a host of difficulties. For one of those difficulties, there is a solution.

The difficulty arises in the way many state and federal assistance programs for the disabled, principally Medi-Cal and Social Security, are administered. These programs are means-tested; in order to qualify for government assistance (usually in the form of a fixed monthly stipend), the applicant must prove that he or she has very little income and very few assets. The applicant must essentially be poverty-stricken to qualify. This does not represent a problem as long as the applicant is under the care of a parent or guardian, since the assets in that case are not considered the assets of the child or other recipient; they are rightly deemed to be the assets of the parent or guardian. A parent may provide a disabled child with any level of support, no matter how luxurious, without making the child ineligible for government assistance.

The problem arises if and when the parent or guardian caring for the disabled child dies. If the child inherits the assets, they are no longer the parent's assets but the child's, and the child will automatically be disqualified for assistance. In the more likely event that the parent created a trust for the care of the child, the funds that the trustee is required to disburse to the child under the terms of the trust will also disqualify the child.

The answer lies in a "special needs trust," a trust like no other you will ever see. Special needs trusts are recognized by federal and state agencies as a legitimate way to preserve a disabled person's eligibility for government assistance.

Most trusts instruct a trustee to pay a certain amount of trust income or principal every month or year to a designated beneficiary, or give the trustee discretion with respect to distributions to the beneficiary. A special needs trust does the opposite: it instructs the trustee not to give anything to the beneficiary unless and until Medi-Cal and Social Security have paid whatever benefits the child is entitled to receive. If, for whatever reason, the government does not pay, the trustee is instructed also not to pay. The trust is designed to pay only for those needs of the child over and above the ordinary care that the government is supposed to pay for, i.e., the child's "special needs." By wording the trust in this fashion, every time the government is scheduled to cut a check to the beneficiary, the beneficiary qualifies, because the beneficiary has no right to any of the trust's assets. Only after the government pays does the trustee's obligation to provide for the child kick in.

A special needs trust can be a stand-alone trust, or it can be a special provision in a parent's living trust or will. An example of the key provisions of a special needs trust is provided on the following pages.

The Anna Adams Special Needs Trust

1. <u>Identification of Beneficiary</u>. This trust is established solely for the benefit of Settlors' daughter, Anna Adams, hereinafter referred to as "beneficiary."

2. <u>Beneficiary's Needs</u>. The beneficiary suffers from a disability which substantially impairs the beneficiary's ability to provide for her own care and custody and constitutes a substantial handicap. It is Settlors' primary concern in creating this trust that it continue in existence as a supplemental (and emergency) fund to public assistance for the beneficiary throughout the beneficiary's life, as Settlors would provide if personally present. Currently, there exist basic living needs, such as dental care and outdoor recreation, which public-benefit programs for the disabled do not provide. During Settlors' lives, Settlors intend to provide for these needs when necessary. After Settlors' deaths, it is vitally important that the beneficiary continue to have these programs in order to maintain a level of human dignity and humane care. If this trust were to be invaded by creditors, subjected to any liens or encumbrances, or cause public benefits to be terminated, it is likely that the trust corpus would be depleted prior to the beneficiary's death, especially since the cost of care for disabled persons (not including any emergency needs) is high. In this event, there would be no coverage for emergencies or supplementation for basic needs. The following trust provisions should be interpreted in light of these concerns and stated intent.

3. <u>Payments of Income and Principal</u>. The Trustee shall pay to or apply for the benefit of the beneficiary, for the beneficiary's lifetime, such amounts from the principal or income, up to the whole thereof, as the Trustee in the Trustee's sole discretion may from time to time deem necessary or advisable for the satisfaction of the beneficiary's special needs, and any income not distributed shall be added to principal. As used in this instrument, "special needs" refers to the requisites for maintaining the beneficiary's good health, safety, and welfare when, in the discretion of the Trustee, such requisites are not being provided by any public agency, office, or department of the State of California, or of any other state, or of the United States. "Special needs" shall include, but not be limited to, dental care, special equipment, programs of training, education, and habilitation, travel needs, and recreation. In making distributions to or for the beneficiary for special needs, the Trustee shall take into consideration the

applicable resource and income limitations of the public assistance programs for which the beneficiary is eligible. In carrying out the provisions hereof, the Trustee shall be mindful that the Settlors' principal desire is the care of the beneficiary and not the probable future needs of the remainderment of this trust.

4. <u>Settlors' Intent Regarding Public Assistance</u>. Settlors declare that it is their intent, as expressed herein, that because the beneficiary is disabled and unable to maintain and support herself independently, the Trustee may seek support and maintenance for the beneficiary from all available public resources, including Supplemental Security Income (SSI), Medi-Cal, Federal Social Security Disability Insurance (SSDI), and the appropriate center for the disabled. All public assistance benefits of the beneficiary shall not be commingled with other trust assets but shall be separately held by the Trustee. Nothing herein shall be construed to require the addition to the trust estate of public assistance benefits received by, or on behalf of, the beneficiary.

5. <u>Trust Corpus</u>. No part of the corpus of the trust created herein shall be used to supplant or replace public assistance benefits of any county, state, federal, or other governmental agency which has a legal responsibility to serve persons with disabilities which are the same or similar to the impairment(s) of the beneficiary herein. For purposes of determining the beneficiary's Medi-Cal eligibility, no part of the principal or undistributed income of the trust estate shall be considered available to said beneficiary. In the event the Trustee is requested to release principal or income of the trust to or on behalf of the beneficiary to pay for equipment, medication, or services which Medi-Cal is authorized to provide (were it not for the existence of this trust), or in the event the Trustee is requested to petition the court or any other administrative agency for the release of trust principal or income for this purpose, the Trustee is authorized to deny such request and is authorized in the Trustee's discretion to take whatever administrative or judicial steps may be necessary to continue the Medi-Cal eligibility of the beneficiary, including obtaining instructions from a court of competent jurisdiction ruling that the trust corpus is not available to the beneficiary for Medi-Cal purposes. Any expenses of the Trustee in this regard, including reasonable attorney's fees, shall be a proper charge to the trust estate. All references in this instrument to "Medi-Cal" shall include any other state's Medicaid program equivalent.

6. <u>Spendthrift Provision</u>. No interest in the principal or income of this trust shall be anticipated, assigned, or encumbered, or shall be subject to any creditor's claim or to legal process, prior to its actual receipt by the beneficiary. Furthermore, because this trust is to be conserved and maintained for the special needs of the beneficiary throughout the beneficiary's life, no part of the corpus thereof, neither principal nor undistributed income, shall be construed as part of the beneficiary's "estate" or be subject to the claims of voluntary or involuntary creditors for the provision of care and services, including residential care, by any public entity, office, department, or agency of the State of California, or of any other state, or of the United States.

7. <u>Savings Provision</u>. Notwithstanding anything to the contrary contained in the other provisions of this trust, in the event that the existence of this trust has the effect of rendering the beneficiary ineligible for Supplemental Security Income (SSI), Medi-Cal, or any other program of public benefits, the Trustee is authorized (but not required) to terminate this trust, and the undistributed balance of the trust estate shall be distributed, free of trust, to Settlors' then-living issue, other than beneficiary, by right of representation. It is Settlors' wish that thereupon the distributee(s) shall conserve, manage, and distribute the proceeds of the former trust estate for the benefit of the beneficiary, to insure that she receives sufficient funds for her basic living needs when public assistance benefits are unavailable or insufficient. This request pertaining to the management of trust proceeds after the termination of the trust is precatory, not mandatory. In determining whether the existence of the trust has the effect of rendering the beneficiary ineligible for SSI, Medi-Cal, or any other program of public benefits, the Trustee is hereby granted full and complete discretion to initiate either administrative or judicial proceedings, or both, for the purpose of determining eligibility and all costs relating thereto, including reasonable attorney's fees, which shall be a proper charge to the trust estate.

8. <u>Distributions Upon Death of Beneficiary</u>. Upon the death of the beneficiary, the Trustee may pay any death taxes that may by reason of said beneficiary's death be due regarding assets passing in accordance with these trust provisions or otherwise, and all expenses of said beneficiary's last illness and funeral, and expenses related to administration and distribution of the trust estate if, in the Trustee's discretion, other satisfac-

tory provisions have not been made for the payment of such expenses. The Trustee shall make no payments for expenses incurred prior to the beneficiary's death if the Trustee shall determine in the Trustee's discretion that payment therefor is the obligation of any county, state, federal, or other governmental agency which has a legal responsibility to serve persons with disabilities which are the same or similar to the impairment(s) of the beneficiary herein. The Trustee shall then distribute the remaining principal and undistributed income of the trust estate to the beneficiary's then living issue, by right of representation, or, if there is no such issue then living, the remaining trust estate shall be distributed to Settlor's then living issue, by right of representation.

9. <u>Distributions Following Death of Beneficiary</u>. Following the death of the beneficiary, the accumulated and undistributed income and all of the principal of the trust shall be distributed to the Settlors' then living children, on the principle of representation, in accordance with the provisions of The AdamsFamily Trust. In the event that the AdamsFamily Trust is not then in existence, the income and principal of the Trust shall be administered and distributed in accordance with the applicable provisions of said trust, as if said trust were in existence.

Asset Protection for Your Children

Most of the asset protection we do at Klueger & Stein LLP is for our clients, the people who have the assets and who wish to protect them. But on occasion, our clients express a desire to protect assets that now belong to them but will one day belong to their children through inheritance. They wish to ensure that the assets they leave to their children cannot ever fall into the hands of their children's creditors. The one creditor they often have in mind is a child's spouse, who may become a creditor in the event of a divorce. This desire is often expressed theoretically, but on occasion is expressed very pointedly, as in, "What can you do to keep my money out of the hands of that no-good bum my daughter married?"

The answer is that we can do quite a bit, but it requires a radical rethinking of the way we usually draft trusts. Most trusts contemplate the eventual distribution of the assets, usually when the children are old enough and mature enough to receive their share of the trust's principal. A trust designed to provide asset protection for the children cannot provide for the outright distribution of trust assets to the child, because once the assets are owned by the child they become subject to the child's creditors, including a spouse in a divorce proceeding. We saw in Chapter 6 that in most separate property states the separate property of each spouse becomes "marital property," subject to equitable division in a divorce. In a community property state such as California, inherited property is not subject to equal division unless a spouse commingled it with the community property, which is not difficult to do. It is not possible to commingle property if you don't own it, and if the property remains in a trust, you don't own it.

Most trusts require the trustee to make distributions of trust principal and income for the beneficiary's "support, health, and maintenance." If asset protection for the child is the goal, such language should be avoided. A trust designed to shield the assets from the beneficiary's creditors must be entirely discretionary, giving the trustee (who should be someone other than the beneficiary) full discretion to withhold any payments to the beneficiary.

Trusts that are drafted to provide asset protection for the younger generation are sometimes referred to as "legacy trusts" or "generational trusts," since they hang around for three or four generations.

CHAPTER 14

Final Thoughts

Is Asset Protection Ethical?

Is it ethical to arrange your affairs so that your creditors cannot get at your assets? We hold aside the question of whether it is ethical to bring a frivolous, meritless lawsuit with the goal of making the ensuing litigation so expensive for the defendant that the defendant will be forced to settle rather than defend the suit. Once the lawsuit is brought, is it ethical to convert nonexempt assets into exempt assets? If no lawsuit has been brought, but one is expected, is it ethical to place assets beyond the reach of the expected defendant's creditors by placing the assets in the hands of a person—such as a spouse—who will not be named as a defendant? If the plaintiff has the ability to game the system by bringing a frivolous lawsuit knowing that the economics of litigation will force a settlement, is it ethical for the defendant to game the system by placing the assets in a Cook Islands trust that owns a Nevis corporation that owns a Swiss bank account, knowing that the economics of litigation will now deter the plaintiff from chasing the assets all over the world?

If whatever the plaintiffs do to reach the assets is not unethical, why should the defendant's efforts to preserve the assets be unethical?

It would seem that these questions should answer themselves, but they don't. Here's why: For one, there is a related but different question as to whether it is ethical not to pay one's debts. If I visit a doctor who in good faith provides me with medical treatment, and who then sends me a bill for his services, most people would agree that it would be unethical for me to make the doctor chase me to the Cook Islands for payment. Ethics and fundamental fairness would seem to require me to simply pay the bill. But life is usually not that simple. Let's assume that the medical services were not billed to me by the doctor, but by the hospital. Let's assume that I didn't have health insurance. When medical insurance is involved, the carrier negotiates with the hospital and receives lower rates than the uninsured. Moreover, the hospital often seeks to recover the losses it sustains when dealing with insurance carriers by overbilling the uninsured. That's why a three-day stay in a hospital results in a six-figure bill, and includes $10 aspirin tablets. The "agreement" I signed making me responsible for whatever the hospital sees fit to charge was signed by me as I was admitted to the hospital, when my choice was agreeing to whatever I would later be charged or dying then and there. Do I owe the $100,000 bill that comes later? Technically—perhaps even legally—I may be obligated to pay it. Is seeking to avoid payment unethical? Is transferring my assets to the Cook Islands in the face of bills for $10 aspirin tablets "fair"? Is being charged $10 for an aspirin tablet while an insured patient in the next room is charged ten cents "fair"? It seems that we have an ethical obligation to pay our just debts. We do not have an obligation to roll over and play dead. Not all thieves wield lead pipes and accost you in back alleys. Some are listed on the stock exchange and employ collection agencies.

The second reason that some people believe that asset protection is unethical is that they believe that asset protection is about hiding assets. If we have made one thing clear in this book, it is that asset protection has nothing to do with hiding assets and everything to do with arranging our affairs so that creditors cannot get at the assets even when they learn where the assets are.

There is nothing unethical about asset protection in general, but certain practices are unethical because they are illegal. We cannot commit perjury to protect assets. We cannot backdate documents to make it appear that a transaction happened long before it actually did. These practices are unethical, and no self-respecting attorney will assist a client who employs these practices.

A Final Final Thought: No Magic Bullets

As I write these words, I have received an e-mail from a client. We transmuted his and his wife's assets from their community property to their separate property, and in the transmutation agreement she obtained sole ownership of a vacation home. She then transferred the vacation home to a limited liability company. The e-mail asks if what we did is "bulletproof."

There are no magic bullets; nothing is certain. Our clients who come to us early in the game have a far better chance of protecting their assets than those who wait until it is too late. The clients who own real estate have a more difficult time protecting their assets than those who own cash. Clients sued by banks have a more difficult time than clients pursued by negligence lawyers. No two people are ever the same.

How secure are your assets from creditors? Go back to Chapter 3, plug in the four variables for your personal situation, and see how you fare. First, who is the likely plaintiff? Is it a lender, a tenant, a former patient, an employee? Second, who is the likely defendant? If the defendant is likely to be limited to your corporation, you might not need to do any more planning. If you are the likely defendant, can we move assets to your spouse or children? If both you and your spouse are the likely defendants, perhaps we should consider an offshore trust for the liquid assets and a limited liability company for the real estate. Third, what is the likely nature of the claim? Will the plaintiff qualify for prejudgment attachment? Finally, what are your assets? Are they exempt because they are in a retirement plan? If not, can we make them exempt? If not, can we move them?

I don't know the answers to any of these questions, because I don't know *you*. But you know you, and now you should know the answers.

Glossary of Terms

Answer The first pleading by a defendant, usually filed and served upon the plaintiff within a strict time limit after a civil complaint or criminal information or indictment has been served upon the defendant.

Appeal A process for making a formal challenge to an official decision. The appeal is taken to an appellate court, usually on specific grounds, including errors of law, fact, or procedure.

Attachment A means of collecting a legal judgment by levying on property in the possession of a third party.

CERCLA Comprehensive Environmental Response, Compensation, and Liability Act, commonly referred to as the "Superfund." The Superfund law was created to protect people, families, communities, and others from heavily contaminated toxic waste sites that have been abandoned.

Closely-held Corporation A corporation where no ready market exists for the trading of the corporation's shares. If there is a ready market for the shares, the corporation is a publicly held corporation or public corporation.

Community Property In a community property jurisdiction, most property acquired during the marriage (except for gifts or inheritances) is owned jointly by both spouses and is divided upon divorce or death. Joint ownership is automatically presumed by law in the absence of specific evidence that would point to a contrary conclusion for a particular piece of property.

Complaint A formal legal document that sets out the basic facts and legal reasons the plaintiff believes are sufficient to support a claim against another person, persons, entity, or entities that entitles the plaintiff to a remedy.

Creditor A person or organization that has a claim to the money, property, or services of another party.

Default Occurs when a debtor has not met its legal obligations according to the debt contract, e.g., it has not made a scheduled payment or has violated a loan covenant (condition) of the debt contract.

Default Judgment A binding judgment in favor of the plaintiff when the defendant has not responded to a summons or has failed to appear before a court.

Defendant A party who is required to answer the complaint of a plaintiff in a civil lawsuit or any party who has been formally charged with a crime.

Depositions Evidence given under oath and recorded for use in court at a later date. Usually conducted outside of a courtroom.

Director A person charged by law with the conduct and management of a corporation's affairs. A director may be an inside director (a director who is also an officer or promoter or both) or an outside, or independent, director. The directors collectively are referred to as a board of directors.

Discovery The pre-trial phase in a lawsuit in which each party through the law of civil procedure can request documents and other evidence from other parties or can compel the production of evidence by using such devices as depositions and interrogatories.

Due Process Clause The Fourteenth Amendment to the United States Constitution provides: "No State shall … deprive any person of life, liberty, or property, without due process of law …"

ERISA The Employee Retirement Income Security Act of 1974, a federal statute that establishes minimum standards for pension plans in private industry and provides for extensive rules on the federal income tax effects of transactions associated with employee benefit plans. ERISA was enacted to protect the interests of employee benefit plan participants and their beneficiaries by requiring the disclosure to them of financial and other information concerning the plan; by establishing standards of conduct for plan administrators.

Foreclosure A proceeding in which a bank or other secured creditor sells or repossesses a parcel of real property due to the owner's failure to comply with an agreement between the lender and borrower called a "mortgage" or "deed of trust."

401(k) Plan A type of employer-sponsored retirement plan, named after a section of the Internal Revenue Code. A 401(k) plan allows a worker to save for retirement while deferring income taxes on the saved money and earnings until withdrawal.

Fraudulent Conveyance Also *fraudulent transfer* is a civil cause of action. It arises in debtor-creditor relation, particularly with reference to insolvent debtors. The usual fact situation involves a debtor who donates his or her assets, usually to an "insider," and leaves himself nothing to pay creditors.

Garnishment The process of deducting money from an employee's monetary compensation (including salary) as a result of a court order. In the United States, such payments are limited by federal law to 25 percent of the disposable income that the employee earns.

Homestead Exemption A legal regime designed to protect the value of the homes of residents from creditors. Laws enacting such protections are found in state statutes or constitutional provisions. They may be limited as to amount or unlimited.

Individual Retirement Account (IRA) A retirement account that provides some tax advantages for retirement savings.

Joint Tenancy (with right of survivorship) A type of concurrent estate in which the joint owners have a *right of survivorship*, meaning that if one owner dies, that owner's interest in the property will automatically pass to the remaining owner or owners.

Lien A form of security interest granted over an item of property to secure the payment of a debt or performance of some other obligation.

Lis Pendens A public notice of litigation that has been recorded in the same location where the real property has been recorded. This notice secures a plaintiff's claim on the property so that the sale or encumbrance of the property will not diminish plaintiff's rights to the property, should plaintiff prevail in its case.

Mediation A form of alternate dispute resolution, it aims to assist two (or more) disputants in reaching an agreement to resolve a dispute prior to trial.

Non-Compete Agreement A contract or agreement, or a provision in a contract, in which one party (usually an employee) agrees to not pursue a similar profession or trade in competition against another party (usually the employer).

Qualified Domestic Relations Order A legal order subsequent to a divorce that splits and changes ownership of a retirement plan to give the divorced spouse his or her share of the asset or pension plan. QDROs may grant ownership in the participant's (employee's) pension plan to an alternate payee, who must be a spouse, former spouse, child, or other dependent of the participant.

Plaintiff Also known as a *claimant* or *complainant*, this is the party who initiates a lawsuit.

Prejudgment Attachment A legal remedy that allows recovery of money damages by levying a security interest on the property of the party prior to the entry of a final judgment in civil litigation.

Promissory Note Also referred to as a *note payable*, this is a contract detailing the terms of a promise by one party (the *maker*) to pay a sum of money to the other (the *payee*).

Self-Settled Trust A trust in which the settlor of the trust names himself or herself as a beneficiary. Under the laws of most states, a settlor cannot avoid creditors by tranaferring assets to a trust in which the settlor is also a beneficiary.

Statute of Limitations A statute that sets forth the maximum period of time, after certain events, that legal proceedings based on those events may be initiated.

Summary Judgment A determination by a court, i.e., a judgment without a full trial. Such a judgment may be issued on the merits of an entire case or on the merits of specific issues in that case.

Summons A document that announces to the person to whom it is directed that a legal proceeding has been started against that person and that a file has been started in the court records. The summons announces a date by which the defendant(s) must either appear in court or respond in writing to the court or the opposing party or parties.

Supremacy Clause Article VI Clause 2 of the United States Constitution, which establishes the Constitution, federal statutes, and U.S. treaties as "the supreme law of the land." The Constitution is the highest form of law. State judges are required to uphold it, even if state laws or constitutions conflict with it.

Tenancy by the Entirety A type of concurrent estate available only to married couples, wherein ownership of the property is treated as though the couple were a single legal person. Like joint tenancy with right of survivorship, the tenancy by the entirety also encompasses a right of survivorship, so if one spouse dies, the entire interest in the property passes to the surviving spouse, without going through probate. For a tenancy by the entirety to be created in some jurisdictions, the party or parties seeking to create it must specify in the deed that the property is being conveyed to the couple "as tenants by the entirety."

Tort A civil wrong providing a cause of action entitling the injured party to a remedy.

Resources

For readers desiring to research one or more of the topics raised in this book, I recommend the following books and websites. The websites selected are those that (1) do not require subscriptions and are readily available and (2) have kept the advertising and promotion to a minimum.

Books

P. Spero, *Asset Protection, Legal Planning and Strategies*. (Warren, Gorham & Lamont, 1997).

This is a treatise designed mainly for attorneys. It contains a comprehensive overview of most statutes dealing for foreign and domestic asset protection issues. It is frequently updated and kept current.

Barry S. Engel, *Asset Protection Planning Guide* 2nd edition. (CCH Incorporated, 2005).

Although not as comprehensive as the Spero treatise, it is more readable.

Websites

Alaska Trusts. For a thorough discussion of Alaska trusts, see *www.fpanet.org*.

Community Property. A survey of state community property statutes can be found at *http://family-law.freeadvice.com*.

Fraudulent Conveyances. For the full text of the Uniform Fraudulent Transfer Act, see *www.law.upenn.edu*. For a list of all of the states that have adopted the UFTA and the Uniform Fraudulent Conveyances Act, and the citation to the state statutes that contain these acts, see *www.law.cornell.edu/uniform*. For a review of recent cases related to fraudulent conveyances, see *www.fraudulenttransfers.com*.

Homestead Exemptions. An excellent review of state homestead exemptions may be found at *http://findarticles.com*.

Limited Liability Companies. For an article on the basics of limited liability companies, see *http://sbinformation.about.com*. For a review of how to organize a limited liability company in any state, including the applicable fees and the addresses of the state Secretary of State, see *www.limitedliabilitycompanycenter.com*.

Mareva Injunctions. A scholarly summary of the state of the law, authored by a New Zealand law firm. *www.waterloochambers.net*.

Offshore Banks. I recommend two offshore banks: Bank Sarasin and Bank Wegelin, both of which are Swiss private banks. Bank Sarasin's website is *www.sarasin.ch*. Bank Wegelin is the oldest Swiss private bank, founded in the 18th century. *www.wegelin.ch*. Both of these sites are informative and keep the advertising to a minimum.

Non-Competition Agreements. A brief survey of some state non-competition statutes can be found at *www.cqc.ct.gov*.

Offshore Trust Companies. I recommend two trust companies in the Cook Islands. The largest trust company in the Cook Islands is SouthPac Trust Ltd. *www.southpacgroup.com*. Asiaciti Trust is one of the most well-established trust companies in the Cook Islands. *www.asiaciti.com*.

Special Needs Trusts. A thorough examination of special needs trusts, authored by an attorney, at *www.nsnn.com*.

Trade Secrets. A listing of all of the states that have adopted the Uniform Trade Secrets Act, and the full text of the act, can be found at *www.ndasforfree.com*.

Sample Agreements and Other Documents

What follows are examples of three types of agreements and other documents you might consider using in protecting your assets. They include a sample irrevocable trust document, an operating agreement, a self-canceling installment sales agreement, and a self-cancelling promissory note. You can use these as models for developing such agreements, but before finalizing them, it's important to check with your attorney to assure that they are appropriate for your specific situation.

Limited Liability Company Agreement of
California Realty Holdings, Llc
A California Limited Liability Company

THIS LIMITED LIABILITY COMPANY AGREEMENT OF California Realty Holdings, LLC (this "Agreement"), dated as of the date set forth below, is entered into by and between Roberto Almaden, an individual residing in California, and Maria Juanita Almaden (sometimes known as Juanita Almaden), an individual residing in California, with reference to the following facts.

RECITALS

The members have formed a limited liability company under the Act (as defined below). The Articles of Organization of the Company filed with the California Secretary of State, are hereby adopted and approved by the members.

NOW, THEREFORE, in consideration of the mutual covenants herein contained, and other good and valuable consideration, the receipt and sufficiency of which is hereby acknowledged, the members hereby agree as follows:

ARTICLE 1. DEFINED TERMS

1.01 Defined Terms.

Unless otherwise clearly indicated to the contrary, the following definitions shall for all purposes be applied to the terms used in this Agreement:

"Act" shall mean the Beverly-Killea Limited Liability Company Act, including California Corporations Code Sections 17000 through 17705, as it may be amended from time to time, and any successor to such statute.

"Additional Member" means a Person admitted to the Company as a Member pursuant to Section 14.01 of this Agreement and who is shown as such on the books and records of the Company.

"Adjusted Capital Account" means the Capital Account maintained for each Member as of the end of each Company taxable year: (i) increased by any amounts which such Member is obligated to restore pursuant to any provision of this Agreement or is deemed to be obligated to restore pursuant to the penultimate sentences of Regulations Sections 1.704 2(g)(l) and 1.704 2(i)(5); and (ii) decreased by the items described in Regulations Sections 1.704 1(b)(2)(ii)(d)(4), (5) and (6). The foregoing definition of Adjusted Capital Account is intended to comply with the provisions of Regulations Sections 1.704 1(b)(2)(ii)(d) and shall be interpreted consistently therewith.

"Adjusted Capital Account Deficit" means, with respect to any Member, the deficit balance, if any, in such Member's Adjusted Capital Account as of the end of the relevant Company taxable year.

"Affiliate" or "Affiliated Person" means, with respect to any Person: (i) any Person directly or indirectly controlling, controlled by or under common control with such Person; (ii) any Person owning or controlling fifty percent (50%) or more of the outstanding voting interests of such Person; (iii) any Person of which such Person owns or controls fifty percent (50%) or more of the voting interests; or (iv) any officer, director, general partner, or trustee of such Person or of any Person referred to in clauses (i), (ii), and (iii) above.

"Agreement" means this Agreement, as it may be amended, supplemented, or restated from time to time.

"Assignee" means a Person to whom any Membership Interest in the Company has been transferred, but who has not become a Substituted Member, and who has the rights solely to the economic interest of the Member, and not the right to vote or participate in the management of the Company.

"Available Cash" means, with respect to any period for which such calculation is being made, the Cash Flow of the Company that the Manager in his reasonable discretion determines shall be distributed by the Company pursuant to Section 5.01 of this Agreement. Notwithstanding the foregoing, Available Cash shall not take into account any disbursements made or reserves established, after commencement of the dissolution and liquidation of the Company.

"Capital Account" A capital account shall be maintained for each Member in accordance with the capital account maintenance rules set forth in Treasury Regulations Section 1.704-1(b)(2)(iv). Without limiting the generality of the foregoing, a Member's Capital Account shall be increased by (i) the amount of money contributed by the Member to the Company, (ii) the fair market value of property contributed by the Member to the Company as determined by the contributing Member and the Company (net of liabilities that the Company is considered to assume or take subject to pursuant to Section 752 of the Code), and (iii) allocations to the Member of Net Income and other items of income and gain, including income and gain exempt from tax, but excluding items of income and gain described in Treasury Regulations Section 1.704-1(b)(4)(i). A Member's Capital Account shall be decreased by (w) the amount of money distributed to the Member, (x) the fair market value of any property distributed to the Member as determined by the distributee Member and the Company (net of any liabilities that such Member is considered to assume or take subject to pursuant to Section 752 of the Code), after adjusting each Member's Capital Account by such Member's share of the unrealized income, gain, loss, and deduction inherent in such property and not previously reflected in such Capital Account, as if the property had been sold for its then fair market value on the date of distribution, (y) expenditures described, or treated under Section 704(b) of the Code as described, in Section 705(a)(2)(B) of the Code, and (z) the Member's share of Net Loss and other items of loss, and deduction, but excluding items of loss or deduction described in Treasury Regulations Section 1.704-1(b)(4)(i). The Members' Capital Accounts shall be appropriately adjusted for income, gain, loss, and deduction as required by Treasury Regulations Section 1.704-1(b)(2)(iv)(g) (relating to allocations and adjustments resulting from the reflection of property on the books of the Company at book value, or a revaluation thereof, rather than at adjusted tax basis). If a Member transfers all or a part of its Membership Interest in accordance with this Agreement, such Member's Capital Account attributable to the transferred Membership Interest shall carry over to the new owner of such Membership Interest pursuant to Treasury Regulations Section 1.704-1(b)(2)(iv)(l).

"Capital Contribution" means, with respect to any Member, any cash, cash equivalents, or property which such Member contributes or is deemed to contribute to the Company pursuant hereto.

"Capital Transaction" shall include any:

(i) Sale or other disposition of all or any part of the real properties owned by the Company;

(ii) Financing or refinancing of such real property;

(iii) Condemnation of all or any part of such real property (except for temporary use or occupancy);

(iv) Payment from insurance on account of a casualty to such real property other than payment for insurance on account of business or rental interruption;

(v) Payment from title insurance on account of a defect in title to such real property or with respect to any other claim under any owner's title insurance policy insuring the Company; and

(vi) Similar items or transactions the proceeds of which under generally accepted accounting principles are deemed attributable to capital.

"Carrying Value" means, with respect to any asset, the asset's adjusted basis for federal income tax purposes, except as follows:

(i) The initial Carrying Value of any asset contributed (or deemed contributed) to the Company shall be such asset's gross fair market value at the time of such contribution, as determined by the Manager in his sole discretion;

(ii) Upon election by the Manager, the Carrying Values of all Company assets shall be readjusted to equal their respective gross fair market values (as determined by the Manager in his sole discretion) at the times, and in the manner, specified in Regulations Section 1.7041(b)(2)(iv)(*f*); and

(iii) If the Carrying Value of an asset has been determined pursuant to clause (i) or (ii) immediately hereinabove, such Carrying Value shall thereafter be adjusted in the same manner as would the asset's adjusted basis for United States federal income tax purposes, except that depreciation deductions shall be computed in accordance with the definition of Depreciation below.

"Cash Flow" shall mean the gross cash receipts of the Company (as appropriate) after deduction of:

(i) All operating expenses of the Company, except to the extent paid by Additional Capital Contributions or out of a reserve and/or an escrow account and excluding any expense not involving a cash expenditure, such as depreciation;

(ii) Interest and principal amortization payments on any loans to the Company, including loans made by Members, except to the extent paid out of a reserve and/or an escrow account;

(iii) Reserves established or payment made into escrow accounts as approved by the Manager for scheduled principal amortization of indebtedness of the Company, working capital, taxes, insurance, capital improvements, and replacements, and any other contingencies of the Company; and

(iv) Capital expenditures, except to the extent paid from a Capital Contribution, a reserve and/or an escrow account for the capital item involved.

"Code" means the Internal Revenue Code of 1986, as amended and in effect from time to time, as interpreted by the applicable final and temporary regulations thereunder. Any reference herein to a specific section or sections of the Code shall be deemed to include a reference to any corresponding provisions of future law or regulation.

"Company" means the limited liability company formed under this Agreement.

"Company Minimum Gain" has the meaning set forth in Regulations Section 1.704 2(b)(2) for the term "partnership minimum gain," and the amount of Company Minimum Gain, as well as any net increase or decrease in Company Minimum Gain, for a Company taxable year shall be determined in accordance with the rules of Regulations Section 1.704 2(d).

"Company Year" means the fiscal year of the Company, which shall be the calendar year.

"Depreciation" means, for each taxable year, an amount equal to the federal income tax depreciation, amortization, or other cost recovery deduction allowable with respect to an asset for such year, except that if the Carrying Value of an asset differs from its adjusted basis for federal income tax purposes at the beginning of such year or other period, Depreciation shall be an amount which bears the same ratio to such beginning Carrying Value as the federal income tax depreciation, amortization, or other cost recovery deduction for such year bears to such beginning adjusted tax basis; *provided, however*, that if the federal income tax depreciation, amortization, or other cost recovery deduction for such year is zero, Depreciation shall be determined with reference to such beginning Carrying Value using any reasonable method selected by the Manager in his sole discretion.

"Entity" means any partnership, limited liability company, corporation, joint venture, trust, business trust, cooperative, association, or other legal business entity.

"ERISA" means the Employee Retirement Income Security Act of 1974, as amended.

"Incapacity" or **"Incapacitated"** means: (i) as to any individual Member, death, total physical disability or entry of an order by a court of competent jurisdiction adjudicating such individual incompetent to manage such individual's person or estate; (ii) as to any corporation which is a Member, the filing of a certificate of dissolution, or its equivalent, for the corporation or the revocation of its charter; (iii) as to any partnership or limited liability company which is a Member, the dissolution and commencement of winding up the partnership or limited liability company; (iv) as to any estate which is a Member, the distribution by the fiduciary of the estate's entire interest in the Company; (v) as to any trustee of a trust which is a Member, the termination of the trust (but not the substitution of a new trustee); or (vi) as to any Member, the bankruptcy of such Member. For purposes of this definition, bankruptcy of a Member shall be deemed to have occurred when: (a) the Member commences a voluntary proceeding seeking liquidation, reorganization, or other relief under any bankruptcy, insolvency, or other similar law now or hereafter in effect; (b) the Member is adjudged as bankrupt or insolvent, or a final and nonappealable order for relief under any bankruptcy, insolvency, or similar law now or hereafter in effect has been entered against the Member; (c) the Member executes and delivers a general assignment for the benefit of the Member's creditors; (d) the Member files an answer or other pleading admitting or failing to contest the material allegations of a petition filed against the Member in any proceeding under any bankruptcy, insolvency, or other similar law now or hereafter in effect; (e) the Member seeks, consents to, or acquiesces in the appointment of a trustee, receiver, or liquidator for the Member or for all or any substantial part of the Member's properties; (f) any proceeding seeking liquidation, reorganization, or other relief of or against such Member under any bankruptcy, insolvency, or other similar law now or hereafter in effect has not been dismissed within one hundred twenty (120) days after the commencement thereof; (g) the appointment without the Member's consent or acquiescence of a trustee, receiver, or liquidator has not been vacated or stayed within ninety (90) days of such appointment; or (h) an appointment referred to in clause (g) which has been stayed is not vacated within ninety (90) days after the expiration of any such stay.

"IRS" means the United States Internal Revenue Service.

"Liquidating Event" has the meaning set forth in Section 12.01.

"Liquidator" has the meaning set forth in Section 12.03(a).

"Manager" means Roberto Almaden, or such other individual or entity as elected by a unanimous vote of the Members. Any reference herein to "Managers" shall include the "Manager."

"Member" means any Person named as a member herein, as this Agreement may be amended from time to time, or any Substituted Member or Additional Member, in such Person's capacity as a member of the Company. Any references to "Members" shall mean "Member" when there is only one member of the Company.

"Member Minimum Gain" means an amount, with respect to each Member Nonrecourse Debt, equal to the Company Minimum Gain that would result if such Member Nonrecourse Debt were treated as a Nonrecourse Liability, determined in accordance with Regulations Section 1.7042(i)(3).

"Member Nonrecourse Debt" has the meaning set forth in Regulations Section 1.7042(b)(4) for partner nonrecourse debt.

"Member Nonrecourse Deductions" has the meaning set forth in Regulations Section 1.704 2(i)(2) for "partner nonrecourse deductions," and the amount of Member Nonrecourse Deductions with respect to a Member Nonrecourse Debt for a Company taxable year shall be determined in accordance with the rules of Regulations Section 1.704 2(i)(2).

"Membership Interest" means an ownership interest in the Company representing a Capital Contribution by a Member, and includes any and all rights and benefits to which the holder of such a Membership Interest may be entitled as provided in this Agreement, together with all obligations of such Person to comply with the terms and provisions of this Agreement.

"Net Income" and **"Net Loss,"** respectively, mean the taxable income or loss, as the case may be, of the Company for a taxable period (or from a transaction) as determined in accordance with Code Section 703(a) (for this purpose, all items of income, gain, loss, or deduction required to be separately stated pursuant to Code Section 703(a)(1) shall be included in taxable income or loss) computed with the following adjustments:

(i) Items of gain, loss, and deduction shall be computed based upon the Carrying Values of the Company's assets rather than upon the assets' adjusted bases for federal income tax purposes and, in particular, the amount of any deductions for depreciation or amortization with respect to an asset for a period shall equal such asset's Carrying Value multiplied by a fraction the numerator of which shall be the amount of depreciation or amortization with respect to such asset allowable for United States federal income tax purposes for such period and the denominator of which shall be such asset's adjusted basis (*provided, however*, that if such asset has a zero adjusted tax basis, then the depreciation or amortization with respect to such asset for purposes of calculating its Carrying Value shall be determined under a method selected by the Manager in accordance with Regulations Section 1.7041(b)(2)(iv)*(g)(3)*);

(ii) Any income received by the Company that would be exempt from the United States federal income tax shall be included as an item of gross income;

(iii) The amount of any adjustments to the Carrying Values of any assets of the Company pursuant to Code Section 743 shall not be taken into account;

(iv) Any expenditure of the Company described in Code Section 705(a)(2)(B) (including any expenditures treated as being described in Section 705(a)(2)(B) pursuant to the Regulations adopted under Code Section 704(b)) shall be treated as a deductible expense; and

(v) There shall be excluded any item of income, gain, loss, deduction, expense or credit that is specially allocated in this Agreement separately from any allocation of Net Income or Net Loss.

"Nonrecourse Deductions" has the meaning set forth in Regulations Section 1.704 2(b)(1), and the amount of Nonrecourse Deductions for a Company taxable year shall be determined in accordance with the rules of Regulations Section 1.704 2(c).

"Nonrecourse Liability" has the meaning set forth in Regulations Section 1.752 1(a) (2) for nonrecourse liability.

"Percentage Interest" means the interest of a Member in a particular the Company as set forth on Exhibit "A."

"Person" means an individual or a corporation, partnership, trust, limited liability company, unincorporated organization, association, or other entity.

"Recapture Income" means any gain recognized by the Company upon the disposition of any property or asset of the Company, which gain is characterized as ordinary income because it represents the recapture of deductions previously taken with respect to such property or asset.

"Record Date" means the record date established by the Manager for the distribution of Available Cash, proceeds from a Capital Transaction, or other amounts.

"Regulations" means the final and temporary Treasury regulations promulgated under the Code (and, to the extent the Manager determines it to be appropriate in its sole discretion, proposed regulations), as such regulations may be amended from time to time (including corresponding provisions of succeeding regulations).

"Substituted Member" means a Person who is admitted as a Member to the Company pursuant to Section 11.05.

"Terminating Capital Transaction" means any sale or other disposition of all or substantially all of the assets of the Company or a related series of transactions that, taken together, result in the sale or other disposition of all or substantially all of the assets of the Company.

ARTICLE II. ORGANIZATIONAL MATTERS

2.01 Organization.

The Company is a limited liability company organized pursuant to the provisions of the Act and upon the terms and conditions set forth in this Agreement. Except as expressly provided herein to the contrary, the rights and obligations of the Members and the administration and termination of the Company shall be governed by the Act. The Membership Interest of each Member shall be personal property for all purposes.

2.02 Name.

The name of the Company shall be "California Realty Holdings, LLC." The Company's business may be conducted under any other name or names deemed advisable by the Manager. The words "Limited Liability Company," the abbreviation "L.L.C.," or the designation "LLC," or similar words or letters shall be included in the Company's name where necessary for the purpose of complying with the laws of any jurisdiction that so requires.

2.03 Registered Office and Agent; Principal Office.

The registered agent of the Company in California shall be Roberto Almaden, whose address is 72 Main St., Whittier, California 90606. The principal office of the Company shall be at any location as designated by the Manager in his sole discretion.

2.04 Statement of Company.

Concurrently with the execution of this Agreement, the Members shall execute and acknowledge, and the Company shall promptly file or record with the proper offices in each jurisdiction and political subdivision in which the Company does business, such articles or certificates as are required or permitted by any limited liability company act, fictitious name act, or similar statute in effect in such jurisdiction or political subdivision. The Members shall also execute and acknowledge, and the Company shall promptly file or record as aforesaid, such articles of organization, or certificates as may from time to time be reasonable and necessary or appropriate to permit the continued existence, qualification, and operation of the Company. The Members further shall execute and acknowledge, and the Company shall promptly file or record as aforesaid, any further documents required by the State of California and shall comply with all applicable requirements of the State of California regarding the continuation and operation of the Company. Subject to the terms of Section 8.04 of this Agreement, the Manager shall not be required, before or after filing, to deliver or mail a copy of the Articles of Organization or any amendment thereto to any Member.

2.05 Term.

The term of the Company commenced as of the date of this Agreement, and shall continue indefinitely, unless the Company is dissolved sooner pursuant to the provisions of Article XIII of this Agreement or as otherwise provided by law.

ARTICLE III. PURPOSE

3.01 Purpose and Business.

The business of the Company shall be to engage in any investment or business activities as may be deemed appropriate by the Manager, including ownership and operation of real estate.

3.02 Powers.

The Company is empowered to do any and all acts and things necessary, appropriate, proper, advisable, incidental to, or convenient for the furtherance and accomplishment of the purposes and business described herein and for the protection and benefit of the Company.

ARTICLE IV. CAPITAL CONTRIBUTIONS

Initial Capital Contributions of the Member.

Simultaneous with the execution and delivery of this Agreement, or as soon thereafter as practically possible, the Members shall make capital contributions to the Company in cash or in kind, as indicated opposite the Member's name on Exhibit "A."

4.01 Additional Capital Contributions.

No Member shall be required to make additional capital contributions.

4.02 General Provisions Concerning Capital Contributions/Security Agreement.

(a) No Third Party Rights. (i) The obligation of the Members to make Capital Contributions hereunder shall not inure to the benefit of, or be enforceable by, any person or entity other than the Company or the other Members. (ii) No Member shall be obligated to make any Capital Contribution in the event that any other Member is in default under this Agreement. (iii) No interest, except as otherwise set forth herein, shall be paid on any Capital Contribution by any Member or on any Capital Account.

(b) No Personal Liability. Notwithstanding any other provision of this Agreement, the obligations of the Members to make Capital Contributions to the Company shall be without recourse to the Members except to the extent of their respective Membership Interests, and no Member shall be personally liable to make any Capital Contributions required of such Member under the terms of this Agreement; *provided, however,* that the foregoing limitation on personal liability shall not relieve a Member of his or her obligations to make Capital Contributions as required by the terms of this Agreement.

(c) Withdrawals. A Member shall not be entitled to withdraw any part of the Member's Capital Contribution or to receive any distributions, whether of money or property, from the Company except as provided in this Agreement.

(d) No Priority of Return. No Member shall have priority over any other Member with respect to the return of a Capital Contribution or distributions or allocations of income, gain, losses, deductions, credits, or items thereof, except as set forth in this Agreement.

ARTICLE V. DISTRIBUTIONS

5.01 Available Cash.

(a) The Company shall distribute Available Cash to the Members, *pro rata*, in accordance with the Members' Percentage Interests; *provided, however*, that the timing for the distribution of Available Cash shall be determined by the Manager in her sole discretion.

(b) Any other provision of this Agreement notwithstanding, the Manager shall not make any distribution of Available Cash to a Member whose interest is being charged pursuant to a charging order, or whose interest is otherwise being pursued in a collection action by any third-party. In the event of a charging order or a collection action the Manager is authorized to make all distributions solely to the other Members; *provided, however*, that the Member whose interest is being charged shall vest in the distribution (*i.e.*, Available Cash shall be distributable to such Member, but shall not be actually distributed until the collection action is terminated).

5.02 Proceeds of Capital Transactions.

(a) The Company shall distribute to the Members, *pro rata*, in accordance with such Members' Percentage Interests, such net proceeds, after payment of transaction costs, from a Capital Transaction (other than in connection with dissolution of the Company) as the Manager determines in his sole discretion are appropriate to distribute.

(b) The Manager is forbidden from making any distributions to any Member whose interest in this Company is subject to a charging order or any other collection action. In the event of a charging order or a collection action against a Member, the Manager is authorized to distribute net proceeds from a Capital Transaction to the other Members, *pro rata*, in proportion to their respective Percentage Interests.

(c) Such distributions made pursuant to this Section 5.02 shall reduce the Capital Account of the recipient Member and shall not be treated as an operating expense of the Company for income tax or financial reporting purposes.

5.03 Amounts Withheld.

All amounts withheld pursuant to the Code or any provisions of any state or local tax law and Section 10.04 of this Agreement with respect to any allocation, payment, or distribution to the Members or Assignees shall be treated as amounts distributed to the Members or Assignees pursuant to Section 5.01 of this Agreement for all purposes under this Agreement.

5.04 Distributions Upon Terminating Capital Transaction or Liquidation.

Proceeds from a Terminating Capital Transaction and any other cash received or reductions in reserves made after commencement of the liquidation of the Company shall be distributed to the Members, *pro rata*, in accordance with such Members' Percentage Interests.

ARTICLE VI. ALLOCATIONS

6.01 Allocations of Net Income and Net Loss.

For purposes of maintaining the Capital Accounts and in determining the rights of the Members among themselves, Net Income and Net Loss shall be allocated among the Members in each taxable year (or portion thereof) to those Members or Assignees who have the right to receive distributions pursuant to Sections 5.01(a) and 5.02(a) (and disregarding Sections 5.01(b) and 5.02(b)) in such a manner so as to cause the Capital Account balance of each Member to equal the sum of (i) Available Cash distributed or deemed distributed to such Member pursuant to Section 5.01 for the Company Year, and (ii) an amount that would be distributed to the Member (a) pursuant to Section 5.01, and (b) on a hypothetical liquidation of the Company, assuming that the Company sells its assets for their adjusted tax basis and distributes such proceeds and its reserves, net of debt repayments, to the Members based on their Percentage Interests.

6.02 Other Allocations.

(a) For purposes of Regulations Section 1.752 3(a)(3), the Members agree that Nonrecourse Liabilities of the Company in excess of the sum of (i) the amount of Company Minimum Gain and (ii) the total amount of gain that would be allocated to all Members described in Regulations Section 1.752 3(a)(2), shall be allocated among the Members in accordance with their respective Percentage Interests.

(b) Any gain allocated to the Members upon the sale or other taxable disposition of any Company asset shall, to the extent possible, be characterized as Recapture Income in the same proportions and to the same extent as such Members have been allocated any deductions directly or indirectly giving rise to the treatment of such gains as Recapture Income.

(c) In the event that a Member acquires an interest in the Company either by transfer from another Member or by acquisition from the Company, the Net Income or Net Loss from operation of the Company for the Company Year in which such acquisition occurs shall be calculated for the portion of the Company Year prior to the date of the acquisition of the interest in the Company by the Member and shall be allocated to the Members who were

Members during such period, and the Net Income and Net Loss allocable to the portion of the Company Year from and after the date of the acquisition of such interest shall be allocated among the Members who were Members during such period; *provided, however,* that Net Income and Net Loss realized from the sale, refinancing, or other disposition of all or a portion of the Property shall be allocated among the Members based upon the actual ownership of interests in the Company on the date of the event giving rise to such Net Income or Net Loss.

(d) Except as otherwise provided in this Agreement, or as required by Code Section 704, 706 or 754, for tax purposes, all items of income, gain, loss, deduction, or credit shall be allocated to the Members in the same manner as are Net Income and Net Loss; *provided, however,* that if the Carrying Value of any property of the Company differs from its adjusted basis for tax purposes, then items of income, gain, loss, deduction, or credit related to such property for tax purposes shall be allocated among the Members so as to take account of the variation between the adjusted basis of the property for tax purposes and its Carrying Value in the manner provided for under Code Section 704(c), using the "traditional method" under Regulations Section 1.7043.

6.03 Overriding Allocations of Net Income and Net Loss.

(a) Nonrecourse Deductions shall be allocated in proportion to the Members' respective Percentage Interests.

(b) Member Nonrecourse Deductions shall be allocated in the manner required by Regulations Section 1.7042(i).

(c) If, during any Company Year, a Member unexpectedly receives any adjustment, allocation, or distribution described in Regulations Section 1.704 1(b)(2)(ii)(d)(4), (5) or (6), and, as a result of such adjustment, allocation, or distribution, such Member has an Adjusted Capital Account Deficit, then items of gross income for such Company Year (and, if necessary, subsequent Company Years), shall first be allocated to such Member in an amount equal to its Adjusted Capital Account Deficit.

(d) Items of gross income shall be allocated in an amount equal to each Member's share of any net decrease in Member Minimum Gain for any Company Year in the manner required by Regulations Section 1.704-2(j)(2)(i).

(e) Items of gross income shall be allocated in an amount equal to each Member's share of any net decrease in Member Minimum Gain for any Company Year in the manner required by Regulations Section 1.704-2(j)(2)(ii).

(f) In the event that Net Income, Net Loss, or items thereof are allocated to one or more Members pursuant to the provisions of Section 6.03(c), subsequent Net Income and Net Loss will first be allocated (subject to such provisions of Section 6.03) to the Members in a manner designed to result in each Member having a Capital Account balance equal to what it would have been had the original allocation of Net Income, Net Loss, or items thereof pursuant to such foregoing provisions of Section 6.03(c) not occurred.

6.04 Intent of Allocations/Cash Savings Clause.

The members intend that the foregoing tax allocation provisions of this Article VI shall produce final Capital Account balances of the Members that will permit liquidating distributions that are made in accordance with final Capital Account balances under Section 5.2 to be made (after unpaid loans and interest thereon, including those owed to Members have been paid) in a manner identical to the order of priorities set forth in Section 5.1. To the extent that the tax allocation provisions of this Article VI would fail to produce such final Capital Account balances, (i) such provisions shall be amended by the Manager if and to the extent necessary to produce such result, and (ii) taxable income and taxable loss of the Company for prior open years (or items of gross income and deduction of the Company for such years) shall be reallocated by the Manager among the Members to the extent it is not possible to achieve such result with allocations of items of income (including gross income) and deduction for the current year and future years, as approved by the Manager. This Section 6.04 shall control notwithstanding any reallocation or adjustment of taxable income, taxable loss, or items thereof by the Internal Revenue Service or any other taxing authority. The Manager shall have the power to amend this Agreement without the consent of the Members, as he reasonably considers advisable, to make the allocations and adjustments described in this Section 6.04. To the extent that the allocations and adjustments described in this Section 6.04 result in a reduction in the distributions that any Member will receive under this Agreement compared to the amount of the distributions such Member would receive if all such distributions were made pursuant to the order of priority set forth in Section 5.1, the Company may make a guaranteed payment (within the meaning of Code Section 707(c)) to such Member to the extent such payment does not violate the requirements of Code Section 704(b) or may take such other action as reasonably determined by the Manager to offset such reduction.

6.05 Disregarded Entity.

At any time when this Company has (i) only a single member, or (ii) husband and wife own all interests in the Company as community property and choose to treat the Company as a disregarded entity pursuant to Revenue Procedure 2002-69, the Company shall be treated as an entity disregarded from its owners for federal income tax purposes, and the provisions of Article 6 and all other provisions of this Agreement that are inconsistent with treating this Company as an entity disregarded from its owners for federal income tax purposes shall be ignored and disregarded.

ARTICLE VII. MANAGEMENT AND OPERATIONS OF BUSINESS; VOTING

7.01 Management.

(a) Except as otherwise expressly provided in this Agreement, all management powers over the business and affairs of the Company are and shall be exclusively vested in the Manager, and no other Member shall have any right to participate in or exercise control or management power over the business and affairs of the Company. If more than one Manager has been appointed, then Managers shall act unanimously, unless provided to the contrary in this Agreement. In addition to the powers now or hereafter granted to the members of a limited liability company under applicable law or which are granted to the Manager under any other provision of this Agreement, the Manager shall have full power and authority to do all things deemed necessary or desirable by them to conduct the business of the Company, and to effectuate the purposes set forth in Section 3.01 of this Agreement, including, without limitation (but in all cases subject to the terms of this Agreement):

(i) the making of any expenditures, the borrowing of money, the assumption or guarantee of, or other contracting for, indebtedness and other liabilities, the issuance of evidence of indebtedness (including the securing of the same by deed, mortgage, deed of trust, or other lien or encumbrance on the Company's assets) and the incurring of any obligations it deems reasonably necessary for the conduct of the activities of the Company;

(ii) the making of tax, regulatory, and other filings, or rendering of periodic or other reports to governmental or other agencies having jurisdiction over the business or assets of the Company;

(iii) the acquisition, disposition, mortgage, pledge, encumbrance, hypothecation, or exchange of any assets of the Company;

(iv) the use of the assets of the Company (including, without limitation, cash on hand) for any purpose consistent with the terms of this Agreement and on any terms the Manager deems reasonably necessary or appropriate for the conduct of the activities of the Company, including, without limitation, the financing of the conduct of the operations of the Company and the repayment of obligations of the Company, the holding of any real, personal, and mixed property of the Company in the name of the Company or in the name of a trustee and the creation, by grant or otherwise, of easements or servitudes;

(v) the management, operation, leasing, collection of rents, marketing, landscaping, repair, alteration, renovation, rehabilitation, or improvement of any real property and the performance of any and all other acts necessary or appropriate to the operation of any real property;

(vi) the negotiation, execution, and performance of any contracts, conveyances, or other instruments that the Manager considers useful or necessary to the conduct of the Company's operations or the implementation of the Manager's powers under this Agreement, including, without limitation, the execution and delivery of leases on behalf of or in the name of the Company, contracting with contractors, developers, consultants, accountants, legal counsel, other professional advisors, and other agents and the payment of their expenses and compensation out of the Company's assets;

(vii) the opening and closing of bank accounts, the investment of Company funds in securities, certificates of deposit, and other instruments, and the distribution of Company cash or other Company assets in accordance with this Agreement;

(ix) the holding, managing, investing, and reinvesting cash and other assets of the Company;

(viii) the collection and receipt of revenues and income of the Company;

(x) the engagement of outside attorneys, accountants, consultants, and contractors of the Company on such terms as the Manager deems appropriate and in the interest of the Company;

(xi) the maintenance of such insurance for the benefit of the Company and the Members as the Manager deems necessary or appropriate (whether or not such is done as part of a group, combined or other policy or policies under which the Company is also insured);

(xii) the control of any and all matters affecting the rights and obligations of the Company, including the settlement, compromise, submission to arbitration, or any other form of dispute resolution, or abandonment of, any claim, cause of action, liability, debt, or damages, due or owing to or from the Company, the commencement or defense of suits, legal proceedings, administrative proceedings, arbitration, or other forms of dispute resolution, and the representation of the Company in all suits or legal proceedings, administrative proceedings, arbitrations or other forms of dispute resolution, the incurring of legal expense, and the indemnification of any Person against liabilities and contingencies to the extent permitted by law and consistent with the terms of this Agreement, including in each and all of the foregoing instances any such matter or thing in which the Manager or its Affiliates have a direct or indirect interest;

(xiii) the determination of the fair market value of any Company property distributed in kind using such reasonable method of valuation as the Manager may adopt;

(xiv) the exercise, directly or indirectly, through any attorney in fact acting under a general or limited power of attorney, of any right, including the right to vote, appurtenant to any asset or investment held by the Company;

(xv) the exercise of any of the powers of the Manager enumerated in this Agreement on behalf of or in connection with any other Person in which the Company has a direct or indirect interest;

(xvi) the exercise of any of the powers of the Manager enumerated in this Agreement on behalf of any Person in which the Company does not have an interest pursuant to contractual or other arrangements with such Person;

(xvii) the making, execution, and delivery of any and all deeds, leases, notes, mortgages, deeds of trust, security agreements, conveyances, contracts, guarantees, warranties, indemnities, waivers, releases or legal instruments or agreements in writing necessary or appropriate, in the reasonable judgment of the Manager, for the accomplishment of any of the powers of the Manager enumerated in this Agreement;

(xviii) the issuance of additional Membership Interests, as appropriate; and

(xix) the filing for insolvency or reorganization of the Company under appropriate federal or state law.

(b) Each of the Members agrees that the Manager is authorized to execute, deliver, and perform the above-mentioned agreements and transactions on behalf of the Company without any further act, approval, or vote of the Members, notwithstanding any other provision of this Agreement, the Act, or any applicable law, rule, or regulation, to the fullest extent permitted under the Act or other applicable law, rule, or regulation. The execution, delivery, or performance by the Manager or the Company of any agreement authorized or permitted under this Agreement shall not constitute a breach by the Manager of any duty that the Manager may owe the Company or the Members or any other Persons under this Agreement or of any duty stated or implied by law or equity.

(c) At all times from and after the date hereof, the Manager may cause the Company to establish and maintain at any and all times working capital accounts and reserves and other cash or similar balances and reserves in such amounts as the Manager, in its reasonable discretion, deems appropriate and reasonable from time to time.

(d) In exercising its authority under this Agreement, the Manager may, but shall be under no obligation to, take into account the tax consequences to any Member of any action taken by it, and may in its discretion make tax elections and take similar actions in respect of tax matters that best serve the interests of the Manager (for example, such a similar action may include causing the Company not to invest in debt securities the interest on which is exempt under Section 103 of the Code). The Manager and the Company shall not have liability to a Member under any circumstances as a result of an income tax liability incurred by such Member as a result of an action (or inaction) by the Manager taken pursuant to his authority under this Agreement and in accordance with the terms hereof.

7.02 Other Matters Concerning Manager.

The Manager may rely and shall be protected in acting, or refraining from acting, upon any resolution, certificate, statement, instrument, opinion, report, notice, request, consent, order, bond, debenture, or other paper or document believed by it in good faith to be genuine and to have been signed or presented by the proper party or parties.

The Manager may consult with legal counsel, accountants, appraisers, management consultants, investment bankers, architects, engineers, environmental consultants, and other consultants and advisers selected by it, and any act taken or omitted to be taken in reliance upon the opinion of such Persons as to matters which the Manager reasonably believes to be within such Person's professional or expert competence shall be conclusively presumed to have been done or omitted in good faith and in accordance with such opinion.

7.03 Title to Company Assets.

Title to Company assets, whether real, personal, or mixed and whether tangible or intangible, shall be deemed to be owned by the Company, and no Member, individually or collectively, shall have any ownership interest in the Company's assets or any portion thereof. Title to any or all of the Company's assets shall be held in the name of the Company.

7.04 Voting.

There shall be only one class of membership and no Member shall have any rights or preferences in addition to or different from those possessed by any other Member. Each Member shall vote in proportion to the Member's Percentage Interest as of the date of the voting. Unless otherwise provided, any action that may or that must be taken by the Members shall be by a majority in interest of Members.

7.05 Term and Appointment.

(a) A Manager shall serve until the earlier of (1) the Manager's resignation, retirement, death, or disability; (2) the Manager's removal by the Members; and (3) until the termination of the LLC. If one Manager is no longer a manager of this Company, the remaining manager shall serve alone. If no manager remain, a new Manager shall be appointed by a Majority of the Members.

(b) If a Manager, at any time, becomes subject to any type of a collection action that may threaten the Company or any of its assets or the Company's ability to conduct its business operations, then such Manager shall be automatically removed as a manager of this Company, and a new manager of this Company shall be selected by a Majority in Interest of the Members.

(c) A Manager may be removed only by consent of those Members holding seventy percent (70%) of the total voting power, and upon the execution and filing of a Certificate of Amendment of the Articles of Organization of the Company in conformity with Act, if necessary, to provide that the Company is to be managed by manager.

ARTICLE VIII. RIGHTS AND OBLIGATIONS OF MEMBERS

8.01 Limitation of Liability.

The Members shall have no liability under this Agreement, except as expressly provided in this Agreement (including Section 10.4 of this Agreement) or under the Act.

8.02 Management of Business.

No Member or Assignee (other than the Manager) shall take part in the operation, management, or control (within the meaning of the Act) of the Company's business, transact any business in the Company's name, or have the power to sign documents for or otherwise bind the Company. The transaction of any such business by the Manager shall not affect, impair, or eliminate the limitations on the liability of the Members or Assignees under this Agreement. Any breach of the foregoing by a Member to whom such powers have not been specifically delegated, which results in a claim against the Company including, but not limited to, claims for brokers' commissions or wages, shall obligate the breaching Member to pay such claim(s) without contribution from the other Member.

8.03 Outside Activities of Members.

(a) Subject to the terms and provisions hereof, it is agreed that any Member and any Affiliate of any Member (including any officer, director, employee, agent, or representative of any Member) shall be entitled to and may have business interests and engage in business activities in addition to those relating to the Company, including business interests and activities that are in direct competition with the Company or that are enhanced by the activities of the Company. Neither the Company nor any Members shall have any rights, claims, or interests by virtue of this Agreement or any relationships, duties, or obligations hereunder (including, but not limited to, any fiduciary or similar duties created by this Agreement, under the Act, or otherwise existing at law or in equity) in any business ventures or investments of any Member, or any Affiliate of any Member. Except as expressly provided below, none of the Members nor any other Person shall have any rights by virtue of this Agreement or the Company relationship established hereby in any business ventures of any other Person, and such other Person shall have no obligation pursuant to this Agreement to offer any interest in any such business ventures to the Company, any Member or any such other Person, even if such opportunity is of a character which, if presented to the Company, any Member or such other Person could be taken by such Person. (b) It is further agreed that, except as otherwise expressly provided above, none of the Members or any of their Affiliates have any duty, obligation, or liability to present to the Company any business or investment opportunity which may arise in the course of activity for or on behalf of the Company, or otherwise, for investment by the Company or any of the Members (even if within the line and scope of the business and affairs of the Company), and instead any Member and any Affiliate may pursue such opportunity for such Member's or Affiliate's own benefit and account, without any participation, right, or claim therein by the Company or any other Member, and without notification or disclosure to the Company or any other Member.

8.04 No Redemption Right.

No Member shall have the right to require the Company to redeem all or a portion of the Membership Interest held by such Member. The Members shall not have any right to resign from the Company, and the Members shall not have any right upon resignation to receive any distributions or the fair value of such Member's Membership Interest.

ARTICLE IX. BOOKS, RECORDS, ACCOUNTING, AND REPORTS

9.01 Records and Accounting.

The Company shall keep or cause to be kept at the principal office of the Company those records and documents required to be maintained by the Act and other books and records which are appropriate with respect to the Company's business, including without limitation, all books and records necessary to provide to the Members any information, lists and copies of documents required to be provided pursuant to Sections 8.04 and 9.03 of this Agreement. Any records maintained by or on behalf of the Company in the regular course of its business may be kept on, or be in the form of, photographs, micrographics, or any other information storage device, provided that the records so maintained are convertible into clearly legible written form within a reasonable period of time. The books of the Company shall be maintained, for financial and tax reporting purposes, on an accrual basis in accordance with generally accepted accounting principles.

9.02 Fiscal Year.

The fiscal year of the Company shall be the calendar year.

9.03 Reports.

All accounting and other professional fees associated with the preparation, compilation, review, audit, and any other matters relating to the Company's records, financial statements and reports, tax returns, and any other Company items described in the preceding paragraphs shall be at the expense of the Company.

ARTICLE X. TAX MATTERS

10.03 Preparation of Tax Returns.

The Manager shall arrange for the preparation and timely filing of all returns of Company income, gains, deductions, losses, and other items required of the Company for federal and state income tax purposes and shall use all reasonable efforts to furnish, the tax information reasonably required by the Members for federal and state income tax reporting purposes.

10.02 Tax Elections.

Except as otherwise provided herein, the Manager shall, in his sole and absolute discretion, determine whether to make any available election pursuant to the Code. The Manager shall have the right to make or not to make, or to seek to revoke any tax election he makes, including, without limitation, the election under Section 754 of the Code, upon the Manager's determination in his sole and absolute discretion concerning what election is in the best interests of the Members.

10.03 Tax Matters Member.

(a) The Manager shall be the "tax matters partner" of the Company, as defined in Code Section 6231(a)(7), for purposes of Code Sections 6221 through 6232 and for state income tax purposes (the "Tax Matters Member"). Each Member shall furnish to the Company the name, address, taxpayer identification number, and profit interest of each of the Members and its Assignees and such other information as is reasonably required to be supplied to the IRS in connection with any administrative proceeding with respect to the Company pursuant to Subchapter C, Chapter 63, beginning with Section 6221, of the Code. The Manager shall cause the Company to elect to be governed by the provision of such Subchapter C, Chapter 63, of the Code if the Company is not otherwise so governed.

(b) The Tax Matters Member is authorized, but not required:

(i) to enter into any settlement with the IRS with respect to any administrative or judicial proceedings for the adjustment of Company items required to be taken into account by a Member for income tax purposes (such administrative proceedings being referred to as a "tax audit" and such judicial proceedings being referred to as "judicial review"), and in the settlement agreement the Tax Matters Member may expressly state that such agreement shall bind all Members, except that such settlement agreement shall not bind any Member: (1) who (within the time period prescribed pursuant to the Code and Regulations) files a statement with the IRS providing that the Tax Matters Member shall not have the authority to enter into a settlement agreement on behalf of such Member; or (2) who is a "notice partner" (as defined in Section 6231(a)(8) of the Code) or a member of a "notice group" (as defined in Section 6223(b)(2) of the Code);

(ii) in the event that a notice of a final administrative adjustment at the Company level of any item required to be taken into account by a Member for tax purposes (a "final adjustment") is mailed to the Tax Matters Member, to seek judicial review of such final adjustment, including the filing of a petition for readjustment with the Tax Court or the District Court of the United States for the district in which the Company's principal place of business is located;

(iii) to intervene in any action brought by any other Member for judicial review of a final adjustment;

(iv) to file a request for an administrative adjustment with the IRS and, if any part of such request is not allowed by the IRS, to file an appropriate pleading (petition or complaint) for judicial review with respect to such request;

(v) to enter into an agreement with the IRS to extend the period for assessing any tax which is attributable to any item required to be taken account of by the Company or a Member for tax purposes, or an item affected by such item; and

(vi) to take any other action on behalf of the Members or the Company in connection with any tax audit or judicial review proceeding to the extent permitted by applicable law or regulations.

(vii) The taking of any action and the incurring of any expense by the Tax Matters Member in connection with any such proceeding, except to the extent required by law, is a matter in the sole and absolute discretion of the Tax Matters Member.

(c) All third party costs and expenses incurred by the Tax Matters Member in performing its duties as such (including legal and accounting fees and expenses) shall be borne or reimbursed by the Company. Nothing herein shall be construed to restrict the Company from engaging an accounting firm to assist the Tax Matters Member in discharging its duties hereunder, including an accounting firm which also renders services to the Manager.

10.04 Withholding.

Each Member hereby authorizes the Company to withhold from, or pay on behalf of or with respect to, such Member any amount of federal, state, local, or foreign taxes that the Manager determines that the Company is required to withhold or pay with respect to any amount distributable or allocable to such Member pursuant to this Agreement, including, without limitation, any taxes required to be withheld or paid by the Company pursuant to Section 1441, 1442, 1445, or 1446 of the Code. Any amount paid on behalf of or with respect to a Member shall constitute a loan by the Company to such Member, which loan shall be repaid by such Member within fifteen (15) days after notice from the Company that such payment must be made, unless: (i) the Company withholds such payment from a distribution which would otherwise be made to the Member; or (ii) the Manager determines, in his sole and absolute discretion, that such payment may be satisfied out of the available funds of the Company which would, but for such payment, be distributed to the Member. Any amounts withheld pursuant to the foregoing clauses (i) or (ii) shall be treated as having been distributed to such Member. Each Member hereby unconditionally and irrevocably grants to the Company a security interest in such Member's Membership Interest to secure such Member's obligation to pay to the Company any amounts required to be paid pursuant to this Section 10.04. In the event that a Member fails to pay any amounts owed to the Company pursuant to this Section 10.04 when due, the Manager may, in his sole and absolute discretion, elect to make the payment to the Company on behalf of such defaulting Member, and shall succeed to all rights and remedies of the Company as against such defaulting Member. Without limitation, in such event the Manager shall have the right to receive distributions that would otherwise be distributable to such defaulting Member until such time as such loan, together with all interest thereon, has been paid in full, and any such distributions so received by the Manager shall be treated as having been distributed to the defaulting Member and immediately paid by the defaulting Member to the Manager in repayment of such loan. Any amounts payable by a Member hereunder shall bear interest at the lesser of (A) the base rate on corporate loans at large United States money center commercial banks, as published from time to time in *The Wall Street Journal*, plus four (4) percentage points, or (B) the maximum lawful rate of interest on such obligation, such interest to accrue from the date such amount is due (i.e., fifteen (15) days after demand) until such amount is paid in full. Each Member shall at its own expense take such actions as the Company or the Manager shall request in order to perfect or enforce the security interest created hereunder.

ARTICLE XI. TRANSFERS AND ASSIGNMENTS OF INTERESTS; WITHDRAWALS

11.01 Transfer.

(a) The term "transfer" when used in this Article XI with respect to a Membership Interest shall be deemed to refer to a transaction by which a Member purports to assign all or any part of its Membership Interest in the Company to another Person, and includes a sale, assignment, gift, pledge, encumbrance, hypothecation, mortgage, exchange, or any other disposition, voluntary or involuntary, by operation of law or otherwise.

(b) No Membership Interest shall be transferred, in whole or in part (including any interest therein), except in accordance with the terms and conditions set forth in this Article XI. Any transfer or purported transfer of a Membership Interest not made in accordance with this Article XI shall be null and void *ab initio*, and the Company shall have no duty or obligation to recognize the transferee as a member or holder of any interest whatsoever in the Company, and the transferee shall have no rights, interests, or claims in or against the Company or any Member.

11.02 Members' Rights to Transfer.

(a) No Member shall be entitled to transfer, assign, convey, sell, encumber, or in any way alienate all or any part of the Member's Interest except with the prior written consent of the Manager, which consent may be given or withheld, conditioned or delayed (as allowed by this Agreement or the Act), as the Manager may determine in his sole discretion.

(b) If a Member is subject to Incapacity, the executor, administrator, trustee, committee, guardian, conservator, or receiver of such Member's estate shall have all of the rights of such Member, but not more rights than those enjoyed by other Members, for the purpose of settling or managing the estate and such power as the Incapacitated Member possessed to transfer all or any part of the Incapacitated Member's interest in the Company. The Incapacity of a Member, in and of itself, shall not dissolve or terminate the Company.

(c) The Manager may prohibit any transfer by a Member of its Membership Interest if, in the opinion of legal counsel to the Company or the Manager, such transfer would require filing of a registration statement under the Securities Act of 1933 or would otherwise violate any federal or state securities laws or regulations applicable to the Company or the Membership Interest

(d) No transfer by a Member of its Membership Interest may be made to any Person if: (i) in the opinion of legal counsel for the Company, it would result in the Company being treated as an association taxable as a corporation; (ii) such transfer is effectuated through an "established securities market" or a "secondary market (or the substantial equivalent thereof)" within the meaning of Section 7704 of the Code; (iii) such transfer would cause the Company to become, with respect to any employee benefit plan subject to Title I of ERISA, a "party in interest" (as defined in Section 3(14) of ERISA) or a "disqualified person" (as defined in Section 4975(c) of the Code); (iv) such transfer would, in the opinion of legal counsel for the Company, cause any portion of the assets of the Company to constitute assets of any employee benefit plan pursuant to Department of Labor Regulations Section 2510.2 101; (v) such transfer would subject the Company to regulation under the Investment Company Act of 1940, the Investment Advisors Act of 1940 or the Employee Retirement Income Security Act of 1974, each as amended; or (vi) such transfer would cause a termination of the Company under Section 708(b)(1)(B) of the Code.

11.03 Right of Redemption and Termination of Interest.

(a) Prior to any transfer of a Membership Interest (or a portion thereof) to an Assignee, or any other transfer assignment, conveyance, or sale (whether arising out of an attempted charge upon that Member's interest in the Company by judicial process, a foreclosure by a creditor of the Member or otherwise) of a Member's interest in the Company which does not at the same time transfer the balance of the rights associated with the Membership Interest transferred by the Member (including, without limitation, the rights of the Member to vote or participate in the management of the business, property, and affairs of the Company), the Company shall have the right to redeem the Member, and the Member shall be obligated to sell to the Company for a purchase price equal to ten percent (10%) of the positive balance of such Member's Capital Account, all of the Member's rights and interests in the Company. Such purchase and sale shall not, however, result in the release of the Member from any liability to the Company as a Member.

(b) Upon the transfer of a Member's Membership Interest in violation of this Agreement or the occurrence of a Dissolution Event as to such Member which does not result in the dissolution of the Company or the withdrawal of a Member in accordance with this Agreement, the Membership Interest of the Member shall either be terminated or purchased by the Company or remaining Members as provided in this Agreement.

(c) Each Member acknowledges and agrees that such termination or purchase of a Membership Interest upon the occurrence of any of the foregoing events is not unreasonable under the circumstances existing as of the date hereof.

11.04 Substituted Members.

(a) No Member shall have the right to substitute a transferee as a Member in the place of the transferring Member, except with the consent of the Manager to the admission of a transferee of the interest of a Member pursuant to this Section 11.04 as a Substituted Member (which consent may be given or withheld by the Manager in its sole and absolute discretion). The Manager's failure or refusal to permit a transferee of any such interests to become a Substituted Member shall not give rise to any cause of action against the Company or any Member.

(b) A transferee who has been admitted as a Substituted Member in accordance with this Article XI shall have all the rights and powers and be subject to all the restrictions and liabilities of a Member under this Agreement.

(c) Upon admission of a Substituted Member, the Company shall amend Exhibit "A" to reflect the name, address and Percentage Interest of such Substituted Member with respect to such Substituted Member's ownership interest in the Company.

11.05 Assignees.

If the Manager, in his sole and absolute discretion, does not consent to the admission of any new Member, Substituted Member, or transferee of an existing Member, whether such admission is voluntary, involuntary, or occurs by operation of law or pursuant to a court order, then any such transferee shall be considered an Assignee for purposes of this Agreement. Such Assignee shall have no voting rights with respect to the Company and shall have no management rights, no right of access to books and records of the Company, no right to receive any distributions of cash or property.

11.06 Right of First Refusal.

(a) If a Member wishes to transfer any or all of the Member's Membership Interest in the Company pursuant to a bona fide purchase offer (and such transfer is approved by the Manager as provided in this Article XI), the Member shall give notice to all other Members at least 30 days in advance of the proposed sale or Transfer, indicating the terms of such offer and the identity of the offeror. The Company shall have the option to purchase the Membership Interest proposed to be transferred at the price and on the terms provided in this Agreement. If the price for the Membership Interest is other than cash, the fair market value in dollars of the price shall be as established in good faith by the Company. For purposes of this Agreement, a bona fide purchase offer means an offer in writing setting forth all relevant terms and conditions of purchase from an offeror who is ready, willing, and able to consummate the purchase and who is not an Affiliate of the selling Member. For 30 days after the notice of the offer is given, the Company shall have the right to purchase the Membership Interest offered, on the terms of the offer for the price stated in the offer (or the price plus the dollar value of non-cash consideration, as the case may be).

(b) If the Company does not exercise the right to purchase the Member's entire Membership Interest, then, with respect to the portion of the Membership Interest that the Company does not elect to purchase, that right shall be given to the other Members for an additional 30-day period, beginning on the day that the Company's right to purchase expires. Each of the other Members shall have the right to purchase, on the same terms, a part of the interest of the offering Member in the proportion that the Member's Percentage Interest bears to the total Percentage Interests of all of the Members who choose to participate in the purchase; *provided, however*, that the Company and the participating Members may not, in the aggregate, purchase less than the entire interest to be sold by the offering Member.

(c) If the Company and the other Members do not exercise their rights to purchase the Member's entire Membership Interest, the offering Member may, within 90 days from the date the notice of the offer is given and on the terms and conditions stated in the offer, sell or exchange that Membership Interest to the offeror named in the notice.

(d) The above notwithstanding, a Member's right to sell, transfer, or assign his or her interest in the Company, shall remain subject to the restrictions of other Section of Article XI.

11.07 General Provisions.

(a) No Member may withdraw from the Company other than as a result of a permitted transfer of all such Member's Membership Interest in accordance with this Article XI or pursuant to any agreement consented to by the Company pursuant to which the Member's interests in the Company are conveyed and the Member's withdrawal is provided for.

(b) Any Member who shall transfer all of its Membership Interest in a transfer permitted pursuant to this Article XI shall cease to be a Member upon the admission of all Assignees of such Membership Interest as Substituted Members.

(c) Transfers pursuant to this Article XI may only be made on the first day of a fiscal quarter of the Company, unless the Manager otherwise agrees.

(d) The Membership Interest of any Member may be transferred without the prior consent of other Members or the Manager (i) by *inter vivos* gift or by testamentary transfer to any spouse, parent, sibling, in-law, child, or grandchild of the Member, or to a revocable trust created for the benefit of the Member or the Member's spouse, parent, sibling, in-law, child, or grandchild of the Member; or (ii) to any Affiliate of the Member.

(e) If any Membership Interest is transferred or assigned during any quarterly segment of the Company's fiscal year in compliance with the provisions of this Article XI on any day other than the first day of a Company Year, then Net Income, Net Loss, each item thereof and all other items attributable to such interest for such Company Year shall be divided and allocated between the transferor Member and the transferee Member by taking into account their varying interests during the Company Year in accordance with Section 706(d) of the Code, using the interim closing of the books method. All distributions of Available Cash attributable to such Membership Interest with respect to which the Company Record Date is before the date of such transfer, assignment, or redemption shall be made to the transferor Member, and all distributions of Available Cash thereafter attributable to such Membership Interest shall be made to the transferee Member.

(f) Upon and contemporaneously with any transfer, assignment, conveyance, or sale (whether arising out of an attempted charge upon that Member's Economic Interest by judicial process, a foreclosure by a creditor of the Member or otherwise) of a Member's Economic Interest which does not at the same time transfer the balance of the rights associated with the Membership Interest transferred by the Member (including, without limitation, the rights of the Member to vote or participate in the management of the business, property, and affairs of the Company), the Company shall purchase from the Member, and the Member shall sell to Company for a purchase price of TEN THOUSAND DOLLARS ($10,000.00), all remaining rights and interests retained by the Member that immediately before the transfer, assignment, conveyance, or sale were associated with the transferred

Economic Interest. Such purchase and sale shall not, however, result in the release of the Member from any liability to the Company as a Member.

ARTICLE XII. DISSOLUTION, LIQUIDATION, AND TERMINATION

12.01 Dissolution.

The Company shall not be dissolved by the admission of Substituted Members in accordance with the terms of this Agreement. The Company shall dissolve, and its affairs be wound up, only upon the first to occur of any of the following ("Liquidating Events"):

(a) an election to dissolve the Company made by the Manager, in his sole and absolute discretion;

(b) entry of a decree of judicial dissolution of the Company pursuant to the provisions of the Act;

(c) the sale or other disposition of all or substantially all of the assets and properties of the Company, unless the consideration received thereupon includes an installment obligation or other right to receive payment in the future, in which case the Company shall dissolve upon receipt of all such payments; or

(d) the occurrence of any other event or the existence of any circumstance constituting an event of dissolution under applicable law.

12.02 Effect of Dissolution.

Upon the occurrence of an event of dissolution described in Section 12.01(a), (b), (c), (d) or (g), the Company's business shall be wound up and all of its assets distributed in liquidation in accordance with Section 12.03.

12.03 Winding up and Liquidation.

(a) Upon the occurrence of any event of dissolution described in Section 12.01 which results in liquidation of the Company in accordance with this Article XII, the Company shall continue solely for the purpose of winding up its affairs in an orderly manner, liquidating its assets, and satisfying the claims of its creditors and Members. No Member shall take any action that is inconsistent with, or not necessary to or appropriate for, winding up the Company business and affairs. The Members shall continue to share profits and losses during the period of liquidation in the manner set forth in Article VI. Any Person selected by the Manager (being referred to herein as the "Liquidator"), shall be fully responsible for overseeing the winding up and dissolution of Company, and shall take full account of the

Company's liabilities and assets and the assets shall be liquidated as promptly as is consistent with obtaining the fair value thereof and the proceeds therefrom (including without limitation any reserves held by the Company) shall be applied and distributed in the following order:

(i) First, to the payment and discharge of all of the Company's debts and liabilities to creditors other than the Members;

(ii) Second, to the payment and discharge of all of the Company's debts and liabilities to the Members; and

(iii) The balance, if any, to the Members in accordance with their respective positive Capital Account balances.

(b) Notwithstanding the provisions of Section 12.03(a) of this Agreement which require liquidation of the assets of the Company, but subject to the order of priorities set forth therein, if prior to or upon dissolution of the Company the Liquidator, determines that an immediate sale of part or all of the Company's assets would be impractical or would cause undue loss to the Members, the Liquidator may, in its sole and absolute discretion, defer for a reasonable time the liquidation of any assets except those necessary to satisfy liabilities of the Company (including to those Members and their Affiliates as creditors) and/or distribute to the Members, in lieu of cash, as tenants in common and in accordance with the provisions of Section 12.03(a) of this Agreement, undivided interests in such Company assets as the Liquidator deems not suitable for liquidation. Any such distributions in kind shall be made only if, in the good faith judgment of the Liquidator, such distributions in kind are in the best interest of the Members, and shall be subject to such conditions relating to the disposition and management of such properties as the Liquidator deems reasonable and equitable and to any agreements governing the operation of such properties at such time; and provided further, each distributee Member shall be afforded by the Liquidator the opportunity to direct the distribution such Member otherwise would receive to entity designed by such Member. The Liquidator shall determine the fair market value of any property distributed in kind using such reasonable method of valuation as it may adopt.

(c) In the reasonable discretion of the Liquidator, a *pro rata* portion of the distributions that would otherwise be made to the Members pursuant to this Article XII may be:

(i) distributed to one or more trust(s) established for the benefit of the Members for the purposes of liquidating Company assets, collecting amounts owed to the Company, and paying any contingent or unforeseen liabilities or obligations of the Company arising out of or in connection with the Company, and which the Manager determines in his discretion will be treated as a grantor "liquidating" trust under the Code. The assets of any such trust(s) shall be distributed to the Members from time to time, in the reasonable direction of the Liquidator, in the same proportions as the amount distributed to such trust(s) by the Company would otherwise have been distributed to the Members pursuant to this Agreement; and

(ii) withheld or escrowed to provide a reasonable reserve for Company liabilities (contingent or otherwise) and to reflect the unrealized portion of any installment obligations owed to the Company, provided that such withheld or escrowed amounts shall be distributed to the Members in the manner and of priority set forth in Section 13.03(a) as soon as practicable.

12.04 Compliance with Timing Requirements of Regulations.

In the event the Company is "liquidated" within the meaning of Regulations Section 1.704 1(b)(2)(ii)(g), distributions shall be made pursuant to this Article XII to the Members who have positive Capital Accounts in compliance with Regulations Section 1.704 1(b)(2)(ii)(b)(2). No Member shall have any obligation whatsoever to cure, or make any contribution with respect to, a deficit balance in such Member's Capital Account at any time.

12.05 Rights of Members.

Except as otherwise provided in this Agreement, each Member shall look solely to the assets of the Company for the return of its Capital Contributions and shall have no right, power, or claim to demand or receive property other than cash from the Company. Except as othe,rwise provided in this Agreement, no Member shall have priority over any other Member as to the return of its Capital Contributions, distributions, or allocations.

12.06 Notice of Dissolution.

In the event a Liquidating Event occurs or an event occurs that would, but for the provisions of an election or objection by one or more Members pursuant to Section 12.01, result in a dissolution of the Company, the Company shall, within thirty (30) days thereafter, provide written notice thereof to each of the Members.

12.07 Termination of Company and Cancellation of Articles of Organization.

Upon the completion of the liquidation of the Company's assets, as provided in Section 12.03 of this Agreement, the Company shall be terminated, a certificate of cancellation shall be filed, and all qualifications of the Company as a foreign limited liability company in jurisdictions other than the State of California shall be canceled and such other actions as may be necessary to terminate the Company shall be taken.

12.08 Reasonable Time for Winding Up.

A reasonable time shall be allowed for the orderly winding up of the business and affairs of the Company and the liquidation of its assets pursuant to Section 12.03 of this Agreement, in order to minimize any losses otherwise attendant upon such winding up, and the provisions of this Agreement shall remain in effect between or among the Members during the period of liquidation.

12.09 Waiver of Partition.

Each Member hereby waives any right to partition of the Company property.

ARTICLE XIII. AMENDMENT OF LIMITED LIABILITY COMPANY AGREEMENT; MEETINGS

13.01 Amendments.

(a) Amendments to this Agreement may be proposed by any Member holding fifty percent (50%) or more of the Percentage Interests. Following such proposal, the Company shall submit any proposed amendment to the Members. The Company shall seek the written vote of the Members on the proposed amendment or shall call a meeting to vote thereon and to transact any other business that it may deem appropriate. For purposes of obtaining a written vote, the Manager may require a response within a reasonable specified time, but not less than fifteen (15) days. Except as provided in Section 13.01(b) or 13.01(c), a proposed amendment shall be adopted and be effective as an amendment hereto if it receives the consent of Members holding a majority of the Percentage Interests of all Members; *provided, however,* that, any amendment which adversely alters the rights of a Member in other than an inconsequential manner, including, without limitation, the right of a Member to receive distributions of Available Cash, proceeds of Capital Transactions or liquidation proceeds or allocations of Net Income, Net Loss, or any other items in the amounts, in the priorities or at the times described in this Agreement, shall require the consent of such

Member in order to become effective.

(b) Notwithstanding Section 13.01(a), the Manager shall have the power, without the consent or approval of the other Members, to amend this Agreement as may be required to facilitate or implement any of the following purposes:

(i) to reflect the admission, substitution, termination, or withdrawal of Members in accordance with this Agreement;

(ii) to set forth the designations, rights, powers, duties, and preferences of other holders of any additional issued Membership Interests;

(iii) to reflect a change that is of an inconsequential nature and does not adversely affect the Members in any material respect, or to cure any ambiguity, correct or supplement any provision in this Agreement not inconsistent with law or with other provisions of this Agreement, or make any other changes with respect to matters arising under this Agreement that will not be inconsistent with law or with the provisions of this Agreement;

(iv) to protect and shield the Company and any of its Members or assets from a claim of a creditor, including the right to amend and revise the provisions of this Agreement dealing with distributions, allocations, buy-outs and redemptions and rights and powers of Members and Assignees; and

(v) to satisfy any requirements, conditions, or guidelines, contained in any order, directive, opinion, ruling, or regulation of a federal or state agency or contained in federal or state law.

(c) Notwithstanding Sections 13.01(a) and 13.01(b) of this Agreement, this Agreement shall not be amended without the consent of each Member adversely affected if such amendment would: (i) modify the limited liability of a Member in a manner adverse to such Member or (ii) alter rights of the Member to receive distributions pursuant to Article V or Article XII, or the allocations specified in Article VI (other than as a result of any adjustments made pursuant to Section 4.03(c)); or (iv) amend this Section 13.01(c); *provided, however*, that this Section 13.01(c) shall not apply to Assignees.

13.02 Meetings of the Members.

(a) Meetings of the Members may be called by the Manager. The request shall state the nature of the business to be transacted. Notice of any such meeting shall be given to all Members not less than seven (7) days nor more than sixty (60) days prior to the date of such meeting. Members may vote in person or by proxy at such meeting. Whenever the vote or consent of the Members is permitted or required under this Agreement, such vote or consent may be given at a meeting of the Members or may be given in accordance with the procedures prescribed in Section 13.01(a) or 13.02(b) of this Agreement. Except as otherwise expressly provided in this Agreement, the consent of holders of a majority of the Percentage Interests shall control.

(b) Any action required or permitted to be taken at a meeting of the Members may be taken without a meeting if a written consent setting forth the action so taken is signed by majority of the Percentage Interests of the Members (or such other percentage as is expressly required by this Agreement). Such consent may be in one instrument or in several instruments, and shall have the same force and effect as a vote of a majority of the Percentage Interests of the Members (or such other percentage as is expressly required by this Agreement). Such consent shall be filed with the Company. An action so taken shall be deemed to have been taken at a meeting held on the effective date so certified.

(c) Each Member may authorize any Person or Persons to act for him by proxy on all matters in which a Member is entitled to participate, including waiving notice of any meeting, or voting or participating at a meeting. Every proxy must be signed by the Member or such Member's attorney in-fact. No proxy shall be valid after the expiration of eleven (11) months from the date thereof unless otherwise provided in the proxy. Every proxy shall be revocable at the pleasure of the Member executing it, such revocation to be effective upon the Company's receipt of written notice of such revocation from the Member executing such proxy.

(d) Each meeting of the Members shall be conducted by the Manager or such other Person as the Manager may appoint pursuant to such rules for the conduct of the meeting as the Manager or such other Person deems appropriate.

ARTICLE XIV. ADMISSION OF MEMBERS

14.01 Admission of Additional Members.

(a) Except as otherwise provided elsewhere in this Agreement, after the admission to the Company of the Members on the date hereof, a Person who makes a Capital Contribution to the Company in accordance with this Agreement shall be admitted to the Company as an Additional Member only upon furnishing to the Company (i) evidence of acceptance in form satisfactory to the Company of all of the terms and conditions of this Agreement, and (ii) such other documents or instruments as may be required in the reasonable discretion of the Manager in order to effect such Person's admission as an Additional Member.

(b) Notwithstanding anything to the contrary in this Section 14.01, no Person shall be admitted as an Additional Member without the consent of the Manager and all Members, which consent may be given or withheld in the Manager's and each Member's sole and absolute discretion. The admission of any Person as an Additional Member shall become effective on the date upon which the name of such Person is recorded on the books and records of the Company, following the consent of all Members to such admission.

(c) If any Additional Member is admitted to the Company on any day other than the first day of a Company Year, then Net Income, Net Loss, each item thereof and all other items allocable among Members and Assignees for such Company Year shall be allocated among such Additional Member and all other Members and Assignees by taking into account their varying interests during the Company Year in accordance with Section 706(d) of the Code, using the interim closing of the books method. Solely for purposes of making such allocations, each of such items for the calendar month in which an admission of any Additional Member occurs may, in the sole discretion of the Manager, be allocated among all of the Members and Assignees, including such Additional Member. All distributions of Available Cash with respect to which the Company Record Date is before the date of such admission shall be made solely to Members and assignees, other than the Additional Member, and all distributions of Available Cash thereafter shall be made to all of the Members and Assignees, including such Additional Member.

14.02 Amendment of Agreement and Certificate of Membership.

For the admission to the Company of any Member, the Company shall take all steps necessary and appropriate under the Act to amend the records of the Company and, if necessary, to prepare as soon as practical an amendment to this Agreement (including an amendment of Exhibit "A") and, if required by law, shall prepare and file an amendment to the Articles of Organization.

ARTICLE XV. GENERAL PROVISIONS

15.01 Addresses and Notices.

Any notice which may be or is required to be given hereunder must be in writing and must be: (i) personally delivered, (ii) transmitted by United States mail, as registered or certified mail, return receipt requested, and postage prepaid, or (iii) transmitted by facsimile (with answer back confirmation) in each case to the applicable party at its address set forth on Exhibit "A." Except as otherwise specified herein, all notices and other communications shall be deemed to have been duly given and received, whether or not actually received, on (a) the date of receipt if delivered personally, (b) two (2) calendar days after the date of posting if transmitted by registered or certified mail, return receipt requested, or (c) the date of transmission with confirmed answer back if transmitted by facsimile, whichever shall first occur. A notice or other communication not given as herein provided shall be deemed given if and when such notice or communication and any specified copies are actually received in writing by the party and all other persons to whom they are required or permitted to be given. Any party hereto may change its address for purposes hereof by notice given to the other parties in accordance with the provisions of this Section 15.01, but such notice shall not be deemed to have been duly given unless and until it is actually received by the other parties.

15.02 Titles and Captions.

All article or section titles or captions in this Agreement are for convenience only. They shall not be deemed part of this Agreement and in no way define, limit, extend, or describe the scope or intent of any provisions hereof. Except as specifically provided otherwise, references to "Articles" and "Sections" are to Articles and Sections of this Agreement.

15.03 Pronouns and Plurals.

Whenever the context may require, any pronoun used in this Agreement shall include the corresponding masculine, feminine, or neuter forms, and the singular form of nouns, pronouns, and verbs shall include the plural and vice versa.

15.04 Further Action.

The parties shall execute and deliver all documents, provide all information, and take or refrain from taking action as may be necessary or appropriate to achieve the purposes of this Agreement.

15.05 Binding Effect.

This Agreement shall be binding upon and inure to the benefit of the parties hereto and their heirs, executors, administrators, successors, legal representatives, and permitted assigns.

15.06 Creditors.

None of the provisions of this Agreement shall be for the benefit of, or shall be enforceable by, any creditor of the Company. No creditor shall have any right to enforce any right of a Member to make any contribution to the Company, and any such obligation of a Member may be compromised upon the approval of the Manager.

15.07 Waiver.

No express or implied consent to or waiver of any breach or default by a Member in the performance by such Member of its obligations under this Agreement shall be deemed or construed to be a consent to or waiver of any other breach or default in the performance by such Member of the same or any other obligations of such Member under this Agreement. Failure on the part of any Member to complain of any act or omission of any other Member or to declare any Member in default, irrespective of how long such failure continues, shall not constitute a waiver by such failing Member of the rights of such failing Member under this Agreement.

15.08 Counterparts.

This Agreement may be executed in counterparts, all of which together shall constitute one agreement binding on all of the parties hereto, notwithstanding that all such parties are not signatories to the original or the same counterpart. Each party shall become bound by this Agreement immediately upon affixing its signature hereto.

15.09 Applicable Law; Consent to Jurisdiction.

This Agreement shall be construed and enforced in accordance with and governed by the laws of the State of California, without regard to the principles of conflicts of law. Each Member and Assignee submits to the personal jurisdiction of the Courts of the State of California in connection with any dispute relating to the Company, this Agreement, or arising in connection therewith.

15.10 Invalidity of Provisions.

If any provision of this Agreement is or becomes invalid, illegal, or unenforceable in any respect, the validity, legality, or enforceability of other remaining provisions contained herein shall not be affected thereby.

15.11 Attorneys' Fees.

The prevailing party in any action brought to enforce any of the terms of this Agreement shall be entitled to such attorneys' fees and costs as a court of competent jurisdiction or any other trier of fact may award.

15.12 Entire Agreement.

This Agreement contains the entire understanding and agreement among the Members with respect to the subject matter hereof and supersedes any other prior written or oral understandings or agreements among them with respect thereto.

15.13 Disposition of Documents.

All documents and records of the Company, including, but without limitation, all financial records, vouchers, canceled checks, and bank statements shall be delivered to the Manager upon termination of the Company.

15.14 Contracts.

Every contract and agreement obligating the Company, or to which the Company may become a party, or by which it may be bound, shall be in writing. The execution of such contracts shall be by the Company, except to the extent that execution is delegated to one of the Members pursuant to this Agreement.

15.15 Disclosure.

Each Member shall give notice to the Manager of its interest, or the interest of any of its Affiliates, in any other business or undertaking which proposes to enter into any business transactions with the Company.

No Member shall disclose the terms of this Agreement without the prior written consent of the Manager, other than to an institutional lender in connection with an application by the Company for financing for the benefit of the Company or an application by a Member for financing to be used to acquire the Property from the Company or the Membership Interest of the other Member, in each case pursuant to the terms of this Agreement.

REMAINDER OF PAGE INTENTIONALLY BLANK

IN WITNESS WHEREOF, the parties hereto have executed this Agreement as of January ___, 2008.

Members

_____
Roberto Almaden

_____
Maria Juanita Almaden

CONSENTED TO ON BEHALF OF THE COMPANY:

Manager

_____
Roberto Almaden

EXHIBIT "A"
NAMES, ADDRESSES, AND PERCENTAGE INTERESTS OF MEMBERs
CALIFORNIA REALTY HOLDINGS, LLC

Name	Percentage Interest	Capital Contribution
Roberto Almaden 72 Main St. Whittier, CA 90606	50%	*
Maria Juanita Almaden aka Juanita Almaden 72 Main St. Whittier, CA 90606	50%	*

* Members are contributing their respective 50% interests in real properties located at:

1. 10 South, Whittier, California

2. 151 Park Place, Whittier, California

3. 111 Henderson Avenue, Whittier, California

Author's Note, Irrevocable Trust

The model irrevocable trust that follows is an irrevocable "grantor" trust. It will remove the property transferred from the estate of the transferor, reducing the transferor's estate taxes. For income tax purposes, however, the trust is tax neutral. Income taxes attributable to the transferred property continue to be taxed to the grantor.

THE ANDERSON CHILDREN'S TRUST

This Irrevocable Trust Agreement, dated as of the date set forth below, is by and between Herbert Paul Anderson, a resident of San Ramon, California (the "Grantor") and Herbert Paul Anderson, a resident of San Ramon, California (the "Trustee"). All references to the term "trust" in this Trust Agreement, unless otherwise stated, shall refer to the irrevocable trust established by the terms of this Trust Agreement and any other trusts created as part of the provisions of this Trust Agreement. All references to the Trustee shall include the initial Trustee's successors.

ARTICLE 1

My Family

I am not currently married. I have two children, now living, Sammy Anderson and Regina Anderson. The intended beneficiaries of this Trust are my children.

ARTICLE 2

Transfers to the Trust

I transfer to the Trustee all the membership interests in Sunshine Sweeteners, LLC, a Florida limited liability company and any other property that may be listed in the schedule to this Trust, and may transfer additional assets, to be held on the terms and conditions set forth in this instrument. I retain no right or interest in any property held by the Trustee under the terms of this Trust.

ARTICLE 3

Irrevocability

This trust is irrevocable, and I cannot alter, amend, revoke, or terminate the Trust in any way.

ARTICLE 4

Common Trust for My Beneficiaries

The Trustee shall hold and administer the Trust assets in trust for the benefit of the beneficiaries named below as provided in this Article 4.

A. Before My Death. Until my death, the Trustee may distribute as much of the Trust's net income to my beneficiaries (as that term is defined in Article 1) as the Trustee shall deem appropriate for any purpose, annually adding to principal any undistributed income. Trustee's ability to distribute is limited by the following guidelines:

   1. The Trustee may distribute income unequally and may make distributions to some beneficiaries and not to others. The Trustee shall never make distributions to any beneficiary who is being pursued by a creditor in a collection action and may only distribute when the threat of the collection action has passed.

   2. The Trustee may consider other income and assets readily available to each beneficiary in making distributions.

   3. The trustee may add to the class of beneficiaries any charitable organization the contributions to which are deductible under Sections 170(c), 642(c), and 2522(a) of the Internal Revenue Code of 1986, as amended, by a writing retained with the records of the trust, designating the date of the addition of the new beneficiary.

B. Upon My Death. Upon my death, the Trustee shall distribute all trust assets to those beneficiaries (from among those designated in Article 1) that I appoint in my will, forthwith and free of trust. The Trustee shall not make distributions to any beneficiary who is being pursued by a creditor in a collection action and may only distribute when the threat of the collection action has passed. It is my intent that the assets of this Trust shall benefit only those beneficiaries who I name in my will, and not any third party, including creditors of my beneficiaries.

ARTICLE 5

Contingent Trust for Certain Beneficiaries

The Trustee shall retain as a separate trust, any principal or income that would otherwise be distributed to a beneficiary before that beneficiary has reached the age of twenty-one (21) years. The Trustee may distribute to or for the benefit of such beneficiary as much of the net income and principal as the Trustee may consider appropriate for the beneficiary's health, education, support, or maintenance, annually adding to principal any undistributed income. When such beneficiary reaches 21 years of age, the Trustee shall distribute to such beneficiary his trust share, outright and free of trust.

ARTICLE 6

The Trustees

A. **Named Trustee.** Herbert Paul Anderson shall act as the initial trustee of this Trust.

B. **Successor Trustees.** Monica Freeman, of San Ramon, California, shall be the successor trustee, to serve if Herbert Paul Anderson is unable or unwilling to serve or to continue serving.

C. **Bond.** No trustee named by me or by another trustee shall be required to provide surety or other security on a bond.

D. **Additional Trustee.** The Trustee may appoint any person as an additional trustee, to serve at the pleasure of the appointing trustee.

E. **Delegation.** The Trustee may delegate to another trustee any power or authority granted by me to the Trustee, to continue at the pleasure of the delegating trustee, unless otherwise agreed. Any person dealing in good faith with a trustee may rely on that trustee's representation that a delegation has been made and remains in effect under this paragraph.

F. **Resignation.**
   1. A trustee may resign by giving written notice specifying the effective date of the resignation to the designated successor.
   2. If no successor is designated, the resigning trustee shall give notice to the then-living adult beneficiaries to whom income may then be distributed.

G. **Vacancies.** A corporation no substantial portion of the stock of which is owned by me or by beneficiaries of this Trust, may be named as successor trustee to fill any vacancy, by majority vote of the adult beneficiaries to whom trust income may then be distributed.

H. **Responsibility of Successors.** No trustee shall be responsible for or need inquire into any acts or omissions of a prior trustee.

I. **Compensation.** In addition to reimbursement for expenses, each individual trustee is entitled to reasonable compensation for services. Each corporate trustee is entitled to compensation based on its written fee schedule in effect at the time its services are rendered or as otherwise agreed, and its compensation may vary from time to time based on that schedule.

J. **Management Powers.** The Trustee may exercise the powers described below, in a fiduciary capacity.

1. The trustee may invest and reinvest the trust (or leave it temporarily not invested) in any type of property and every kind of investment, in the same manner as a prudent investor would invest his or her own assets.

2. The trustee may sell or exchange any real or personal property contained in the trust, for cash or credit, at public or private sale, and with such warranties or indemnifications as the trustee may deem advisable.

3. The trustee may borrow money (even from a trustee and from any beneficiary of the trust), for the benefit of the trust and secure these debts with assets of the trust.

4. The trustee may grant security interests and execute all instruments creating such interests upon such terms as the trustee may deem appropriate.

5. The trustee may compromise and adjust claims against or on behalf of the trust on such terms as the trustee may deem appropriate.

6. The trustee may take title to any securities in the name of any custodian or nominee, without disclosing this relationship.

7. The trustee may determine whether receipts are income or principal and whether disbursements are to be charged against income or principal, to the extent not established clearly by state law. Determinations made by the trustee in good faith shall not require equitable adjustments.

8. The trustee may make all tax elections and allocations the trustee may consider appropriate; however, this authority is exercisable only in a fiduciary capacity and may not be used to enlarge or shift any beneficial interest except as an incidental consequence of the discharge of fiduciary duties. No tax elections or allocations made by the trustee in good faith shall require equitable adjustments.

9. The trustee may employ such lawyers, accountants, and other advisers as the trustee may deem useful and appropriate for the administration of the trust. The trustee may employ a professional investment adviser in managing the investments of the trust (including any investment in mutual funds, investment trusts, or managed

accounts), delegate to this adviser any discretionary investment authorities, and rely on the adviser's investment recommendations without liability to any beneficiary.

10. The trustee may divide and distribute the trust in kind, in money, or partly in each, without regard to the income tax basis of any asset and without the consent of any beneficiary. The decision of the trustee in dividing any portion of the trust between or among two (2) or more beneficiaries shall be binding on all persons.

11. The trustee shall distribute any of the trust to a minor by distributing it to any appropriate person (who may be a trustee) chosen by the trustee, as custodian under any appropriate Uniform Transfers (or Gifts) to Minors Act, to be held for the maximum period of time allowed by law. The trustee may also sell any asset that cannot legally be held under this custodianship and invest the sales proceeds in assets that can be held under this custodianship.

ARTICLE 7

Overriding Purposes

This article states some of my purposes in creating this Trust, and all provisions of the Trust shall be construed so as best to effect these purposes. No trustee shall exercise any discretion in a manner that could reasonably be expected to frustrate the effectuation of these purposes.

A. **Income Tax.** The trust shall be a grantor trust deemed owned by me for federal income tax purposes.

B. **Gift Tax.** All transfers to the trust shall be incomplete gifts for federal gift tax purposes.

C. **Estate Tax.** The assets of the trust shall be included in my gross estate for federal estate tax purposes.

D. **Limited Power to Amend.** The Trustee may, by an instrument in writing, amend this agreement in any manner required to meet the tax objectives set forth in this article. No amendment under this paragraph may increase the class of beneficiaries or provide me with any beneficial interest or economic benefit in this Trust. This power to amend may not be exercised by any trustee who is me, or who is appointed by me as successor trustee.

ARTICLE 8

Trust Administration

A. **Spendthrift Limits.** A beneficiary may disclaim or release his or her interest in principal or income, but no beneficiary shall anticipate, assign, encumber, or subject to any creditor's claim or to legal process any interest in principal or income before its actual receipt by any beneficiary. The beneficial and legal interests in this Trust, its principal, and its income shall be free from interference or control of any beneficiary's creditor and shall not be subject to claims of any such creditor or liable to attachment, execution, bankruptcy, or other process of law. If a creditor obtains a writ of attachment, garnishment, or like process against a beneficiary, then, until its release, the Trustee shall pay to such beneficiary only such sums as are necessary for his or her reasonable health, education, and support according to his or her accustomed standard of living, and the remainder of his or her interest shall be accumulated.

B. **Protection from Creditors.** If the Trustee shall determine that a beneficiary would not benefit as greatly from any outright distribution of trust income or principal because of the availability of the distribution to his or her creditors, the trustee shall instead expend those amounts for the benefit of the beneficiary. This direction is intended to enable the trustee to give each beneficiary the fullest possible benefit and enjoyment of all of the trust income and principal to which he or she is entitled.

C. **Merger and Consolidation.** The Trustee may merge or consolidate any trust into any other trust that has the same trustee and substantially the same dispositive provisions.

D. **Division of Trusts.** The Trustee may divide any trust into multiple separate trusts.

E. **Accountings.** The Trustee shall not be required to file annual accounts with any court or court official in any jurisdiction.

F. **Change of Situs.** The Trustee may change the situs of the trust, and to the extent necessary or appropriate, move the trust assets to a state or country other than the one in which the trust is then administered if the trustee shall determine it to be in the best interests of the trust or the beneficiaries. The trustee may elect that the law of such other jurisdiction shall govern the trust to the extent necessary or appropriate under the circumstances.

G. **Disabled Beneficiary.** The Trustee may distribute income, principal, or both for a disabled beneficiary to his or her guardian or other legal personal representative, to his or her parent, guardian, personal representative, or the person with whom the beneficiary resides, without looking to the proper application of those payments.

H. **Additional Transfers.** Any person may transfer property to the Trustee at any time. The Trustee may refuse to accept a transfer if the trustee deems that acceptance is not in the trust's best interests. The trustee may accept a gift subject to one or more conditions imposed by the donor or the trustee if it is in the best interests of the trust and the beneficiaries and if the condition does not change the rights of a beneficiary with respect to any prior gift.

I. **Tax-Sensitive Powers.** The Trustee may make no distribution or expenditure that discharges a legal obligation of mine or gives me any pecuniary benefit or incident of ownership in any life insurance policy held by the trust. The trustee may not participate in the exercise of any discretion to distribute principal to himself or herself other than for his or her health, education, support, and maintenance, or any of them, nor may any trustee participate in the exercise of any discretion to distribute or expend principal or income in a manner that would discharge a trustee's personal obligation to support the beneficiary. If this paragraph precludes all of the then-serving trustees from exercising a discretion otherwise granted them, an independent person may be named by the trustee as an additional trustee, with the sole authority to exercise these discretions.

J. **Income Taxes.** The Trustee shall not pay or reimburse me for the payment of any incremental income taxes imposed upon me with respect to income or gains received by the Trust, whether or not distributed to me.

ARTICLE 9
Definitions and Miscellaneous

A. **Survivorship.** No person shall be deemed to have survived me for purposes of this trust unless he or she is living on the date ninety (90) days after the date of my death.

B. **Tax-Related Terms.** All tax-related terms shall have the same meaning in this Trust that they have in the Code.

C. **Trust.** "Trust," without further qualification or specification, shall refer to all trusts under this instrument.

D. **Trustee.** "Trustee" shall include each trustee individually, multiple trustees, and any successor.

E. **Absence of Beneficiaries.** If all of the beneficiaries of this Trust should die before the trust assets have vested, the trustee shall distribute all of the remaining assets of that trust to my legal heirs who would have inherited my personal estate, and in such shares as they would have inherited it, had I died without a valid will, determined on the later of the date of my death or the date of the death of the last of the beneficiaries to die.

F. **Copies.** There is only one signed original of this Trust. Anyone may rely on a copy of this Trust certified by a notary public or similar official to be a true copy of the signed original (and of any amendments) as if that copy were the signed original. Anyone may rely upon any statement of fact certified by the person who appears from the original document or a certified copy to be a trustee.

G. **Number.** Whenever the context of the will requires, the singular number includes the plural and the plural the singular.

H. **Applicable Law.** This trust shall be governed by and construed according to the laws of the state of California.

I. **Contest Clause.** In the event any beneficiary under this Trust shall, singly or in conjunction with any other person or persons, contest in any court the validity of this Trust or shall seek to obtain an adjudication in any proceeding in any court that this Trust or any of its provisions is void, or seeks to nullify or set aside this Trust or any of its provisions, then the right of that person or any of such person's descendants to take any interest given to him or her by this Trust shall be determined as it would have been determined had the person predeceased me, without descendants. The Trustee is hereby authorized to defend, at the expense of the Trust, any contest or attack of any nature on this Trust or any of its provisions.

I CERTIFY that I have read the foregoing Declaration of Trust and Trust Agreement and that it correctly states the terms and conditions under which the Anderson Children's Trust is to be held, managed, and administered by the Trustee. I approve the Anderson Children's Trust in all particulars.

[SIGNATURES APPEAR ON FOLLOWING PAGE]

DATED: November 6, 2007

_____

Herbert Paul Anderson
Grantor

ACCEPTED:

DATED: November 6, 2007

_____

Herbert Paul Anderson
Trustee

STATE OF CALIFORNIA

COUNTY OF LOS ANGELES

On November 6, 2007, before me, _____, a Notary Public, person-
ally appeared Herbert Paul Anderson, personally known to me (or proved to me on the
basis of satisfactory evidence) to be the person whose name is subscribed to the within
instrument and acknowledged to me that he executed the same in his authorized capacity,
and that by his signature on the instrument the person, or the entity upon behalf of which
the person acted, executed the instrument.

WITNESS my hand and official seal.

_____

Notary Public

Author's Note, Self-Cancelling Installment Agreement and Note

The two Appendixes that follow are a model Self-Canceling Installment Agreement, and the actual Self-Canceling Installment Note. The first represents the obligation of both parties to sell the subject property. The second is the buyer's binding obligation to pay for the property. The key provision in the Note is the provision that terminates the buyer's obligation to pay in the event of the death of the seller.

Self-Canceling Installment Sales Agreement

This Agreement is made and entered into on or as of April ___, 2007, by and between June Smith, Trustee, The June Smith Trust of 1977 (the "Seller"), and Forever More, LLC, a California limited liability company, the Buyer.

RECITALS:

A. Seller is the owner of all that certain parcel of real property described in Exhibit A, attached hereto and incorporated herein by this reference, and commonly known as 35 Coast Drive, Malibu, CA 90265, herein, the "Property."

B. Buyer desires to purchase an undivided one-half interest as tenant in common in the Property on the terms and conditions hereinafter set forth.

C. A word or phrase initially capitalized and set forth within quotation marks shall be a defined term and shall have the meaning first indicated unless the context clearly indicates otherwise. The following definitions shall apply:

1. "Agreement" means this document.

2. "Closing" means the meeting for the consummation of the transactions intended under this Agreement.

3. "Effective Date" means April 30, 2007.

D. The parties hereto have engaged a qualified appraiser to appraise the Property.

E. The appraised value of the Property is $4,200,000.00.

F. This transaction is not being made for the purpose of income tax avoidance by either party to the transaction.

THEREFORE, the parties hereto, with the specific intention of being legally bound hereby

---

and of so binding their respective heirs, personal representatives, successors and assigns, agree as follows:

ARTICLE I

Purchase and Sale

1.01 The recitals set forth above are true and correct and are incorporated herein.

1.02 Seller agrees to assign unto Buyer (the "Assignment"), and Buyer agrees to purchase from Seller, an undivided one-half interest in the Property, in accordance with the provisions set forth herein:

1.03 The consideration for the Assignment shall be the gross sum of Two Million One Hundred Thousand Dollars ($2,100,000.00) (the "Purchase Price").

1.04 The Purchase Price, subject to adjustments hereinafter set forth, shall be payable as follows: The Purchase Price shall be evidenced by a Note in the form attached hereto and marked Exhibit "B" (the "Note"), which shall be executed by Buyer at the Closing.

1.05 It is understood that the Purchase Price is based upon an appraisal of the Property. If within one year from the date of this Agreement it shall be discovered that an error was made in the valuation of the Property, all necessary adjustments shall be made to cure any undesirable results caused by such error.

1.06 Upon the death of Seller, all sums due hereunder, whether principal or interest, shall be deemed canceled and extinguished as though paid. The parties intend this to be a contingent payment sale. The purchase prive of the Property is variable, and will be somewhere between 0 and $2,100,000.00, depending upon how long the Seller lives. A condition precedent to each contingent payment is that seller be alive on the scheduled payment date. Consequently, if Seller dies before any scheduled potential payment, the obligation to make such payment does not come into existence.

ARTICLE II

Title

2.01 Title to the interest in the Property being conveyed shall be by a Grant Deed.

2.02 Prior to delivery of the Assignment, Seller shall not suffer or permit any lien or encumbrance against the Property without the consent of Buyer.

ARTICLE III

Representations and Warranties

3.01 Seller represents to Buyer that Seller has good and unencumbered title to the Property.

3.02 Buyer represents that Buyer has made its own investigation of the potential value of the Property and that Buyer is entering into this Agreement as a result of Buyer's own investigations and knowledge and not in reliance upon any oral representation made by anyone acting or purportedly acting on behalf of Seller which is not set forth in this Agreement.

ARTICLE IV

Closing

4.01 The Closing shall be held at a time and at a place in Los Angeles County, California, to be designated by Buyer. Written notice of the exact time, date, and place shall be delivered to Seller at least two days prior thereto.

4.02 Buyer shall be responsible for the cost of preparation and recordation of the Deed.

4.03 At the Closing, Buyer shall execute the Self-Canceling Promissory Note and the Deed of Trust. The Seller shall execute the Grant Deed.

ARTICLE V

Miscellaneous

5.01 This Agreement embodies the entire agreement and understanding between the parties hereto and supersedes any prior agreements, representations, and understandings relating to the subject matter hereof. This Agreement may not be modified or extended except by an instrument in writing signed by all parties; any alleged extension or modification, expressed or implied, which is not confirmed by a writing signed by all parties, shall be deemed to be null and void and unenforceable.

5.02 Buyer's right to acquire title under and pursuant to this Agreement may be assigned by it, but the obligations and liabilities of Buyer hereunder may not be assigned or discharged by an assignment without the consent in writing of Seller.

5.03 Any notices required hereunder shall be sufficiently given if delivered personally or sent by certified mail to the following addresses and/or to such persons and at such addresses as any party may designate and require by notice in writing to the other parties as follows:

Seller: June Smith, Trustee
3504 Coast Drive
Malibu, CA 90265

Buyer: Forever More, LLC
22 Deerborn St.
Woodland Hills, CA 91367

5.04 Buyer represents that Buyer has not dealt with or obtained any information from any broker or agent and agrees to indemnify Seller against and hold Seller harmless from any loss, liability, cost, and expense arising out of or resulting from any claim for a commission by any broker or agent based upon a claim that Buyer dealt with such person in connection with the Property.

5.05 Seller represents that Seller does not have any exclusive listing agreement with any broker or agent for the Property and agrees to indemnify Buyer against and hold Buyer harmless from any loss, liability, cost, and expense arising out of or resulting from any claim by any broker or agent on the basis of an exclusive listing agreement.

5.06 The division of this Agreement into articles and sections and the use of headings for such articles is for the purpose of convenience only and not for the purpose of construing this Agreement.

5.07 If any provision of this Agreement shall be determined to be void or invalid, such determination shall not adversely affect any other provision of this Agreement or the validity or enforceability of the remainder of this Agreement.

5.08 This Agreement and the rights and obligations of the parties hereunder shall be governed by the applicable laws of California.

5.09 Dates and times set forth in this Agreement shall not be deemed to be of the essence. Performance shall be completed within a reasonable time.

IN WITNESS WHEREOF, the parties hereto have set their hands and seals on or as of the date first above written.

Seller:

The June Smith Trust of 1977

By:

_____ By _____ (SEAL)

June Smith, Trustee
Buyer:
Forever More, LLC

By:

_____

James March
Manager

_____

Suzanne March
Manager

Self-Canceling Promissory Note

ABV Holdings, LLC (the "Debtor") promises to pay Nancy Marshall, Trustee, The Nancy Marshall Trust of 1977 (the "Creditor") the sum of Two Million One Hundred Thousand Dollars ($2,100,000.00), plus interest as described hereinbelow.

1. PAYMENTS

1.1 Amortized Payments. Debtor will make seven annual payments to Creditor in the amount of Four Hundred Forty Five Thousand Two Hundred Twenty Four Dollars ($445,224.00) according to the amortization schedule ("Amortization Schedule") attached hereto as Exhibit "A." These annual payments shall be due on the last day of each year commencing December 31, 2009 with the last scheduled payment being due on December 31, 2015 (the "Maturity Date"). Creditor and Debtor agree that the Amortization Schedule is accurate and will control, absent any prepayment. The parties agree to report the interest and principal payments for tax and financial purposes according to this schedule. The parties further agree that this note is pursuant to a contingent payment sale, in accordance with the Self-Canceling Installment Sales Agreement ("Agreement"), which Agreement is incorporated herein by this reference.

1.2 Prepayment. Debtor may prepay all or any portion of the principal of this note at any time, without penalty or premium.

1.3 Where Payments Made. Payments shall be made to Creditor at 111 Highline Drive, Pacific Palisades, CA 90265. Creditor may change the place of payment at any time by giving written notice to Debtor of the new address. Such notice shall be effective as of the next payment which is due if given at least ten (10) days prior to such payment date. Otherwise, it shall be effective as of the next successive payment.

1.4 Form of Payment. Payment may be made by cash, personal check, certified check, cashier's check, money order, or any other additional means acceptable to Creditor.

1.5 Timeliness of Payment. A payment is timely made if it is actually received by Creditor on or before the date on which it is due, or if it is mailed using the U.S. Postal Service and is postmarked at least one day prior to the date on which it is due. If the date a payment is due falls on a Saturday, Sunday, or a day that is a legal holiday under the laws of the United States, that monthly payment shall be due on the next succeeding business day.

1.6 Notices. Any notices which Creditor is required to give to Debtor shall be mailed or delivered to Debtor at Street Address, City, State, Zip, or such other place as Debtor may designate by notice to Creditor.

1.7 Cancellation of Payment. Unless sooner paid, upon the death of Creditor all sums due hereunder, whether principal or interest, shall be deemed canceled and extinguished as though paid, and the final monthly payment, if any, that is due to Creditor hereunder shall be prorated based on the number of days during such year that Creditor survived. In consideration of the complete cancellation of this Note in the event of Creditor's death before the repayment of all sums due hereunder, the interest rate hereunder includes a risk premium.

2. DEFAULT

2.1 Definition of "Default." The Debtor will be in default if it fails to pay any installment of principal or interest when due and does not cure the deficiency within ten (10) calendar days after being notified of such default by Creditor or Creditor's legal representative.

2.2 Interest on Past Due Amounts. Interest or principal not paid when due shall draw interest thereafter at the lesser rate of percent ten percent (10%) per annum, or the maximum legal interest, until paid.

2.3 Acceleration. Whenever Debtor is in default, as defined at Paragraph 2.1, Creditor may declare the entire principal balance in default, and immediately due and payable.

2.4 Remedies. Upon default, the Debtor does hereby empower any attorney of any court of record, within the United States or elsewhere, to appear for the Debtor and, with or without declaration filed, confess judgment against the Debtor and in favor of the Creditor, as of any term, for the above sum, interest, costs of suit and reasonable attorney's fees, hereby authorizing the issuance of a writ or writs of execution thereon forthwith, agreeing to condemnation of real estate levied upon, releasing and waiving inquisition, errors, stay of execution, exemption now and hereafter allowed by any law, trial by jury and any right of appeal. The Debtor knows that it has Constitutional rights to notice and a hearing before the seizure or deprivation of its property by an execution on a judgment which it is authorizing by this paragraph, but, after having obtained such advice as it deems necessary from its legal counsel, knowingly waives such Constitutional rights. Further, the Debtor acknowledges that it has been advised to seek legal advice and, to the extent it deems necessary, it has obtained advice of its legal counsel with respect to the provisions contained in this paragraph. Use of this warrant of attorney shall neither exhaust the same nor affect the power to thereafter confess judgments, as a continuing remedy, to be used as often as may be required, and notwithstanding any law or rule to the contrary, a reproduced copy of this instrument certified by an attorney of any court of record to be true and correct shall be sufficient evidence of the contents hereof for the purpose heretofore set forth. It is agreed that the rate of interest on any judgment shall be the same as the rate of interest on the note set forth above.

3. SECURED PROMISE

3.1 Security. Debtor's promise to pay is secured by that certain Deed of Trust, of even date, securing an interest in that parcel of real property commonly known as 111 Highline Drive, Pacific Palisades, CA 90265.

4. MISCELLANEOUS

4.1 Governing Law. This note and the rights and obligations of the parties hereunder shall be governed by the applicable laws of the State of California

DATED as of the _____ day of April, 2007.

ACV Holdings, LLC

_____
John White
Manager

_____
Suzanne White
Manager

Index